THE DIRECTOR'S CUT

THE BEST OF PROJECTIONS

by the same author

in the same series

PROJECTIONS 1
John Boorman fires the starting-gun for the series; includes interviews with Michael Mann, Gus Van Sant by River Phoenix and Demme on Demme

PROJECTIONS 2
Interviews with George Miller, Willem Dafoe, Jaco Van Dormael, as well as Altman on Altman

PROJECTIONS 3
The diaries of Francis Coppola, interviews with Quentin Tarantino, Chen Kaige, Sally Potter, as well as Kasdan on Kasdan

PROJECTIONS 4
James Toback's diary, an interview with Gene Kelly, Lindsay Anderson's tribute to John Ford, Walter Murch on sound design, Arthur Penn on Arthur Penn and poetry by Viggo Mortensen.

PROJECTIONS 4$^1/_2$
What is your favourite film? Answered by Clint Eastwood, the Coens, Elia Kazan, Mike Leigh, Stephen Frears, Steven Soderbergh, among others

PROJECTIONS 5
Animation issue. Also includes Jamie Lee Curtis talking to her father Tony Curtis, Quentin Tarantino and Brian De Palma, and Jimmy Stewart's last interview

PROJECTIONS 6
Pieces by Mike Figgis, Eleanor Coppola, Tom DiCillo, Robert Towne and interviews with Vittorio Storaro and Stanley Donen

PROJECTIONS 7
Scorsese issue; also includes Jamie Lee Curtis talking to her mother, Janet Leigh, Willem Dafoe with Frances McDormand and an interview with Robert Mitchum

PROJECTIONS 8
International critics answer the question: Does film criticism have any value today? Also, Christopher Doyle's diary of his work with Wong Kar-Wai and interviews with Abbas Kiarostami and Abraham Polonsky

PROJECTIONS 9
The legacy of French cinema from Robert Bresson to Matthieu Kassovitz's *La Haine*

PROJECTIONS 10
The Hollywood issue. Mike Figgis explores the System in conversation with Mel Gibson, Salma Hayek, Paul Thomas Anderson and others

PROJECTIONS 11
The New York issue. A companion issue to the Hollywood one in which Spike Lee, Tim Robbins, Jim Jarmusch, David O. Russell and Wes Anderson provide an alternative to Hollywood film-making

PROJECTIONS 12
Are film schools necessary? Former film students such as Lynne Ramsay discuss the pros and cons. Interviews with new directors: François Ozon, Pawel Pawlikowski, Bruno Dumont and Walter Salles; Peter Weller's diary of working with Antonioni; images by Richard Linklater and a story by Ethan Hawke

PROJECTIONS 13
Anna Karina talks about life and work with Jean-Luc Godard; Katia Lund, co-director of *City of God* discusses how the film was created; interviews with Ingmar Bergman and David Gordon Green; Pauline Kael on Renoir and John Boorman on Conrad Hall.

THE DIRECTOR'S CUT

The Best of Projections

Edited by John Boorman and
Walter Donohue

faber and faber

First published in 2006
by Faber and Faber Limited
3 Queen Square London WC1N 3AU

Published in the United States by Faber and Faber Inc.
an affiliate of Farrar, Straus and Giroux LLC, New York

Typeset by RefineCatch Limited, Bungay, Suffolk
Printed in England by Mackays of Chatham, plc

A CIP record for this book
is available from the British Library

ISBN 0–571–23315–5
ISBN 978–0–57123315–1

2 4 6 8 10 9 7 5 3 1

Contents

FILM-MAKING

Introduction

The process. That is what we filmmakers are concerned with, what we argue about, what we struggle to understand; and that was, and is, the purpose of Projections, to provide a forum for discussing that process.

We have done fourteen years. Here is a selection of some of the most insightful material about acting, directing, writing – not an instruction manual on how to make a movie, but the fumbling, groping steps that talented filmmakers take in their quest for magic.

Although this moviemaking process is largely technical, it is also essentially mysterious. After all, a movie is made up of nothing but waves – light waves, sound waves – insubstantial, without mass. Waves and imagination and money, those are the ingredients.

Today those waves are mostly digitalised, they pass through computers and can be moulded and manipulated. The boundaries to the imagination have come crashing down. But the downside is down indeed. These new powers have been seized by the mainstream. Computer special effects offer construction and destruction on a cosmic scale. We cower before sound effects that register on the richter scale. We drown in a tsunami of music. They overwhelm us, intimidate. We grow to fear the movies. Full of sound and fury, these CGI monsters signify very little. Facing huge production, marketing and overhead costs, the big studio pictures are made in a funk of fear. Most of all they fear an R rating, for they claim it reduces income by 30 per cent. Directors of big pictures have to bland them into PG. This has changed Hollywood moviemaking more than any other factor, but is something even more sinister happening? Is the computer eating movies from within, sucking out their humanity?

The High Definition image strives for reality. The film emulsion transforms reality, blinds the elements in the heft of its chemicals, but the digital image wants to *be* reality, to clone it. Whether we shoot on digital tape or film, we mostly now digitalise before going back to film and we enjoy the range of tricks we can apply, but whatever may be added, I have a sense that something is taken away. When we convert back to film it reacts against the digital image like a body rejecting an organ transplant.

I am not a luddite. I have cut on an Avid for many years. I shot my new film, *The Tiger's Tail* on the new Sony/Panavision digital camera, the Genesis, a device that mimics the film camera, like one of those movies where the aliens look like human beings but under the skin there are only computer chips and circuits. It captures vivid images, but converting them back to film something is sucked out – we need to find a drug that will prevent rejection.

For better or worse, once digital projectors are installed in cinemas, film will die. It is, after all, a nineteenth-century invention. When I was invited to make a film on the original Lumière camera I examined it with great fascination. A claw pulled a frame down, held it steady, the shutter opened and closed and the next frame was pulled down. Add a few gadgets and you have the modern film camera.

Technology has always influenced content – the advent of sound, of colour, of wide screen, of dolby sound, the digital image, and potentially the most revolutionary, distribution by internet.

If Projections survives for another dozen years, it will be fascinating to find out where all this leads.

Acting

1 De Niro and Me

by Martin Scorsese

Mean Streets

Mean Streets: 'All the abandon of a trapped animal.'

The pool table. What he did was jump on to the table. I remember him behaving with all the abandon of a trapped animal; I thought the bravado of jumping up and dancing on the table was great. I don't remember if I planned it; I do remember that I had planned Johnny would do something like that – the last part of a candle flame burns the brightest just before it goes out. And that's what he was doing here. I know that the shot was planned very clearly, tracking all around the table. I even have storyboards of this. I don't remember if I planned him getting on the table. I remember him breaking the cue stick and falling

Mean Streets: 'There is nothing more to say: you start pulling guns.'

off the table, and the other guys coming over and smashing him . . . I – forget if it was an improv. But I think it was part of a long take we did. Also, he kicks. That was the main thing in the streets: you had to learn how to kick. Because if you weren't powerful enough with your hands, you'd always kick – kick people in the head, or between the legs, or in the chest to save yourself. So it's all authentic that way. I always had asthma, so I couldn't get into fights. If I did, first I needed the guts to do it (because a lot of these guys were very tough). Secondly, if you didn't have asthma and there were too many people, you could get a few good kicks in there. They used to say, 'Give a few good kicks and then run!' Well, I couldn't run! I had to figure out something else. I can get a kick in, but then if I stay there I'm going to get kicked! So no thank you!

And this is right before the end of *Mean Streets*. It's a series of three scenes which become more and more intense as the film goes on, until finally it resorts to holding a gun. The first scene is Michael 'telling' Charlie (Harvey Keitel), 'Your friend Johnny hasn't paid.' Charlie tells him, 'I'll take care of it.' The next thing is, Johnny (Robert De Niro) comes in, Charlie takes him aside and says, 'You haven't paid.' Johnny says, 'I know, I should have done it; I'll do it next time.' Afterwards they go out, they all have a drink. Charlie: 'Michael, I talked to Johnny, everything is going to be fine.' 'Great, let's all drink on him.' Those three scenes are repeated, and each time the same themes are repeated till it gets more complex: as the options are cut away, people start dealing with each other in a less friendly way. Finally, there is nothing more to say: you start pulling guns. I remember that my father used to say, 'There was a certain time when so many words had been said that no more words were left, you had to pick up a bat and hit somebody . . .' It's beyond words; it goes into hitting. But this was even beyond hitting. Johnny picks up a gun and in doing such a thing – they're not gangsters, they're just kids – he simply crosses the line of the code of behaviour. What's very important in this scene is that, among the guys we grew up with, a lot were like Michael. Michael the loan shark is a sweet guy basically, dressed in a velvet coat. Johnny expresses his contempt for somebody like that – because he doesn't give a damn about anything, he doesn't care if he gets killed. Johnny what's going to happen to him; but Charlie has to live there and he's trying to hold all these elements together. Michael may behave like he's a made man, that he's in the organization, that he put his finger in the blood and that he signed the oath. But we know that not only is he not made, but he probably never will be, because he doesn't have the guts, he doesn't have the brains. Charlie is saying to Johnny: But why let him know that? If Michael is disrespectful to me, I can deal with him in a certain way. But he's not disrespectful of me, so why make a fool of him? You're only causing trouble because then you're going to force him to act in a way where he has no choice; which is the gun. And that's what he does. There is a line of dialogue we wrote there which is hysterically funny to me. Johnny says to Michael, 'I borrowed money from everybody in the neighbourhood. Everybody knows not to give me money. So who's the last jerk who would give me money? It's you!' Michael is basically a sweet man, a nice guy, but he doesn't belong there. That's what Johnny knows. Johnny knows that Michael is not made to be in this world – in which he's behaving like he's a wise guy, like a made man. Michael tends to put on airs that way. Johnny resents it, and he tells the truth. But sometimes it's not very wise to tell the truth in this way. He burns his bridges behind him, and Charlie tries to balance it up: 'I know that Michael will never make it . . . but Michael has never disrespected me. If he's disrespected you, it's because you disrespected him by not paying him back.' That's how it all goes, that's how we grew up.

Robert De Niro was aware of all this. He used to hang out with a group of guys like this. And I was with another group. The streets were four blocks away. I was on Elizabeth Street between Prince Street and Houston. Broom Street and Grand was where De Niro was hanging out. This was when we were fifteen or sixteen years old. We never crossed paths socially; we never went to dinners or had drinks together. We were in clubs – kind of speakeasies – and I'd see him there, but he was with another group. The one thing I remember is that everybody liked him because he was a sweet guy. I chose him for *Mean Streets* because De Palma told me about him. I didn't remember him, but he remembered me. I went to a Christmas dinner at Jay Cocks's, and after dinner I sat down in the living room and De Niro looked over and said, 'You used to be with so and so, and so and so . . .' I said, 'Yeah!' And he said, 'Do you remember me?' And I went, 'Oh yes, your friends were so and so, and so and so. Yeah, that's right, I remember!' We were at the same dances at Webster Hall, a dance hall my father and mother went to when they were courting in the 1920s. We went there in the 1950s. We shot *Raging Bull* in there, the scene where he sees Vicki dance with the other gangsters. And I remember De Niro at certain dances which were run by the parish priests for Italian-Americans. I said to him that I had made one movie called *Who's That Knocking on my Door?* about the neighbourhood. He said he'd like to see it, so I arranged a screening for him and he liked it. He said he knew that I knew . . . and I knew that *he* knew. So when it came to *Mean Streets*, I said, 'It's a perfect part for him.' He had an apartment down on 14th Street at the time, and he had clothes from the old days. I remember him putting a hat on. And I said to myself, 'Oh it's perfect!' I didn't tell him that, I just said, 'Oh it's good, it's good.' But when I saw the hat, I knew it was . . . *him*. Just leave him alone, don't touch him.

Taxi Driver

Taxi Driver: De Niro with Scorsese.

This particular scene is a favourite of mine. I always liked how Bob is standing here. Keitel's body position is hostile, ready to hit. Bob's frozen like a shield, like somebody who is ready to accept it: 'I may get hit, but you are going to go down with me.' There's just something about the way he froze like this. He just knew how to do anything. He suddenly put himself in that body posture, and Keitel then knew exactly how to move. And it's a very funny scene, because Keitel improvised some of it. He says, 'It's entrapment already?' Meaning that if you're a cop, it's entrapment already. Like this (*makes gesture*). He got that from my mother. She used to do it to say someone's behind bars – it's a little sign they used to make. 'Where is he?' 'He's in prison!' Also, he says, 'I had a horse once. It got hit by a car.' I loved that, because I always wanted a horse when I was a kid, and my mother said, 'Yeah, right, I'll get you a horse and we'll keep it in the apartment.' So to have Harvey say, 'I had a horse in Coney

Taxi Driver: Harvey Keitel, hostile; De Niro, frozen like a shield.

Island, it got hit by a car' – I always loved that. I remember the shooting on that day, it was real nice. Harvey improvised all the sexual things he could do with Iris (Jodie Foster): 'You can do this, you can do that. Screw every way you want . . . but no rough stuff.' It was like a litany, a profane litany. The humour is street humour, but you know, many people don't find it funny. I didn't think that *Taxi Driver* was going to do anything. We just made it as a labour of love. But Bob knew, he felt kind of strongly about it. I just thought I had to make it because I had felt so strongly about Schrader's script and the character.

The mohawk: it's because of a friend of mine named Victor Magnotta. We went to NYU together. He was going to be a priest, but when Vietnam broke out he went into the Special Forces. He came back from Vietnam, and we met with him one night for dinner. He told us some of the things that he had done or had happened to him – horror stories. He then became a stunt man in movies. He's in this picture; he's in practically every one of my films up to a certain point. During dinner, Bob was asking him questions about being in the Special Forces. He told us that, in Saigon, if you saw a guy with his head shaved – like a little mohawk – that usually meant those people were ready to go into a certain Special Forces situation. You didn't even go near them. They were ready to kill. They were in psychological and emotional mode to go. He showed us a picture: the mohawk was shorter than the one in the film, but pretty close. And Bob had the idea. This is a story where Bob says, 'I had the idea,' and I go, 'No, *I* had the idea.' I'll give it to him! But both of us looked at each other. It was one of those things that started to happen with the two of us: we'd both get the same idea – literally. It happened again as recently as *Cape Fear*. I was away in the country for two days, which I never do. He was calling me, and I didn't return the calls until I got back. And he said, 'What's the matter with you? I was trying to reach you.' 'Well,' I said, 'I wanted to take a break for two days. Let me tell you what I did. I took the tape of *Cape Fear* – the original film [1962] – and I played it one night. I was with my friend Illiana (Douglas). And Illiana and I looked at each other, and I said, "That's the music! It's Bernard Herrmann's music. We should just use the old music." ' And he said. 'That's why I was calling you. I had the same idea.' It has always been like this with Bob, and it started around that time.

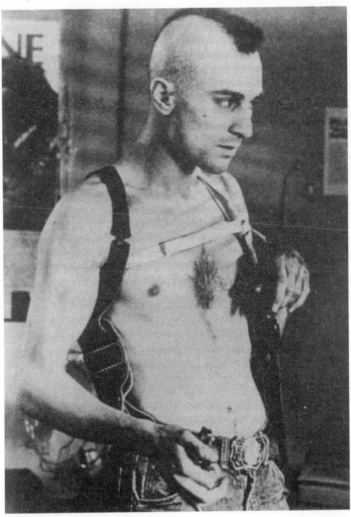

Taxi Driver: the mohawk.

Victor Magnotta then died in a stunt. It's just crazy. It was going to be the last stunt of the day: going off into the Hudson River in a car. It was in 1988, I think. He was with another stunt man. And they flipped a coin. He got the job, went in and never came out. That was the end.

New York, New York

I must say – maybe because I expect a lot from people – that Bob just seemed like a fellow who had a big range. And I never really understood what an actor has to go through to in order to get that sort of range. So I learned a lot from *New York, New York* because we pushed and pushed and pushed. And we tried to go in all different ways. But people can only really go so far. And I was not even sure where I wanted to go. I did *New York, New York* in a very different way. I didn't plan it. Usually I plan everything as much as possible: I draw every picture, in most cases. These days I draw pictures – and often when you get there, you change it because of the locations. But some things you've got to get. But here I was trying to improvise the whole thing. And I'm not good that way. I wasted money and time. Bob was so remarkable from *Taxi Driver* and *Mean Streets* that I thought if I kept pushing, he might do something really unique each time, each take. But after a while, you can only do so much. I did some acting in *Taxi Driver*, and since that film I have tried to make it a point to 'act' every now and then in a movie, to be in front of a camera. Just to keep remembering what it's like: waiting in the trailer, changing lines at the last minute. I want to learn about the limitations, and how much I can really expect from a person. Some people, you can change lines at the last minute and they'll do it. For most people it's very hard – improvising and staying in character. Even the 'acting' I do is not even acting, it's just being myself. I'm on front of a lens, I can sense the lights, and so I can tell an actor, 'Feel the light on your right. That's where we want you.' It's as simple as that. It's about learning the craft.

I expected a lot from Bob and Liza Minnelli. And I got it, actually. If I had worked it better, they could have had even more room to expand their range. It shaped very well in three scenes. The first sequence, where he tries to pick her up in the night-club, worked out nice. The second was the scene where he proposes to her in the snow and breaks the car window by accident. We improvised it and improvised it until we really got it right. And the third one was the best, I thought – I should have had the whole film that way and I couldn't. It was a scene where they are rehearsing the band together. She counts off the band, 'One, two . . .' and he goes to her and tells her, 'Excuse me, but you don't count off the band. I count off. You don't do that.' And he gets mad and throws a table. He gives her a little tap on the behind. He humiliates her. And then he argues with

New York, New York: De Niro and Liza Minnelli.

the drummer. It's about rehearsal, about working together, about jealousy; it's about competition, envy, trying to create something. His music goes one way, hers goes another way completely. That's what the movie should have been about – those three scenes – but it didn't come together. The best stuff in the film is De Niro, Minnelli, the other actors – who I thought were terrific – and the *Happy Endings* sequence, because that was written by John Kander and Fred Ebb. I just told them I wanted something in that style. The image of her as a usherette came from Boris Leven, from the Edward Hopper painting of the usherette – we opened the scene the same way. Boris Leven designed every set: so, basically, all I had to do was figure out a way to place the camera to get the set. I had the right music, a great choreographer. It was easy. It was the first ten days of the shoot. It was one of the happiest ten days I ever shot a movie. And after that, it was not good for me . . .

Raging Bull

Bob really wanted to make *Raging Bull*. I didn't want to make it. I didn't understand anything about boxing. I mean, I could understand that it's like a physical game of chess. You have to be like a chess player in your mind, but you're doing it with your body. A person can be totally uneducated but can be brilliant, almost a genius, to fight according to these rules. When I was a kid I watched fights on a big screen; it was always done from one angle, and I couldn't tell who the fighters were. It was very boring to me. So I didn't understand it. I understood the character a little, and why Bob liked the idea of playing Jake La Motta because he came from a lower working-class Italian-American background. And he and his brother were thieves when they were young kids – it was a story of brothers.

But I wanted to go in another direction; I wanted it to be more a story about the Italian-American experience – which eventually became the story of my parents that Nick Pileggi and I put together: the Italian-American experience in Sicily, then coming to America; my mother and father meeting, then going through the Italian-American experience in the 1920s, 1930s, 1940s and 1950s, and ending around the mid-1960s when my grandparents all died. So I was going to go more in that direction, and I spent two years working on this script.

During those two years we did *New York, New York* and *The Last Waltz*. *New York, New York* was a flop; my second marriage had broken up; my second child was born; I started living with Robbie Robertson, and went through so many drugs that I almost destroyed myself completely. And then, just before I almost totally collapsed, we asked Paul Schrader to write a version. And Schrader did a brilliant thing: he started in the middle. We had started all the way back in the beginning, but Schrader started in the middle. Jake is obviously winning a fight; he knocks the guy down . . . but he loses. Why? Because he's not going to give in for the wise guys. Not because of honour, but because he doesn't want them to share his money. OK. With that, he goes home and says he doesn't like the way his wife cooks his steak. Well, that means tables are going to go flying and his brother is going to come up; he's going to try and talk, try to calm him down . . . so then you have a movie. You have everything going. And Schrader gave us all that. He had the whole dramatic progression of the picture. We were so close, but I wasn't really interested. I was more interested in fooling around and having fun. And I didn't know any more what kind of movies I wanted to make. I knew *Taxi Driver* was the right thing to do after *Mean Streets*. I also knew that *Alice Doesn't Live Here Any More* was the right thing to do; but there were reasons for that – the studio, working with women. After *Mean Streets* they said I couldn't direct actresses, so I said, 'No, no, no, I'll show you,' and I tried improvisatory situations like John Cassavetes. So after *New York, New York*, the only thing I had in mind was *Gangs in New York*, a fantasy about the old gangs of New York in the 1820s. I didn't know what I wanted to say any more. And the failure of *New York, New York* was received with such gleeful joy in Hollywood that I said, 'OK, let's go to hell for a while. Let's see what happens . . .' I was young enough to think I couldn't die . . . so who cares? It was 1977–78. There were a lot of drugs. And the word got around Hollywood and the international film scene. And so there was even more against me. The more I got around, the more I did it. Robbie kept saying to me, 'Marty, there is this great party in Paris. You want to go?' and we'd go to Paris to a party, to Rome to a party, to London to a party, to LA to a party, to New York – it was always the same party! Are you going to meet the love of your life? Are you going to have the greatest sexual encounter? I doubt it! At least, the way I operate. The rock 'n' roll guys got everything! They were having a great time. I was just foolin' around, moving, following them, trying to find someone. I got some companionship at the time, but it was nothing compared to these guys. They were used to living that way. I was not. What was happening to me was that I was no longer able to concentrate on work. Rather than building life experiences, foolishly, I was no longer really able to work. I got to a point where four days a week I was in bed sick because of asthma, because of the cocaine and pills. Also, during that period I was very upset with myself because I felt I had failed with *New York, New York*. What did I want to do? I knew I wanted to make movies, but I didn't know what. What the hell did I want to say? Not in the pretentious way of 'I have something to say' – I don't have anything to say. It's the idea of a situation with certain kinds of people.

And then I made this wonderful film, *The Last Waltz* [1978]. I can say it's good becasue most of it is the work of other people. It's the work of Robbie Robertson, it's the work of Bob Dylan, it's the work of Van Morrison, it's the work of Joni Mitchell. And I was able to do it in a certain way, experiment with it. It worked out real nice with the editors: Yeu-Bun Yee, a Chinese-American, and Jan Roblee made a beautiful job in the editing. It took two years to supervise; it's obviously a film that I directed, but it's really more their work. And I remember looking at it on the opening day at the Cinerama Dome. I knew that it was probably the best film I had made up to that point – I thought – and I still wasn't happy. Not that you have to be happy every minute in

Raging Bull: 'I only have a few more years during which I can do this to my body.'

your life, but there was no sense of creative satisfaction. And then I knew I was in trouble because there was a void, there was nothing there any more. So I took more drugs! And finally I collapsed.

At the same time I met somebody who was really nice: Isabella Rossellini. And I was trying to put myself together, but it was too late. My body gave way. I was 109 pounds (I'm 155 pounds now) and couldn't get myself back together physically and psychologically. I remember being at the Telluride Film Festival and not being able to sit through a terrific Wim Wenders film. Wim was there, and I had to tell him; I had to get up and leave because I couldn't stay in the room, I couldn't function, I didn't know what was happening to me. Basically, I was dying; I was bleeding internally all over and I didn't know it. My eyes were bleeding, my hands, everything except my brain and my liver. I was coughing up blood, there was blood all over the place. It was Labor Day weekend of 1978. I wound up in Las Vegas with Tom Luddy, two Czechoslovak film-makers, Wim Wenders and Isabella Rossellini. It was like a nightmare. I made it back to New York; they put me in bed, and next thing I knew I was in the emergency ward at the New York Hospital. The doctors took care of me for ten days. And Bob came to visit me. Now we had Paul's script, but I couldn't get myself together. We were casting the film, but I wasn't really paying attention. Sometimes I was so exhausted I couldn't even talk in the casting sessions. But Bob was just hoping I was going to pull myself together. I still couldn't see what the hell he saw in it. I knew that he wanted to gain the weight. The two of us were thirty-five or thirty-six years old at that time, and he kept saying, 'I only have a few more years during which I can do this to my body. We've got to do this.' He had his own thing about what he wanted to do, and I had no idea what it was until he came to visit me and said, 'What's the matter with you? Why are you doing this to yourself? Don't you want to make this picture? You can do it better than anybody.' And I said 'Yeah' – and then I knew what it was, I realized that I was *him* (points at picture of De Niro as La Motta). I could do it then; I'd make the movie about me. I didn't need to tell Bob that it was about me . . . he knew it. At that point he was just trying to get a commitment from me: are you going to direct this or not? And somehow I just snapped and said, 'Yeah, I'll direct it. OK, let's go.' He told me, 'Go and visit your friend [Isabella Rossellini] after the hospital, go to Rome for a few days and relax. And then come back and maybe we should work on the script together.' And I said, 'OK, let's do that.'

When I was discharged from the hospital, I went to Rome, I went up to northern Italy and visited Rossellini up there and the

Raging Bull: Scorsese with De Niro in the ring.

Taviani brothers (they were doing *Il Prato*). Then I came back, and Bob and I went off to an island and rewrote the script. We did the whole movie during those two and half weeks on the island – just the two of us, on the island of Saint Martin. And oddly enough, a couple of years later one of the producers, Peter Savage, had a heart attack playing roulette on that island. He's in the movie and he's in *Taxi Driver* too. Anyway, when I came back from the island, I stopped taking drugs. During that period I remember talking with Robbie Robertson. He got up and went to the bathroom a few times, and I said to him, 'You don't need to go to the bathroom, you can take drugs in front of me.' And Robbie said, 'Marty, I'm not taking any drugs; I don't want any. Why should you want me to take them? You did them all! You did every one of them.' I said, 'I know, I know.' He was exaggerating, but it was such a waste of time and energy. I didn't care about it any more. Basically, I got back into what I wanted to do, what I wanted to say. And I didn't care if anybody liked it . . . I didn't give a damn. I never expressed that kind of thing to Bob. He knew what he wanted to do in the film; and I knew what I wanted to do. And so on the island we rewrote everything and it came together very clearly. It was so precise: getting each shot and lighting it wasn't easy, but it was driven with such conviction on my part because I knew what I wanted. Like on *Taxi Driver* and on *Mean Streets*, but even more so. Finally I felt comfortable again. I designed all the fight scenes on paper. Little drawings and designs. I remember Bob showing me the moves. He was actually fighting in a ring for me on 14th Street, and they had worked out all the moves. I sat there and I looked away for a second. Bob came out of the ring and said, 'Are you watching me?' And I said, 'Yes.' 'I'm killing myself, I'm going down and . . .' And I said, 'Yeah, yeah, I'm watching.' He said OK and got back in the ring. I realized that I couldn't shoot it like that; I told myself, 'I can't shoot it just flat. We have to be inside the ring. This is going to have to be some-thing very intricate and really worked out.' He could show me all the moves he wanted that day; or he could put it on videotape (which is what he did) so I could run it back and forth and try to design it. It wouldn't show me much. I could look at him physically, that's all. But I couldn't explain that to him. What had hit me was the enormity of having to design the picture. Not just *make* the movie, but *design* it, design the fights. We did the fights first for ten weeks, and then we did ten weeks with the actors. That was hard, but that was normal film-making; you had the normal problems. But in the fight scenes the cinematographer, Michael Chapman, and I had enormous problems each day, physically, to devise the machinery to get the shots. We had to be very careful of Bob's physique too. You could only do so many takes. But he was in such good shape that he was amazing in the ring. The making of the fight scenes themselves was like doing ten movies in one.

King of Comedy

At the end of *Raging Bull* you have Jake La Motta looking in the mirror and doing the speech from *On the Waterfront*. For me, here was a person who had gone through terrible times, had treated himself badly, treated everybody else around him badly, and had then evolved to a point where he was at some sort of peace with himself and the people around him. But I didn't get there. I had become manic again. I thought that *Raging Bull* was kamikaze film-making: we threw everything I knew into making it, and I really thought that was the last movie I was going to make. I thought I was going to go and do documentaries in Rome based on the lives of the saints – because I had found out certain historical details about the different legends of the saints. I wasn't being very realistic about what I wanted to do, but I started to think that I wasn't going to make any more features. Anyway, I was still a little displeased with myself. I liked *Raging Bull*, but all the energy I had put into the movie didn't stop when I finished it. I still kept going, but I had no place else to go. Bob jumped in again and said, 'Why don't we just do *King of Comedy*? It's a New York movie, we can do it real fast. You could do what you want to do.' And I said, 'Oh yeah, OK, OK.' I thought about it and came up with the idea of Jerry Lewis. I met Jerry in Vegas, found Sandra Bernhard and did the whole thing. I was still kind of run down from doing *Raging Bull*. I had a little touch of pneumonia that I lost while I was in Rome. We started pre-production and shooting earlier than planned because of an imminent directors' strike.

And this is what made me realize that I'm not a director, because a director is a professional. He gets up in the morning and goes to work. I don't want to do that, I'm lazy. And I didn't feel right. ' "Didn't feel right"! You have a $20 million movie to make and you don't *feel right*! If you didn't feel right, why did

King of Comedy: De Niro as Rupert Pupkin.

King of Comedy: De Niro with Jerry Lewis.

you agree to make the movie?' I didn't feel comfortable with it. Bob had given me the script ten years earlier, and I didn't see anything in it. But then during those ten years, we had lived through some of it, we had become some of it – not all of it, but aspects of it. Aspects of Jerry and aspects of Rupert. Bob had felt that in the beginning, because as a movie star he would get people coming up to him. I had a different thing, so it took me longer to get to that point and begin to understand. With *King of Comedy* I wanted to do two things: to make a film as fast as I could, and to break the style down to very flat, very simple compositions, which enclose the characters in the same frame. There's a tension because they can't get out of each other's frame. I was a little annoyed at the time by critics who said about the movie, 'You can take a frame from this movie and put it on a wall like a painting.' I thought about the movies we liked from the old days of Hollywood, where the lighting is flat and yet the movie is very powerful. Like the movies of Ozu, for example, which are very powerful and simple-looking. I was saying, let's go back to a period where you don't try to impose certain camera techniques on the audience. It was the perfect style for the film because it was a comedy of manners. It had to be formal. The frames had to look – a little – like television. It was very hard. Michael Chapman agreed with me; he didn't shoot the picture but he talked to me about it: 'It's difficult to shoot it like television because your eye is too sophisticated.' He was right, so it became something else. In any event, what happened was that I certainly didn't make the film fast enough. I went on too long and I lost my energy. Every day I had to get myself back into why I wanted to make the picture. And I realized something then for the first time in my life: it's going to get harder. We're getting older. We just can't make a movie like we could when we were thirty-two years old: 'Let's make a movie fast and move on.' No, *King of Comedy* was something that De Niro liked and I had to be convinced to do. If I have to be convinced to do something, I shouldn't do it. It deosn't mean I won't make a good movie, it doesn't mean that I won't get terrific performances – but it's harder for me to do. And I realized that I only want to do pictures that come from me.

But it's a good picture, and the actors are wonderful. The next thing was supposed to be *The Last Temptation of Christ*; that was planned, that came from me. And then I was destroyed in 1983. *ET* came out, and *Star Wars* had been out (*New York, New York* opened a week or two before *Star Wars* and we were killed). In the 1980s it was like a diaspora, I had to figure out how to survive. I tried to think my career all over again. I did two movies that didn't come from me – *After Hours* and *The Color of Money* – to try and discipline myself, to try at last to become a director – and this is not false modesty – who could do other people's material, but see how much I could make it my own.

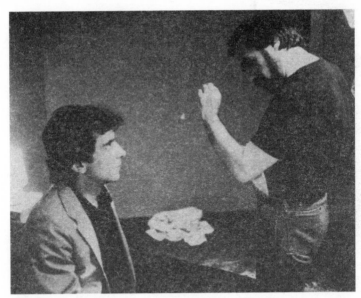

'Two movies that didn't come from me' – *After Hours*
(with Griffin Dunne) . . .

. . . and *The Color of Money* (with Paul Newman).

GoodFellas

There was a lapse of eight years between *King of Comedy* and *GoodFellas*. Michael Powell said about a collaboration, 'When one partner starts to get more out of it than the other, then you should break it.' Bob may not feel that way, because he might not have been aware of it. But the reality was that I wasn't as satisfied as he was. Not because of him. He was great in *King of Comedy*. Everybody was terrific, but it didn't come from me. I said I wanted to do *The Last Temptation of Christ*: Paul Schrader wrote a terrific script, we started preparing it and then it was cancelled, totally destroyed, taken away. I was left with nothing.

Within a two-day period I was offered a couple of films in Hollywood, which I turned down. And I wound up doing an independent film called *After Hours* [1985], which allowed me to do several things. One, to tell a story that was very different; you couldn't tell how it was going to end up. Two, it was a story you could control economically: one man running at night in the streets, and along the way he meets different people. You don't have big crowds, you don't have big car scenes, it's very simple. Three, to learn how to work faster. This was the most important part: to work slow wasn't going to do me any good in the future. I had to learn how to work faster, and that's how I met Michael Ballhaus. With him, I was able to do twelve to sixteen set-ups a day. Forty days of shooting (forty nights, actually). And when we finished that, we just upped it one more notch with a more polished Hollywood film, *Color of Money*. It had a movie star, Paul Newman. Luckily, Tom Cruise also became a star when we were editing the film; *Top Gun* was released during that period. It took about a year to make *Color of Money*, which is very fast for me. Tom Cruise became a star, Paul Newman was a star. That was that.

At that point I met Mike Ovitz, who said, 'What picture do you want to make? I think you should join my company.' I said,

GoodFellas: De Niro with Ray Liotta.

'I want make *The Last Temptation of Christ*.' And he said, 'OK, we'll get that going.' I didn't believe him, but he did it. A year later we were shooting it. Granted, we did it for no money. Granted, when I look back at it now – and even then – I wish I'd had another two weeks of shooting. But I didn't. And I wish I'd had another two months of editing. But I didn't – we had to release it because of the controversy. That's not to excuse it: there are a lot of things I added that I shouldn't have. But there are some nice things in the film.

With *Last Temptation* I felt I was back on track. At the time of *Color of Money*, I saw Nick Pileggi's book *Wise Guy*. I said, 'It's interesting. I haven't done a story about wise guys in a while. Let me find out about that.' I enquired, and Irwin Winkler called me, 'You like that book? I'll buy it for you.' Then it took from 1986 to 1987, two years, for Nick and me to do the script. And once I had the script solid, I knew it was a project I could fall into. A number of people questioned this. I remember Marlon Brando asking me, when we were down on his island in 1987, 'Why do you want to do a gangster film? You've already done that.' Even Michael Powell was saying it. After a while, I too began to wonder why I should make another gangster picture . . . maybe I should do something else. I became fascinated by *Age of Innocence*, a book Jay Cocks had given me. I was going to start to work on it with Jay; we would discuss it at night when he'd come over to my house.

Michael Powell wanted to look at the gangster script, but as he couldn't read any more Thelma Schoonmaker read it to him. It was a really good script, I thought, very tight. But I went off to do *Last Temptation* and *New York Stories* [1989] because I thought, 'Maybe I shouldn't do it. Maybe they're right.' But when Thelma read it to Michael, he immediately called me from the apartment and said, 'Now I see why you want to do it. Make that film, the script is terrific. It's another way of looking at gangsters. It's a whole other thing. That's the way you should do it.' And I said, 'OK, we'll make it.' And then I went to Warner Brothers. *GoodFellas* had been at Warners, but they waited for me to do *Last Temptation*. So I came back to Warners, but they wouldn't make it unless I had a movie star in it. And I asked Bob who could play the part of Jimmy. He had read the script a year before. He asked me a few questions: 'Is that the part of the older guy, and he's only in a few scenes?' 'Yeah.' And he said, 'Why don't I do it?' And I said, 'Well, that would be great!' And when they got Bob's name on it, we were able to get the six million dollars to make the whole film.

Bob was only there three weeks, but he gives a solid centre to the picture. It's Uncle Jimmy! And Uncle Jimmy is killing everybody! How did that happen? It was so funny that we started laughing. That's why we took so many stupid still photographs with the cheapest camera you could get: at birthday parties, vacations in Hawaii. You look at those photos and you see this guy who killed all these people – and he's baptizing babies! What kind of a world is this? It's Uncle Jimmy's. He understood that immediately.

Also, Bob had changed a lot during those nine years since *King of Comedy*. He had started to do much more work. In other words, he would be in *Once Upon a Time in America*, which is a big epic, then *The Mission*, which is another epic, then a quick cameo in *Brazil* – continually working and experimenting with different directors, different films. So he was used to working for the short time that I needed him on *GoodFellas*. We had evolved a different kind of relationship. He'd just say, 'What do you need?' and I would say, 'I need this and that,' and he'd say, 'OK, let's try that.' We used to laugh sometimes in the trailer afterwards, saying, 'Do you remember years ago? We used to talk so much! What were we talking about?' I'd say, 'I don't know!' It's like two people getting older. We'd start laughing, remembering the old days. But invariably you do talk a lot with him; that happened in *Cape Fear* and it happened in *Casino*.

Cape Fear

First of all, about the rape scene. The character played by Nick Nolte was not supposed to be having an affair with the Illiana Douglas character. We even said it in the movie. But reviewers and the public invariably thought, 'Oh yeah, that's the girl he's having an affair with.' He was not. Of course, that demonstrates what I wanted to do about the guilt of the husband: no matter what he did earlier in the marriage, there's no way that he could ever be pardoned by the family. He's lost their respect. There's nothing he can do. All he needs is for Max to come in and finish it off. With De Niro we did research on rapist killers, and we found a deposition in court which described the biting of the cheek. By the way, that is only considered 'aggravated assault'. It's amazing, isn't it? The rapist said, 'Got you, you bitch!' when he bit the cheek off, and it was considered aggravated assault! We were shocked by how a woman is totally screwed in a situation like that. In the film, she's a nice kid. She's not somebody who goes out and gets into a difficult situation all the time. She was just a little drunk.

In any event, I didn't want to make this picture, but it came down to a series of events involving a deal I had with Universal. On the basis of *GoodFellas* and *Last Temptation of Christ*, I said to myself, 'Let me try to be a director again, if I can.' I promised Universal I'd make them a picture. I'm not excusing the film; I tried a lot of things with it – some of them successful, some not – and, quite honestly, I don't know if it works or not.

De Niro's character was over-the-top. That was his intention, and I thought it was good. Because we had to dispel notions of the earlier film, which is a gem. One has to be careful: Robert Mitchum was very low key. That's the only way we could go, not just for the sake of being different but to get into another kind of mindset, to get into that religious mind. There was also the idea of an avenging angel, the idea of a person paying for their sins. Also, the script by Wesley Strick was already formed in a kind of operatic way.

Spielberg was going to direct *Cape Fear* and I was going to direct *Schindler's List*. When *Last Temptation of Christ* opened, Tom Pollock called me up and said, 'Would you like to try *Schindler's*, because Steven doesn't feel he wants to do it now.' But I knew that Steven had had the idea of doing *Schindler's List* for as many years as I had the idea of doing *Last Temptation of Christ*! So I read the book and I said, 'This is terrific stuff!' I don't know why Schindler did it. But who cares? He did it! Let's just forget about trying to explain why, let's just go from here to here. I talked to Steve Zalian, who then did the script. But when he finished, I looked at it and felt like I was coming in and taking someone's pet project. It had to go back to Steven. Of course, he read it and changed it and did it his own way; I had nothing more to do with it. In any event, I said, 'Let me try a studio picture. Let me try a Spielbergian storm sequence where I can design the shots

Cape Fear: De Niro as the avenging angel.

and do real good action sequences.' I designed the shots, not some storyboard artist – like I did with *Raging Bull*, where a storyboard artist would work from my drawings. We did about 200 drawings, but dropped some of them as we were shooting. I worked with Freddie Francis, a real cinematographer from another era. The whole film was like that: Elmer Bernstein reworked the original Bernard Herrmann score, Henry Bumstead was the art director, Gregory Peck and Robert Mitchum were in it. I wanted the film to be like a cross between the old and the new.

There was a lot in De Niro's acting; each scene was unique in its way. His character was relentless: no matter what you do to him, he comes back. I don't mean just the end sequence, when he goes into the water and comes back: that was for the genre, and done with religious overtones. But there was something determined about him: 'You hurt me. Now you have to pay. There's nothing you're going to say or do that's going to change me or change my path. You can talk law? I can talk law better than you. You can go to the police? I can go to the police. You can get a lawyer? I'll get that lawyer. He'll work for me. There's nothing you're going to say or do. You're going to have to pay up. You know you're wrong.' It was a matter of keeping him like a knife. There are two bolts of lightning tattooed on his body; it's like his body is a lethal weapon. He is going to go straight down his path. His own destruction is in that, but it doesn't matter. In a way he's doing Nick Nolte's character a favour. He's making Nolte face himself. Bob had the idea of hanging on to the bottom of the car: from that point, the movie changes and becomes the genre of today, like *The Terminator*. What he had in mind was that the man just keeps coming back and there's nothing you can do to him. And not just as a cyberspace thing. There was a moral issue: guilt. And when I figured that out, when I saw that Bob's character was determined in that way, then I said that the only way to do it is to change things. In the old script, the old movie, they had Bob's character chasing the girl at school. He meets her at school and chases her downstairs, and they had a scene with her hanging on to a shade. She slips and she's holding on, but one support pops off and then the other pops off. And he's there, he's going to grab her. But something happens: she's saved and he leaves. There's a similar scene in the old film, but simpler: she gets frightened, but it turns up to be the janitor. And I said, 'I can't do that kind of thing. Spielberg is the best at that. I'll be lucky if I can do the storm sequence at the end. That's really like going back to school for me.' The only way for me to do it would be for him to seduce the young girl and destroy whatever feeling, whatever belief, whatever trust she had in her father. And Steven Spielberg said, 'Why don't you just work with the writer, Wesley Strick, for a couple of weeks?' And I said, 'Who's Wesley?' 'He's sitting at the other end of the table. Do me a favour: just work with him for a week.' So I came up with the idea for the scene that night at dinner. I said to Wesley, 'What do you think of that?' He said OK and we talked about it, then we met with Bob and talked about how the movie should come out of that scene. Wesley started writing the scene and did a beautiful job. And so we changed many things – we changed the family – but we didn't change the end. It was an experiment. And of all my movies, it's the one that made the most money: $87 million, domestic. *GoodFellas* only made $50 million, domestic. So for De Niro and myself, it was a good collaboration doing a studio movie.

Casino

De Niro in *Casino* – in control.

When it came to the world of *Casino*, I thought about two characters: one is controlled, the other is dangerous. I could only think of two people: Bob and Joe Pesci. Why force yourself to go around looking? I don't make movies as fast as they used to make them in the old days, like Hawks or Ford, who could make Westerns with John Wayne and Ward Bond. They'd make two pictures a year; I make one every two years. So why look any further? If I can get something in a role for Bob that is different from what he and I have done before, that's interesting. When we met Frank Rosenthal, we realized that the character was very different from anything we had previously done. He's a man who doesn't let his emotions show. And his way of dressing was perfect for me; and for Bob too. We just loved the clothes.

As usual, I invited him into the scripting stage. We never really had a full story: as we were writing the script, we were getting more information. When I'd get something new I'd pass it on to Bob, who'd then ask Rosenthal. Then Rosenthal would tell a story to Bob, or to Nick (Pileggi) on the telephone. And we'd write it down. From Rosenthal and others, we found the best incidents to chart the rise and fall of Bob's relationship with Ginger. They were true incidents, but we redesigned them, put them in different places. It was a very long, very difficult process. We were scheduled to make the film at the end of the year, whereas with *GoodFellas* we had two years to write the script. I also felt that I didn't want to make a movie about the mob in Vegas with characters like a family group; it had to be a bigger thing which took in the whole mechanism, the whole machine, which reflected America then and now. Whatever implications people want to find in it, they're there. It's basic: it comes down to two people married to each other, chasing a bag of money. De Niro's performance had to be low-key. There's no sense in us doing a story unless we can do something new. Otherwise we'd get bored.

There's no doubt that I feel more comfortable speaking through him as an actor. I've been lucky over the years, because he isn't afraid to look unpleasant, to be mean, to be a person that nobody likes. We don't care. And yet what's interesting is that in reality he's a loving, compassionate person. And the audience somehow knows that. He gets this over as Travis Bickle (*Taxi Driver*). I don't know how he did it, but he did.

There are so many things that we don't have to talk about, that we just know: trust, guilt, pride. And it cuts through a lot of the nonsense we have to deal with.

2 Some Like it Dark

Tony Curtis talks to Jamie Lee Curtis

Editor's Note

Tony Curtis was sleeping late. His daughter, Jamie Lee, had just got back from a hot summer in London shooting the sequel to *A Fish Called Wanda*. At our request, she took a tape recorder with her when she went to see him.

JAMIE: *So, this is Jamie and Tony. Say 'hello'.*
TONY: Hello, Jamie.
JAMIE: *Tony, it's lovely to meet you.*
TONY: That's the truth.
JAMIE: *After all these years.*
TONY: It's been a privilege. I've heard so much about you.

Tony Curtis with his daughter Jamie (photo by Jamie Lee Curtis)

JAMIE: *Yes, you too.*

TONY: And I'm at last in your presence –

JAMIE: *Yes?*

TONY: – in your sweet presence.

JAMIE: *Well, we're sitting in . . .?*

TONY: Bel Air – on a very hot day.

JAMIE: *In a beautiful room on a big white bed.*

TONY: A big white bed. The room is somewhat white. White, white, white.

JAMIE: *And it's a little dark.*

TONY: A little dark.

JAMIE: *But it's nice. Actually, believe it or not, like a movie theatre.*

TONY: I have found that in the environment that I live, the less light the better. You walk outside, out in the middle of the hot sun and somebody is sure to give you a piece of information like, 'You got cancer.' Whereas if he could wait till you get into a little low-lit apartment somewhere, he might glance up at you and say, 'Maybe, I'll tell you something.' I find almost all the time I try to control where I sit and in what kind of lighting, and how intense the light is.

JAMIE: *I have reasons for asking this question. I, being an actor and a woman, am very conscious of light and how faces photograph. Now, my face – I have the thinnest face in show business. Thank you very much, by the way . . .*

TONY: You're welcome.

JAMIE: *. . . for that wonderful gift. They call me hatchet face.*

TONY: Please, it's the least I could do.

JAMIE: *I'm always conscious of light and how I'm being photographed, but you are a man and you were beautiful. Were you aware of how they were lighting you?*

TONY: I was. Right from when I started out in movies. It was astounding how critical I became of my looks when I saw it blown up thirty-five feet. I looked in the mirror a lot, turned my head left and right, or took another mirror and held one in the front of me and one on the side of me so I could see the profile, then I could see the back of my head. I made a study of my head as a boy. I loved my looks. I would always be looking at myself from different angles – looking up, looking down, and I never let anybody catch me doing it, you know [*chuckles*], but I enjoyed it. I just really enjoyed it.

I always dreamt that one day I would be in the movies. I'm in the Navy, in Tokyo Bay, the war is over, and I'm on this Japanese base, I'm a Signalman. And they've got one of those big arc lights, and when that thing was lit, I would go bah bah bah bah, bah dah dah dah dah.

JAMIE: *Semaphore?*

TONY: Morse Code. Inside of it was a big mirror, concave. When I stood in front of that mirror, it was to die for.

JAMIE: [*laughs*]

TONY: I went from this diminutive, charming, handsome Jewish boy to this movie giant. I looked at myself. My face was magnified three times in that mirror but in proportion, perfect. I'll never forget that. I've never told it to anybody. That convinced me to be in the movies, 'cause I knew that my looks would be good in the movies, that I would look good. Then I felt good and loved it. So that's how I started. I got myself in the movies, right? I just came out of nowhere.

When you get your first acting job, they push you around more than they push extras, furniture, props, anything. Nothing is as low as an actor coming in for his first day's work. Not an extra, but a Screen Actor Guild member who's never done that fucking work before. To walk into that environment is like going inside the entrails of a monster machine, and there you are, inside of the machine. Inside the machine. As I got to know more about movies, the more I realized how inside you are. Even if the set is tiny, you are still inside the mechanics of making that film. That first day I went over to the camera, which was a three-strip Technicolor camera. I couldn't believe it. Irving Glassberg was the cameraman. I'd already been on to the lot, but this was the first time I'd been on a set for a long period of time, and wasn't kicked off or looked at in a funny way or nothing. They were beginning to get to know me a little bit. I was standing there and Irving says, 'Hi, kid.' I said, 'Hi.' 'You come here, do you want to take a closer look?' I said, 'Uh, yup.' So I walk up there and I'm watching them changing the film. It was three pieces of film of primary colours which were run together and it was so noisy that they had to put it in a lead box – a big, blue lead box. And three strips of film went through that camera simultaneously. How intricate that was. And only when they took those three pieces of film and developed them, then made one matrix, it was only then they ended up with a film. I went up to this camera which was grey and white and beautiful and Technicolor, and nobody was looking and I put my arm around the lens. The camera was as close to me as I'm close to you now, and I said, 'I'm your pal. I love you. I want to do this for the rest of my life. If there's anything you want to tell me to do, just tell me, I'll do it. I'll know that you are my pal. I want you to know that I need your help.' I never forgot it. All of a sudden I'm talking to a fucking camera. You know? No, excuse the language, not a fucking camera. I'm talking to the machine of my life.

JAMIE: *We started talking about lighting and the idea of the image, right?*

TONY: I could see that the lighting is key. And it wasn't just opening up a light and shooting whatever fell in front of it. It needs so much more to make an image. Right at the beginning when I started in the movies, one of the stages at Universal had a big hallway up on the top of the roof with an opening that they used to go in and out of. And I remember one day it was open. A shaft of light came shooting down into this black studio and rests itself on a piece of cracked floor. I looked at that image for so long and thought, 'Why, pray tell, why is that piece illuminated out of everything else because of a shaft of light? Look at the way the light breaks around that edge.'

I then began to realize when I saw Barbara Stanwyck working at Universal and Yvonne De Carlo and Shelley Winters and Dana Andrews, and Jimmy Stewart – they'd all go a little ape shit whenever the lights were on them and that camera was in front of them. They didn't just get in front of a camera, they related to it. Take Claudette Colbert, she had a good side. That side was so good, everything else in the world was bad. If you didn't photograph her from her good side, from this particular position, nothing worked. Cars had to enter that way. Sets were built to suit it. I mean, the stuff that went on, because an actor had a good side and a bad side.

When I was doing *The Prince Who Was a Thief*, I had big rings under my eyes. So the producer comes up to me, and says, 'What are you doing every night, kid?' I said, 'I'm in the bathtub, I'm sleeping or trying to sleep.' So I went to a doctor and I said, 'How do I get rid of these circles under my eyes?' He says, 'Use make-up.' I said, 'Yeah, I know, but they seem to think I'm staying out late – is there something in my system?' He says, 'No. Your eyes are cast that way. Try to get a little more sleep, maybe you're not sleeping enough.' I was unable to sleep in those days. It was hard to sleep. So I began to see how light carved out of the environment the very thing that it wanted to show, the thing that wanted to be seen. So it's a monumental experience, particularly in movies when someone's face ends up bigger than thirty feet, twelve feet from one eye to the other. With that closeness, the slightest twitch can be seen. Impossible to hide from it, impossible to hide your emotions. The people that don't make it don't have emotions, or they have emotions, but they don't have them where they need it. So, a director has to be very, very intelligent, more than intelligent. Now, suppose the director – suppose Tim Burton, or, uh, Orson Welles is watching a take –
JAMIE: *Isn't he dead?*
TONY: Who?
JAMIE: *Orson Welles?*
TONY: He's –

JAMIE: *He's pretty dead, isn't he?*

TONY: No, no, there's no one better.

JAMIE: *He's dead, though.*

TONY: Yeah – no, no, he's dead.

JAMIE: [*laughter*] *There's a car wash on Santa Monica Boulevard, they have all these pictures of actors and we play a game, 'dead, not dead'.*

TONY: [*laughs*]

JAMIE: *They have glossy pictures of all these celebrities, so you walk along and see a picture of somebody, you point to it, you look at your friend and say, 'Dead, not dead.'*

It's sort of terrifying, that being a celebrity can boil down to that. No matter how hard you work, no matter how much money you've given to charity, no matter how good a human being you've tried to be, all of it can be reduced to a game at a car wash in West Hollywood: 'Dead, not dead'. One day they'll look at my picture and go, 'Dead, not dead.' 'No, she's dead.' 'No, I don't think she is dead.'

TONY: There used to be a place in the Valley called Nudie's – N-U-D-I-E-S.

JAMIE: *Sure. A country and western store.*

TONY: Well, yeah, it's country and western. An Iranian-Jewish guy – that's who Nudie was. Tiny little Jewish guy who got caught up with Southern Baptists. So that, uh, Roy Rogers and his wife, Dale Evans, and all these other big-time cowboys, if they wanted a Christian cowboy from wherever, that's where they went. So, that's the way it was. And in his shop –

JAMIE: *There were pictures.*

TONY: In a special section.

JAMIE: *Right.*

TONY: In there were all the dead.

JAMIE: *He had a little shrine?*

TONY: Yeah, all the dead. Only the dead. Outside were the living. And there was Nudie's picture too, on the outside, alive.

JAMIE: *Right, of course.*

TONY: I mean a whole slew of them. And I'd go out and see who had been moved from the outside to the inside.

JAMIE: [*laughs*] *Oh, great. Yeah.*

TONY: It went on after Nudie died. Sure enough, Nudie was in with the 'dead'.

JAMIE: *'Dead, not dead.' That's going to be the name of the autobiography.*

TONY: [*laughs*]

JAMIE: *Now, do you know that it was actually on Santa Monica Boulevard at the corner of La Cienega that you gave me the only piece of advice you've ever given me about show business.*

TONY: On where?

JAMIE: *Santa Monica Boulevard at the corner of La Cienega. There used to be a bowling alley. It started out as a bowling alley, it turned into a roller derby –*

TONY: Yeah, I know – I know the place you mean.

JAMIE: *We pulled up to that light, we were in some convertible of yours, some fabulous car you had, and you looked at me and said, 'Never let them shoot you with anything less than a fifty.' Then you drove off. And I just loved it, because it was so correct.*

TONY: So much part of our lives. You've told me that before.

JAMIE: *I just loved that.*

TONY: And it means a lot to me.

JAMIE: *You know what it did? It made me realize what I inherited from you.*

TONY: Right.

JAMIE: *Because I didn't really know you all that much growing up –*

TONY: Yeah.

JAMIE: *– it's not like I got it from watching you every day.*

TONY: Yeah, right.

JAMIE: *I inherited this from you. Genetically. The idea that this work is all encompassing. That it isn't –*

TONY: Right.

JAMIE: *– just performing.*

TONY: Yeah.

JAMIE: *That it is a knowledge.*

TONY: Oh?

JAMIE: *You're a photographer. I love to take pictures.*

TONY: Yeah, right.

JAMIE: *I love light. You love light.*

TONY: Yes.

JAMIE: *The pictures you took of us when we were babies – they're beautiful, Poppa, the light is always beautiful.*

TONY: Yes.

JAMIE: *The capturing of the light.*

TONY: Right.

JAMIE: *And what that bit of advice taught me was that you pay attention to the same aspects that I do.*

TONY: Yes.

JAMIE: *That you were not oblivious to the camera.*

TONY: No. No.

JAMIE: *That you were aware of what was going on around you at all times.*

TONY: Right. I was. Right from the beginning. The only thing that fucked me up was my family problems. When I first started in movies, my mother, my father and my kid brother moved out here three months later. I had to find a job for my father, a place for my mother, my crazy brother. On the one hand, I'm trying to balance that; on the other hand, I meet your mother, fall in love, and want to have a career. Then on top of that, I'm standing around waiting to see where the 50mm is going to be, or what size lens they're putting on, and in that unwritten book in my brain, I said, 'Don't ever let them shoot you full face, on a wide-angle lens, you'll end up looking like Dumbo.'

JAMIE: *[laughs]*

TONY: You know you, you'll end up looking like a mouse.

JAMIE: *[laughs]*

TONY: Don't ever do that. Whenever they'd put on a thirty-two, or even a twenty-two, I would go home. You could follow me with that lens. That lens was so wide you couldn't get out of the shot: you would do your scene, exit, start taking off your wardrobe, have a drink of coffee, take off your trousers, the hair person would come over to fix up your hair and it was all in the shot. [*laughs*] You know, you really had to get in your car to get out of that shot.

JAMIE: *What you've brought up is very important. Most people see somebody in the movies and they don't want to know what's going on in that person's life, which is yielding that work.*

TONY: Right.

JAMIE: *They just want to believe you're that guy looking cute, driving that car, smooth, scamming some chick, and being that guy in the movie. Whatever is going on in your personal life isn't important, and yet, you're dealing with an oppressive family –*

TONY: Right.

JAMIE: *– trying to make a relationship with this woman, and at the same time trying to love and enjoy your work and be funny in the part and great and all of those struggles –*

TONY: . . . at the same time.

JAMIE: *When John first asked me to participate in* Projections, *I thought, OK, I'm going to do* A Fish Called Wanda II *this summer. I'll write a journal. It's eight years later and I'm going back to England to do the sequel. I'll just write my thoughts and feelings. But many things started to happen that were very tough. One of which was a very, very dear friend of mine was critically ill with AIDS, and I had to leave him here and go over there to do a comedy – make this comedy film as well as taking my daughter out of school, and all of the dramas in my personal life – and I realized, you know, people say, 'Oh, I saw* A Fish Called Wanda. *Oh, it's so fabulous. You must have had the greatest time.'*

TONY: Yes, right.

JAMIE: *When I remember that time – what I remember of it – yes, the time was lovely, yes, we had some laughs, but I remember that my baby was six months old, and all I felt was guilt.*

There wasn't a day when I was at work – that first movie – when I didn't say, 'What am I doing? I have a baby at home.' Marilyn Monroe, in her last interview in Life *magazine, said about making movies: You're never allowed to have a cold. You're supposed to be an artist.*

TONY: Yeah.

JAMIE: *But you're never allowed to have a cold.*

TONY: Right, yeah, yeah, yeah.

JAMIE: *It's a business. If you have a cold, they say, 'Fuck you, show up to work.' You know, you have to get a doctor to say you're on your death bed before they won't let you come to work.*

TONY: And then when you do the scene, you hope your concentration is strong enough so that you're not thinking of your brother Bobby and what mental institution he should be in, or about calling your friend Nicky to go pick him up because he got busted on a bicycle. And there you are standing in front of Piper Laurie saying, 'Yonder lies the castle of my father.' I mean, how I did it, I'll never know. And I look at some of the films that I've made that they show on television . . .

JAMIE: *What was the one where you were on the lake? You were on a lake in a boat and there were a bunch of rich women. It was like you were a busboy, a waiter?*

TONY: Oh, yeah, that's *Mr Cory.*

JAMIE: *I loved it. That was good.*

TONY: *Mr Cory,* that was a good one. These pictures, *Sweet Smell of Success, The Defiant Ones,* the dramas where my intent had to be so clean – I was having fucking trouble with the woman I was married to at the time, the girl I was going with was giving me trouble. Another one said she was pregnant. This guy said I owed him five hundred bucks because he did something that he thought I wanted him to do. Then Edie Wasserman didn't invite me to their dinner party because she was pissed off at me because I wasn't talking to your mother. And there was an agent trying to steal me from MCA. I'm telling you, these were the facts that were going on. There was a producer's wife, Howard Koch's wife, who, if you didn't treat her like the princess she was, you'd never work for her husband. He never made me a presenter at the Academy Awards after he became the president of the Academy because of the day when I took you and your sister to the place where they have those horses. It was a Sunday – when I was busy on a picture I only got you guys on the weekend, and I was miserable, you know, feeling terribly unhappy. And she says, 'Hello, Tony.' And I said, 'Oh, hi, nice to see you.' I was distracted. The fact that I wasn't exuberant – 'Oh, my darling, am I happy to see you today' – was enough for her to cross me off her list. So, you see, these were all of the things that went on when they call you to work in the morning, and you look at the girl and say, 'Yonder lies the castle of my father, my darling. I'll get you some tea.' Oh, what charm in one section of your brain. In the other is your personal life, and at an additional level is the gyroscope. That's the mechanic. That's the genius. That's the engineer. That's the pilot. That's the astronaut. That's the scientist. That's the mathematician. That's the part of the brain that's guiding you across the room – taking you across the room, delicately pulling up your pants so that you don't look too much like a fool, walking you across the room very, very delicately and lying you down on a couch – that is the brain of the movie, the most important part in film-making. I don't give a fuck about anything else. How to get where you're going within the time allotted and, within the time allotted, give the emotion that is absolutely necessary in order for it to go to the next one. That's what you've got to do. And you'll do it, and the director will say, 'Cut. Um, I don't know, let's do it again.' And you know what he's talking about. You took an eighth of a second too long in the turning. I get it. You come in and so you turn a little quicker, so the scene comes down a little shorter. He looks at it, and he says, 'I like it. Cut. Print.' What you've done for him is given him a smooth transition, nothing clumsy, nothing that looks like you're being directed by the camera. That's why with every camera I used to put my arm around it, look at the lens, hoochie, coochie, touchie. I don't know, I just felt so perfect counting the distance. I sound like I'm fucking crazy. Like I'm in a nut house. I mean, there I am standing in the middle of the room, beautifully dressed, handsomely attired with everything going for me, on a yacht with this big beautiful fabulous blonde woman with the biggest pair of tits you've ever seen, you know, who's sticking her tongue down my throat to Calcutta. I tried to get me a hard on so that – uh – well, she thinks that's going to make the scene work. And there I am, flotsam and flitsom, and there we are, Cain and Abel, Mork and Mindy, right? That's what's going on. In a darkly lit room, press a button and the lights go on. Turn the radio on – there's no sound. There's a prop man touching two wires together, then the light on the radio dial brightens up and you know now the radio is on. And there's no music, there's nothing. It's all quiet. Nothing. And she starts swaying and dancing and coming up closer to you, and then closer to you, and then closer to you, and then finally comes the time for the kiss. The camera's here, she's there, you're there. She's the woman. Her name is Marilyn, so you don't want to, in any way, be ungentlemanly, number one, and number two, she deserves the right for her face to be seen and if the camera is there, I can't swap it way over this way. I've got to manoeuvre my body in the most delicate manner, twisting it this way so that she's kissing here and you're able to see her completely, not the back of her head. Now what the fuck did I just go through with you? Intelligence. Dumb people can't do that. You couldn't work in movies if you couldn't do that. You could be the most beautiful person in the world, the most emotional person in the world, the finest actor that has ever lived in the world. You could be able to do emotions that would tear down brick shit houses. But if you don't where the fuck to stand, if you don't have a relationship to the objects around you, then forget it.

JAMIE: *You know the person who says, 'Let's do it again,' and doesn't really say much to you, but you know what he or she wants, then you do it and they go, 'Great, print'? Is there any-*

body that you can think of who really was great – an unbeliev-
ably great director – because I've not heard you talk about that.
TONY: I don't have a lot of respect for most of them and I don't
give a fuck what I say. I'm telling you, out of the 107 movies,
there may be three guys out of 107 that I've worked with who
I thought had some knowledge of the camera and how it should
be used – one of them was Billy Wilder. That doesn't make him
a good director – because he doesn't direct you, he casts you
properly in a film. If he casts you right in the part, then you're
going to be great in the part. Dick Quine is the most delicate,
elegant film director I have ever known. I loved him. He and
Blake Edwards were buddy-buddy. Once, Dick Quine says to
me, 'You know what the definition of "success" is?' I says,
'What?' He says, 'To be doing better than your best friend.'
Took my fucking breath away. These two guys, Edwards and
Quine, were alternating, right? He's directing, writing, directing. I knew them both in those early days.

Nic Roeg – untouchable. His material – that's what makes him
so odd. He's like a half a dozen guys who know, just by some little delicacy, how to give you confidence. I had that once or twice
with Blake Edwards, but no more than that, and I made four or
five pictures with him, so I don't put him in that category.

Carol Reed. *Trapeze*. Ooh, sweet, fabulous film director.
English directors – I found the English were more sensitive. I
don't know why. Maybe it's because it's such a small country
and it makes everybody so introspective, throws everybody
inside each other. That's why the Irish grow great moustaches
and the English wear those beautiful clothes – they've got to do
something to express themselves. If they were living in Wichita,
Kansas, they'd schlep around with their Levi's and a hat, dirty
boots, and they wouldn't mind it. But in England, in those tidy
little streets, everybody's got to have his own little funny thing
going on.

JAMIE: *You filmed in England a lot.*
TONY: Yeah.

JAMIE: *You lived in England.*

TONY: I lived in England maybe a total of six or seven years. You know, my sweet daughter, out of 107 films, I would say almost seventy of them were made in Europe. I would work all over. And Lew was the one who organized all of that.

JAMIE: *Wasserman? Your agent?*

TONY: Yes. He said these foreign countries would pray to Allah: 'Please send me a movie star for next month's movie.' And who did they pray to? To God. Lew Wasserman. MCA. Got him on the horn. 'Mr. Wasserman – I'm – listen –' 'Yeah, hun. What is it about?' As an introduction, he said, 'When can you get a script here?' 'I'll have it to you on Monday.' And he says, 'Would you like Tony Curtis?' 'Tony Curtis! You can get me Tony Curtis?' He says, 'Uh, uh, when are you supposed to start?' He says, 'In October.' 'He will be available. You send the material. If he likes the script then we'll talk deal.' He says, 'I'll give you whatever he sends you.' 'We'll talk deal slowly that way.' Hang up the fucking phone. He always gave me the information the day he'd get it. That's why I love Lew. He also gave me a little hope, you know? He didn't hold back. And four or three weeks later I'm in a gin joint somewhere, or on a dance floor, and a girl says, 'Oh, you're going to do a picture with my boyfriend, the producer?' I said, 'I am? What picture is that?' 'Oh, you know, the one where you capture the girl and bring –' There was no such story, you know. Because it wasn't true unless I heard it from Lew Wasserman.

JAMIE: *Hmm.*

TONY: I love talking to you like this. I hope you don't mind.

JAMIE: *I knew this would be good.*

TONY: Uh, I'm enjoying it. And so it was Lew, that's the way it was done. In that way I went to every country: Italy, Greece, Turkey –

JAMIE: *France?*

TONY: France, definitely France – Austria, Hungary, part of Poland for some exteriors, all the Scandinavian countries for *The Vikings.* All of England and then some. Then when I finished all of that, I did North Africa and went into Egypt, then went to Israel, worked in the Red Sea, the Dead Sea, the Live Sea, the Up Yours sea. There wasn't a sea I didn't work in.

JAMIE: *I love the look on your face in* Taras Bulba, *when they're about to chop your arm off.*

TONY: *The Vikings* was the one movie that took seven countries to make.

JAMIE: *And would you travel by plane?*

TONY: Well, in those days I hated planes, so I used to go by boat, and when I did *Taras Bulba*, they got so fucking mad at me, UA. This is Argentina. This is the other end of the world. If there was a train that could do it, but there are no trains. You're going to have to go by boat, train, then take a ferry, and then there's a little train that links up to another big train that's got to go twelve hundred miles inside the country to get you to the picture. I says, 'I'm going by train.' So I went by train. I travelled always on the ground. Or by boat. I was on the *Queen Mary*. I was on the *Ile de France* and the sister of the *Andrea Doria*, the *Christopher Colombo*, a beautiful Italian ship, on the *America*, on the two Elizabeths. With forty-four pieces of luggage. And you guys – whatever batch was around at the time.

JAMIE: *I was in the first batch.*

TONY: With your mother everything was itemized: wig, buckle, knee pad –

JAMIE: [*laughter*]

TONY: – the eyeglasses – where are the eyeglasses? I – but – but – but – check the eyeglasses. Which ones are you talking about? The eyeglasses we need for Tony.

JAMIE: [*laughter*] *I love her. She is so good. You know why? She gave it to me. It's a gift. It is a gift from her to me. My friends hire me to move them into new houses –*

TONY: You've got it.

JAMIE: *– because I do it so well.*

TONY: You got it. And when we first were married I was crazy. Uh, I'm going to tell you a story. We got to LA, we were living on Wilshire Boulevard where one of these big high rises are now. We had this nice little apartment, clean as a whistle – smooth. We were just back from our honeymoon, we're settling in and getting ready to work. I was lying on the couch reading the paper, and I said, 'Darling, may I have a glass of water?' She said, 'Sweetheart, of course.' I went back to the paper. And while I'm reading, she ran and she rinsed out a glass, put water and some ice in it, brought it and put it on the glass table right in front of me. I said, 'Thank you, my dear.' She says, 'Oh, please, my love.' And I went back to reading the paper. Then I took a sip of the water – hmm, delicious – put it back down on the table. I opened a page, turned a page, looked at both sides of the page. I went back and the fucking glass was gone. And it was wiped dry. Had I knocked it down? She's going to fucking kill me.

The Black Shield of Falworth: Tony Curtis with Janet Leigh.

JAMIE: [*laughing*]

TONY: Ja – Ja – Janet? Did – uh – I knock the water over? She said, 'No, darling, I thought you were done.' [*both laughing*]

JAMIE: *I love her. It's just good.*

TONY: It was her compulsiveness that sometimes used to drive me crazy. But I couldn't understand where it came from, you know? And so once her mother said, 'When Janet was a little girl, she went away to camp.'

JAMIE: [*laughs*]

TONY: 'And she packed herself. And that suitcase was packed perfectly. Stockings rolled up here. Toothbrush. Paper. Underwear. And I instantly saw that it looked exactly like the inside of your body. Liver. Gallstones. Oesophagus. Lungs. Everything exactly where it belonged.' And that's –

JAMIE: – *That's Momma. Everything is where it belongs.*

TONY: And that's Momma – Mommie dearest, did I tell you. It's one of the most endearing qualities about her.

JAMIE: *Oh, it's lovely.*

TONY: And that's what travelling was like in those days, you know. It took a little longer, right? But you know, they'd say, 'Where you been?' 'Oh, I went to London, did a picture, now I'm back. Great.' Wait a minute. It's not that easy. You got to get passports. Somebody gives you a job. Somebody's got to go scout ahead and find a place where you're going to stay. When are you leaving? When does the picture start? Where do you do the wardrobe? I mean, you know, there are a hundred and fifty questions in that big, 'Where were you?' Well, I went to London, did a movie, and I'm back. The experiences you are having now, OK? Every part of your body has been through this London trip, you can write a book about it.

JAMIE: *Oh, absolutely.*

TONY: Absolutely.

JAMIE: *My impression of you is somebody who knows how to put things, objects in a room, in just that perfect place – to be able to take somebody's business card and stick it in a lamp in a way that is absolutely right. I also have this impression of you as a great businessman, because you always talked about the business side. I'm a dreadful businesswoman. I'm a technical actor, but I'm a dreadful businesswoman. So I'm just curious as to how that business acumen was developed. Did you go to somebody for advice, or did you just figure it out?*

TONY: I learned it step by step. I learned it by experience and by what was meant by commitment: a shake of a hand, a paper commitment, a contract, taking care of everything – Wait a minute, he didn't say anything about six weeks' location in Utah. He says he's got this picture he wants to do, but he never mentioned that. Well, that's got to be included too. You got to include everything involved with making a picture. And I learned early, and I learned under the auspices of Lew Wasserman, because when he drew up a contract for me, I could see I was in good hands. I wasn't in good hands for the first three or four years I was in the business. Your mother and I broke our ass, but we were always almost dead broke, and her father was one of her advisors.

Morgan Marie was another advisor, somebody at Blum was another advisor, these are business advisors that took a percentage of your salary, right? And they were the ones that were, if not stealing, then making mad, stupid decisions about where to put the money. And so I decided – I didn't even decide. I was just looking and listening and saying, 'Um, no, I – I don't want to buy that house.' 'Why don't you want to buy it?' I didn't want to buy a house down in a valley with a mountain running down so when it rains the water runs down into your house. You can't get up your driveway; you can't go anywhere. Put the house high. Let the driveway come down. Let the house sit on its own bedrock.

JAMIE: *But for a long time, you were buying premier properties and selling them for profit. I mean, you really were a businessman.*

TONY: Yeah, I was doing that.

JAMIE: *Did you ever make money from movies? Besides your salary? Profit participation?*

TONY: No, no. They gave you nothing then. I get it now.

JAMIE: *In residuals.*

TONY: Because now they can't steal it from me. Now it's too late.

JAMIE: *Right.*

TONY: Now those pictures are out.

JAMIE: *But, then, I mean, when you hear about big movie stars owning 10 per cent of the gross, 20 per cent of the gross.*

TONY: Yeah, there may be a number. Now the businessman, when he talks, you got to define what you mean by gross; what they mean by gross.

JAMIE: *First dollar.*

TONY: See they'll get first dollar, but it's first dollar after what? After negative cost? After double negative? After prints, advertising, then double negative? Then the distributor takes out his piece, then you get from the first dollar?

JAMIE: *But the definitions now for the big movie stars are pretty clear.*

TONY: When they're making fortunes.

JAMIE: *Oh, they're making fortunes.*

TONY: It was different then. I was a gun for hire, but I had my percentage. I still have that. You know, I have thirty-four movies that I collect on. I'm the only one still collecting on *Some Like It Hot*. Billy Wilder sold his. From *Some Like It Hot* I made two and a half million dollars.

JAMIE: *You know, some people didn't reap the rewards –*

TONY: *Taras Bulba, Trapeze, The Great Race, Sweet Smell of Success, The Defiant Ones*, all the United Artists movies. I had a piece of them, of the action; I had 5, 7 to 10 per cent of the gross of those films. And that was from the first dollar.

JAMIE: *Right.*

TONY: Some of it went to pay off the costs of the publicity, which was always a big, touchy point –

JAMIE: *Right.*

TONY: – but without that, I got a gross position. I was the only one that was getting it. Jack Lemmon didn't get a penny from *Some Like It Hot.*

JAMIE: *Really?*

TONY: Not a penny. He got a salary, but no points. When we did *The Great Race*, Jack Warner said he wouldn't make the movie unless I was in it. Blake Edwards and Jack were all teamed up, ready to go, but he just wouldn't do it. He said, 'It's no movie without Tony. It's no movie without these two guys.' So I got them raises. And we ended up with a percentage of it, which we still collect money on. So there are some thirty-odd movies that I own. Perhaps this will be of interest to you, the business end of it, you know. When *Some Like It Hot* was put together, it was put together as a $2 million production, of which I was given 5½ per cent of the gross, Marilyn got 10 per cent of the gross, that's fifteen and a half – the studio wouldn't give you any more than that. United Artists owned the movie in distribution. So a chunk of money comes in every so often – some comes in for $3,000, some comes in for 35 and 40 grand. I mean, there's a huge amount of money that I'm able to accrue each year without doing anything, and that's because of Lew Wasserman's ability to get me a percentage of the gross. I did a movie called *Captain Newman* with Gregory Peck where I'm an owner, because I was under contract to Universal and they gave me that piece of the action to get me to work with Gregory Peck. With *Some Like It Hot*, Marilyn and I owned the movie. She owned ten. I owned five and a half. We were paid two-fifty each, salary. $250,000 against 10 and 5½ per cent of the gross after the picture breaks even. The picture cost $2 million to make. It broke even in a week and a half, and started generating money. And they tried to steal some of it. Then the agency jumped in and stopped it. There we go. We were getting our residual cheques. And whenever they sent to Marilyn, they sent to me. So she always knew and I always knew exactly what we were getting, because we would get the same printouts. Marilyn dies and leaves her percentage of *Some Like It Hot* to the Actors Studio.

JAMIE: *Lee Strasberg? Yeah.*

TONY: Right. They turn around almost immediately and sell it to an attorney for a chunk of dough. She leaves it to them, and they turn around and they sell it to this attorney that I happened to know, only because we're in business together. So every time I get a cheque for *Some Like It Hot*, I know that this attorney is getting that money. Billy Wilder sold his interest. One day he walked away with, what, $4 million? He sold eight of his movies.

JAMIE: *Hold this thought. I'm just getting a tape.*

TONY: Go ahead.

JAMIE: *Just let me show you how much Janet Leigh's daughter I am, look – extra batteries.*

TONY: [*loud laughing*]

JAMIE: *Extra tape. Now I have to pee.*

TONY: Go ahead, Honey.

JAMIE: *It's dark.*

TONY: The light's in there somewhere.

JAMIE: *It's a black hole.*

TONY: [*to the tape machine*, sotto voce] Oh, dear. She's in the bathroom. She's the cutest kid I've ever seen in my life. I love her. I love talking to her. She makes me feel like a kid.

JAMIE: [*coming back in*] *It's fine. Let me just change the tape. Where were we?*

TONY: We were talking about gross percentages.

JAMIE: *What have you ended up with from being an actor in the movies after all these years? How many years?*

TONY: Forty-five years now. Since 1948–'58, '68, '78, '88, '98 would be fifty years. It's '95 now?

JAMIE: *In 1998 it will be fifty years you've been in the movie business?*

TONY: Yes.

JAMIE: *Fuck. That's fabulous.*

TONY: Incredible.

JAMIE: *Isn't it great?*

TONY: Fifty years. Three years from now. And I haven't got a penny of the money I earned in those years. It all was used to live on. I'm doing great because of these monies from real estate, but money from films – a chunk of that salary never ended up in the savings account; it always ended up for my daily living expenses.

JAMIE: *But my question is: what have the movies meant to you? I mean, truly – I'm not being facetious.*

TONY: Movies – movies have given me the privilege to be an aristocrat, to be the prince. That's what it's given me. It gets me great tables at restaurants, beautiful cars to drive around in, a lovely woman to take out to dinner, to sit around and talk with some of the most intelligent brains that are around, to be recognized everywhere, to be loved by so many people, to lie here in bed, turn on the television, and there I am. Yes, and there I am. Some nights I turn on the television, and it's a movie made by somebody else, and they've got a film clip of me in the movie. There's a movie out called *Clueless*. In it they got two shots of me from *Spartacus*. [*laughs*] I love it. I've always loved that part of it. You know, Jamie, I would never tell you differently. Always loved that part of it. The part that I didn't like, that I wasn't able to handle was the enemies that I found in this town; the out and out hate and anger that I felt from people. When I was married to your mother, we were almost shunned by certain groups in this town, and your mother, who was very social (and I was too) – we were stunned that we were not invited to these places. We were so fucking popular. We were so famous. We had everything. Jamie, we had everything, your mother and I. When we got married, when we hit, and those magazines carried us, right after us were Eddie Fisher and Debbie Reynolds. They could have been our cook and butler for all the attention they got. I mean, it was incredible. That's what it was. And life was easy. I was fucked up. I had this terrible family problem that I was dragging with me everywhere I went. It was like – like Ebenezer Scrooge in the movie where you see his partner, Marley, dragging those chains. That's the way I felt. I had a horrible time. There were years that I was so unhappy; I couldn't shake that part of it. And then your mother and I started having trouble. There was so much envy in this town. I could feel it, I could see it. I was at a party – Charlie Feldman gave a party, and Monty Clift was there, and I just was starting. I think he had just started too. I don't know if he was ahead of me or not. And I was the king of the fucking city. And this guy gets up at this dinner table and says, 'Look at her. She thinks she's the king. Can you match her looks with mine?' Now, I mean I never heard such overt anger at someone else. And that was Monty Clift.

JAMIE: *Talking about who?*

TONY: Me.

JAMIE: *Oh, he called you a her?*

TONY: Yes, and right there I started to cry sitting at the table. People laughed. I fucking wept. I hated him from then on in. He embarrassed me. I didn't have any social graces. I came out of New York City, right out of that pot, went into the Navy, came right out of the Navy, went into an acting school, right out of that, and there I am, thrown into Hollywood, sitting next to Janet Leigh, David Selznick – I've got to watch very carefully who picks up what knife where – I'm not joking now, I'm telling you the truth – where to put the napkin. Now, every now and then, I look at your mother across the table. She'd look at me and I'd go, 'Oh really? Ha ha hoo, oh, charming. No, no, no champagne for me, thank you.' These are the parties we had to go to, and then the next morning I had to be up at five-thirty or six to go to work. There I was with these fucking angry people, you know? Kirk Douglas comes up to me at a party one night. I'm standing there with Burt Lancaster. This is right after *Trapeze*. He says, 'You think you're pretty good, don't you, you little prick.' I didn't know what to say to these people. And that was no joke. He didn't do it as a joke. He meant it. That frightened me a lot. And then on top of that, I had to go on the set in the morning and work with some actors who really hated my guts. Who'd do anything but fucking kill me. Audie Murphy was one. I did a Western with him. I played a minor role in it. But I was getting all the action by then. By that time every movie magazine had my picture on the cover and I was getting third, fourth, fifth billing in this movie, and by then nobody gave a shit about Audie Murphy. They'd loosen the saddle, the stirrups underneath, so that when I took off, the saddle would slide off and I would slide off with it. They picked up the tail of my horse and shoved a stick with kerosene soaked in it right up its ass and pulled it out. That fucking horse would go crazy with me on it. Camera rolling. Action. And we'd take off. I mean, I had to fight for my life out there.

JAMIE: *Oh, they were envious, but it wasn't just because you were beautiful, Poppa.*

TONY: I don't know what it was.

JAMIE: *It's because you were you. It was because you can't combine somebody who's beautiful with somebody with great charm. It just isn't found. It's rare. And, you have it in spades. You had that and they didn't.*

TONY: I was labelled the worst fucking actor that ever came down the pike since day one. '[*heavy Brooklyn accent*] Hey, hey, Charlie! Come over here and take a look at Willie here on the tenth floor.' Everybody was doing that accent. They said that was my accent. Meanwhile, every motherfucker grew his hair long, put a lot of pomade in it, curled it in the front, and there were eight hundred Tony Curtises roaming the city.

JAMIE: *But you had comedy. You can make people laugh. You can make fun of yourself.*

TONY: I didn't even know that.

JAMIE: *You didn't?*

TONY: I didn't.

JAMIE: *And when did you figure that out?*

TONY: I didn't figure it out for a very long time.

JAMIE: *Really?*

TONY: A very long time.

JAMIE: *Did somebody help you figure it out?*

TONY: No, it just slowly came to me. I began to invent little things on the set that kind of tickled me. I thought they would be funny.

JAMIE: *And they got a nice reaction?*

TONY: Yeah, right. I'll make a confession to you. When I did *Some Like It Hot* I held back a lot, you know? I didn't want to overwhelm Jack Lemmon. I didn't want to overwhelm Marilyn. I didn't want them to be mad at me. I didn't want them to be angry on the set or envious or anything. Now this may be the most egotistical thing anybody has ever said in their lives. Billy Wilder catered to Jack Lemmon all through the whole film. And to Marilyn. Those were his – what would one call it? – priorities, you know, not me. I don't mind. I mean, I have moments in that movie that are as good as anybody's moments anywhere in the whole world, and they're not from Billy Wilder. The Cary Grant piece was my idea, and it's so perfect because today nobody knows who Cary Grant is any more. All of a sudden, there's a guy acting like some New York Englishman, or what he thinks is a New Yorker's fancy schmancy. You know, it's funny, now, talking about him like that. See, the very thing we talked about at the beginning is now coming out. All of the intricacies of making the movie is coming through now, and the movie still remains the ebullient, floating beauty that it is when you turn on the television set or you go to the movie theatre – scene by scene, the beautiful music, people looking at each other intensely. It takes a bit of doing. You can't be faint hearted and do it. You can't be faint hearted when you take a beautiful bosomy woman that you just met four days earlier and have this big love scene and you're swapping spits and – uh – tits are pressing against tits, and then at the end of the day, say, 'Doll, I liked what we did today.' She says, 'Yeah, I do too, I thought it was a little different or it had a little different air.' How do you do that? It's not easy, you know? It's not easy. You're dealing with every part of you when you look at somebody in a moment of peak – in a moment of love – in a moment of concern. 'Oh, maybe I'll fake her out by

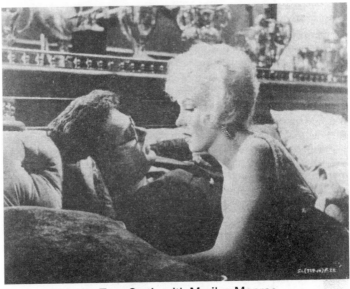

Some Like It Hot: Tony Curtis with Marilyn Monroe

touching her hair a little bit. Ha ha.' One of your charming smiles. [*laughs*] Meanwhile the audience is still figuring: did she or didn't she? That's got to be on the fucking screen. You can't do that any other way. I remember one director once in a movie, I don't remember where it was. Uh, I came into the movie and he said, 'Tony, this is your brother. This is your brother's wife. You know she wants you. And you're not sure you can hold out too long, so when you see her, I want to see in your face that this is true and then when you go by your brother, I don't want your brother to even have an inkling of what it is.' I said, 'Does that mean you want me to come in faster or slower?'
JAMIE: *We both subscribe to the same craft.*
TONY: Hey, hey.

JAMIE: *We think about it. We're always thinking.*

TONY: Always.

JAMIE: *Our antennae are always out there.*

TONY: We don't need direction any more.

JAMIE: *Oh.*

TONY: You know, what you accomplished in *True Lies* was an extraordinary performance on your part. You went the range of comedy from Mae West, to Carol Lombard, all the way through to Lucille Ball. The whole spectrum was in there. Every bit of it. You didn't give a motherfucker a chance. There isn't a girl in this town that could ever, ever repay you for what you showed them in that movie: how to play with the guys and win.

See, it's easy to play certain beats. The other day on television I saw the movie where I played Ira Hayes, the Indian boy who raised the flag on Iwo Jima. I love that movie, I do a good job. It was such an intense and wonderful movie, and nobody fucking ever heard of it. Now, they're playing it on air, on GMC, AMC, and I'm getting calls from all over the place. So, you see, I'm lucky. I'm lucky. You know why? Because while I'm sitting here talking to you, I'm reaching in my bag here, and I'm coming up with a movie called *No Room for the Groom.* You ain't seen that one yet.

JAMIE: *No.*

TONY: That's a twenty-year wait.

JAMIE: *What's the next one?*

TONY: *The Kansas Raiders.* Oh, no, no, no, no, no, you ain't going to see it, no way, my dear. So there's a whole slew of stuff. A hundred and seven movies, some odd pieces in there – in forty-seven years – and with it, families, great disappointments, terrible disappointments, ending up an alcoholic drug-abused person. At a period of time when I could have been more useful, I wasn't. The pictures that I wanted to do, I wasn't getting. Lew Wasserman wasn't my agent any more. I shouldn't talk like this. Now all of a sudden I'm in a conversation about what I never had.

JAMIE: *That's not how it will be perceived.*

TONY: Listen, nobody's got it better than me now. Nobody. I don't know any guy my age, in his seventies, who's doing the work I do, who does it any better if they can stand up. I'm not going to die. You know that story? A prostitute dies and they decide to give her a funeral. There's one girl there bawling her eyes out who knew her all those years, just crying and crying, and another girl on the other side starts to cry too. She says, 'Oh, Alice is gone – she's –' 'Well, you didn't know Alice like I did. Alice, she was one of the great people of our time.' And a voice in the back says, 'You know, she was the greatest cocksucker in our place.' And the one that knew her for years says, 'Ah, you had to wait till she died before you said something nice about her.' [*laughs*]

JAMIE: [*laughing*] *Thanks, Dad*

Jamie Lee Curtis with Janet Leigh (photo by Jamie Lee Curtis).

3 Jeanette Helen

Janet Leigh talks to Jamie Lee Curtis

JAMIE LEE CURTIS: *Hello, Jeannette Helen.*

JANET LEIGH: Jeannette Helen Morrison, yes.

JLC: *How long have I called you Jeannette Helen?*

JL: Since you were old enough to know what my real name was.

JLC: *Why do you think I call you Jeannette Helen?*

JL: I don't know. Instead of calling me Mom, it's more like you're saying 'I know who you are, we're kind of on the same level, we're more like friends than like mother-daughter'.

JLC: *What's interesting to me is that I also refer to you as Janet Leigh.*

JL: I know.

JLC: *And Jeannette Helen. But it's very specific when I refer to you as Jeannette Helen and when I refer to you as Janet Leigh. To the lay person, of course, hearing that I would ever refer to you as Janet Leigh would be kind of odd. But I think it's because I recognize very clearly that something happened to you in your life at some point and you truly changed your name. Both you and Dad changed your names. You became a different person. Now, that's not saying that internally you became a different person.*

JL: Well, when I wrote my autobiography I started to write it in the third person. I referred to Jeannette Helen Morrison as 'she'. But when I got to the part in my life where I signed a contract at MGM and got the new name, I started to write 'I'.

JLC: *Well, the way I look at it is that I was raised in Los Angeles, and I was raised –*

JL: Surrounded by this business.

JLC: *Yes, surrounded by this business, but also in very comfortable circumstances, and obviously you weren't. And I think that Jeannette Morrison has stayed with you throughout your career. I mean, a lot of people know you as Janet Leigh, and revere you as Janet Leigh; men lust for you as Janet Leigh and women have great admiration for you as Janet Leigh. But my truest admiration for you is as Jeannette Morrison because I think that the mind-fuck – excuse my French – of that experience is so profound. Since 1946 you have navigated your way through show business from a place that most people don't realize you've come from. So just briefly tell me how it began: how old you were, where you were living, and how you came to be discovered by Norma Shearer. Where were you raised as a child?*

JL: I was raised in the small town of Merced and then Stockton, and then back to Merced and then back again to Stockton. My parents were very young; we were very poor, and it was not an easy life for them. There were happy times, there were happy family times, but it was always wanting – I mean, always needing – never knowing if we'd have ten cents to go down and buy two eggs for dinner.

JLC: *You were that destitute?*

JL: At times, yeah.

JLC: *And what did your dad do?*

JL: Well, a lot of different things. He worked in an electrical store – Mr Grider's electrical store – for many years –

JLC: *As a salesman?*

JL: A salesman.

JLC: *Right. So it was minimum wage.*

JL: It was during the Depression – but I think he got ten dollars a week.

JLC: *So you had no money.*

JL: We never owned a house; we always rented, usually an apartment. When I went to college, both my mom and dad worked all the time, and I worked whenever I could – you know, after school and on Saturday and during the summers – to save money. It was their dream and mine that I'd go to college. It was a state school, but it was a college. And that was very important to them – and to me – because neither of them had gone to college. I had come too early, and they never had a chance to get further schooling. I think that always lay heavy on them because they weren't able to move as far ahead as I think they could have – which is a shame. There was great potential there that wasn't ever able to materialize.

JLC: *OK, go on.*

JL: Well, anyway, when I was eighteen and a senior in college (I went through school very quickly – I graduated from high school in three and a half years) I got married. Mom and Dad had never been free, so they just took off. They went up and got a job at the Sugarbowl Ski Lodge in northern California. They had never seen snow. Daddy was the assistant desk clerk. Mom was a waitress, and doubled as a maid sometimes. So my husband Stan and I went up to see them, and Daddy took a picture of me in the snow, and he put it in his little cubicle. And Norma Shearer always spent the month of February at this particular lodge. She saw the picture and said, 'May I bring it back to Hollywood?' My dad said, 'Of course.' She had eight by tens made. She had dinner with one of the MGM executives, and the photo ended up in the hands of Mr Lew Wasserman at MCA, who gave it to a Lewis Green who was the head of the new talent department. He wrote me a letter. Meanwhile, Stan and I had come to Los Angeles because he had had a band in college – it was a good band – and he wanted to go for the big time. We sold everything that we had, he took out a $10,000 GI loan, and we went to Los Angeles. He got a band together which was very good. The man at MCA came to hear the band and was very impressed. But we didn't know that it was the end of the big band era.

JLC: *But when did they call you?*

JL: Well, the letter was written to Stockton, but was forwarded to this hotel I was staying at in downtown LA. It said, 'We would like to see you if you are ever in the vicinity. Please call Lewis Green at MCA.' I called. I thought it was a joke. And it was MCA. I made an appointment for the next day. The day after, he took me to MGM and that afternoon I signed a contract, a seven-year contract, but with three-month options for them. Then they took me to Miss Burns – you know, our Lillian, Mrs Lillian Burns Sidney – and she gave me a scene to read from *Thirty Seconds Over Tokyo*. I came back the next week, read it with her. She called in the director and producer of *The Romance of Rosy Ridge* because they were looking for this young, dumb, innocent, naïve mountain girl, and . . .

JLC: *. . . they found her.*

JL: They found her in Jeannette Helen.

LC: *Do you remember who your first phone call was to when you got the job? Where were you when you found out you actually got it?*

JL: Well, OK. They told me I was going to do a screen test.

JLC: *Who did you do the test with?*

JL: With Lena Royal, who played the mother. Roy Rowland directed. And it was about ten days after I did the test . . .

JLC: *That's lot of time.*

JL: Well, they had to edit it.

JLC: *I understand.*

JL: But I didn't know that. And so I really thought that that was it, because in my mind I didn't know about having to cut it together. What do I know about that? I thought all they did was they took it home that night and looked at it.

JLC: *Right. So then you just felt that they probably looked at it and you weren't going to get it.*

JL: Yeah. And I had a lesson with Miss Burns, and I was waiting in the little anteroom – her office was in the back – and I was early. I was always early. It was just fun to sit there and watch people come in and out. And I had to go to the ladies room, so I went, and I'm washing my hands and I hear some-body pounding on the door. It's Harry Friedman, my agent. He said, Jeannette, are you in there? Jeannette? Jeannette? I said, Harry, what are you doing? I'm in the ladies room. He burst in the door, got my hand, ran back to Lillian's office, and the door's open and Lillian's there, and Jack Cummings is there and Roy Rowland is there and Harry dragged me into the room and sits me down, and says, you've got the picture!

JLC: *Ah.*

JL: I started to cry. I've got goose bumps right now. I'll never forget it as long as I live; every time I go by Lillian's picture in my dressing room, I think of that day.

JLC: *Do you remember who you called first?*

JL: Well, I didn't get a chance at that moment. The first thing they did was bring me to wardrobe. And after I got back from wardrobe I went to Miss Burns's office and I called my husband, Stan, at my aunt's house, and then I called Mom and Dad. That's when Stan and I lived in the back of their garage. It was their laundry room, but it was big enough so that we could get a bed in there.

JLC: *Do you remember what you said?*

JL: I just said – I'm going to be in a movie.

JLC: *And all because of Norma Shearer? Did you ever meet her?*

JL: I met her after, yeah – I hadn't before then. I had done the test and Mr Mayer decided to go with the new kid. You know, it was like the miracle of all miracles, and when Norma Shearer heard about this, she came on the lot to pose for pictures with Van Johnson and me. That's the one I have upstairs. And that was the first time I ever met her.

JLC: *And Van Johnson is the equivalent today of whom? Tom Hanks?*

JL: Tom Hanks. Tom Cruise. He was the highest-paid actor in Hollywood. He was number one. He could have had anyone in Hollywood, so for him to agree –

JLC: *But I'm still trying to find out where Jeannette Helen is in all this.*

JL: Jeannette Helen never left.

JLC: *I know she didn't. That's why I call you Jeannette Helen.*

JL: Yeah.

JLC: *So I'm now Jeannette Helen Morrison, being told I'm going to act with Van Johnson –*

JL: You know one thing, Jamie? I didn't know enough to be scared, to be nervous.

JLC: *That makes sense.*

JL: I mean, it was such a fairy story, it was almost unreal. I didn't know that they had scheduled some of the harder scenes, so that if I hadn't cut it they would have replaced me just like that. But I didn't know that. I didn't know the workings of anything.

JLC: *How quickly did your marriage break up?*

JL: Well, it was broken up before we ever got married, but it was a year and a half after I was discovered.

JLC: *I think that one of the hardest things – and I'll refer to Tony as well because there are similarities between your stories in the sense that both of your backgrounds were meagre – was that you were both discovered and so were both thrust into a new world. You were given new names, and I find that fascinating because, of course, I wasn't. I was born into this world. I kept my name. I have always been Jamie Curtis.*

JL: Right.

JLC: *And so I'm fascinated with this idea of you being somebody else. And the reason I'm bringing it up is because the pulls on you from your old life must have been profound. The pulls from your parents, for instance. I'd like to talk a little about your parents, about how your success affected them. From* The Romance of Rosy Ridge, *your career escalated pretty fast.*

JL: Right.

JLC: *From that beginning to when you were at the top of your game – how many years is that?*

The Romance of Rosy Ridge: Janet Leigh with Van Johnson.

JL: I'm just trying to think. In *Little Women* I was billed above the title.

JLC: *Right.*

JL: And that was my sixth picture in two years.

JLC: *In just two years, OK. I'm interested in the effect it had on your relationship with your family, the responsibility you started to feel for them, and on your marriage, because I know the pull of Hollywood, the pull of people saying come on, come to this party, come here, come; the literal suck, if you will, of show business into that world is profound and very powerful.*

JL: Let me say one thing here, Jamie: you must understand that Hollywood when I entered it was not the Hollywood you entered.

JLC: *I know that.*

JL: So the scrutiny, the pull, as you say, of PR – I can't even give you the percentage of what it is today as compared to what it was then. The approach to personal lives was much different from the approach today. It seems to me that today they try to tear you down, but when I started they were trying to build you up.

JLC: *Right.*

JL: And I think that had a tremendously different effect.

JLC: *How did it feel when you started making more money than your parents?*

JL: I was making more money than my parents when I started at the studio.

JLC: *That's my point.*

JL: Fifty a week.

JLC: *From the moment the changeover from Jeannette Morrison to Janet Leigh began, was there the pressure to feel responsible for your parents?*

JL: Well, I just felt so grateful that I had something I could share with them, something that could help them, that we could have a better life. It isn't like I said, well, now I have to take care of them, you know, because Dad worked. The problem with Stan was that he never worked.

JLC: *Right.*

JL: And I just lost respect for him. He was perfectly willing to be Mr Janet Leigh, and that bothered me tremendously. It wouldn't have mattered if he'd worked and earned twenty dollars a week, I would have had respect for that.

JLC: *Had you been a fan of the movies?*

JL: Always.

JLC: *Who were your favourites?*

JL: Oh golly, Spencer Tracy and Katherine Hepburn and Judy Garland and, oh, before that even. I just loved the movies.

Mom and Dad always put me in the movie house on Saturday and Sunday so that they'd have free time in the afternoon and evening.

JLC: *It was a baby-sitter.*

JL: Absolutely. I lived for the movies: I travelled all over the world, I wore beautiful gowns. It was the dream world of everyone's life. You have to realize that there was no other form of visual entertainment. Yet I never thought that I'd be in it.

JLC: *When your marriage broke up and you were newly under contract and making movies – you know, there's always the new kid on the block, there's always that rush of excitement, women want to have a new friend, men . . .*

JL: . . . want to have a new girl.

JLC: *It goes without saying that you were renowned as a great beauty. So tell me a little about what that felt like. Where did you live? I don't know any of this part of you.*

JL: Stan had borrowed money from the government – you know, his GI loan – and he'd also borrowed money from his parents. Well, when we separated, since I was the only one who was making any money I assumed the government debt because I didn't want to owe anything. It's always been this way with me because I remember from my childhood living with my dad's next week's salary already spent.

JLC: *I understand.*

JL: I hate debt. I don't want to buy anything unless I can pay for it – and that's obviously where it stems from. That reminds me of that funny story with Hedda Hopper. Do you remember?

JLC: *Hedda Hopper, no, but tell me anything you want to.*

JL: Well, I lived with Mom and Dad after the separation. They moved to LA. I rented a house in the San Fernando Valley and we stayed there. I was working, so they would keep house; they'd cook and everything. Daddy was looking for a job and finally found one. I forgot what he did, but he did find a job.

JLC: *Tell me the Hedda Hopper story.*

JL: Well, I was living with Mom and Dad, and Dad managed my salary; he was like a business manager. And I was in a store doing a photo shoot and I saw this sweater. It had a little trim of fur around the collar. And I thought, oh, I'd love to have that. I think it was sixty dollars, which at that time was a lot.

JLC: *Mom, you don't spend sixty bucks today on a –*

JL: I do too.

JLC: *You do not.*

JL: I do too, I do too.

JLC: *You do not.*

JL: I do, I do, I do.

JLC: *I'm just saying that if you and I walked into a store and did a cost of living increase on that sweater – what it would cost now – you wouldn't buy it.*

JL: If I liked it, as I long I knew I could pay for it –

JLC: *– if that sweater was three hundred dollars?*

JL: I'd think about it.

JLC: *That's my point.*

JL: So Hedda Hopper was at the store, and I called Dad and said, 'Daddy, can I afford this sweater?' And her jaw dropped. She said, 'I have never heard of that in my life.' And every time I ever saw her after that, she would say, 'I don't believe you.'

JLC: *I have referred to you as 'Pollyanna goes Hollywood' for a long time because you have a genuine naïveté. You were green as green could be. Hedda Hopper hearing you saying 'Daddy, can I afford this sweater?' – that's a perfect example of your naïveté. And you know, I've certainly taken a little of that from you. I am your daughter in many, many respects, and that is one of them – but I'm a lot more savvy than you were.*

JL: Oh, much more.

JLC: *That's why I'm really interested in Jeannette Morrison's introduction to Hollywood. Did you date actors?*

JL: Actually, the first person I dated was Barry Nelson.

JLC: *And then?*

JL: Arthur Lowe.

JLC: *Right.*

JL: Then I dated Lex Barker a couple of times. And then there was the time when Howard Hughes was chasing me.

JLC: *Let's talk about Howard Hughes for just a minute.*

JL: [sighs] No.

JLC: *I know you've talked about him until you're blue in the face. I mean, the idea that Howard Hughes was 'chasing' you is funny. Today, if somebody obsesses about someone it would be called stalking. Today, he would be arrested because it's illegal.*

JL: He had me tailed.

JLC: *That's what I'm saying – he stalked you. How did he first see you? What was the first encounter?*

JL: The first time I met Mr Hughes was at a wrap party for *Little Women*. At Mervyn Le Roy's house. And I brought Barry Nelson with me. Mr Le Roy said, 'There's someone I'd like you to meet, Janet,' and took us into the library, and there was Howard Hughes. Now I had read about Howard Hughes, I had seen a picture.

JLC: *How old was Howard Hughes at the time?*

JL: I was twenty-one and he was probably forty.

JLC: *OK, so you're at this party and you walk in and the guy says, Howard Hughes.*

JL: And that was fine. The first manipulation came: Barry Nelson got a call from his agent saying that he had an offer to do a picture for a tremendous amount of money in – I forget where, but it was somewhere like Timbuktu. The offer was from RKO, from Mr Hughes. He wanted Barry out of the way. This happened all the time. Anybody I dated, suddenly they'd disappear. I was dating a dancer, Bobby Shearer, when we were doing *Two Tickets to Broadway*, and Hughes sent him to Vegas when he found out we were dating. He had his spies on the set where we were rehearsing. I mean, it was really bizarre.

JLC: *Did you ever go out with him?*

JL: Once.

JLC: *Did you fuck him?*

JL: Oh God, no. He was always where I was. I mean, I'd have a date and he'd show up.

JLC: *This sounds more and more like O.J., but we won't go into that.*

JL: No, he was not violent. It wasn't like that at all. He just was manipulative.

JLC: *He was stalking you, Mother. See, you call it 'manipulative' – that's where you're naïve. That's where you're Jeannette Helen.*

JL: OK.

JLC: *So you went out with him?*

JL: This is how it happened. He had me followed. And then he called me in. I was going with Arthur Lowe, and he was trying to discredit Arthur. He called me in and said, 'I just want you to see this.' He hands me these papers, and I said, 'What is this?' He says, 'Well, I have ways of getting a hold of this kind of information. And I want you to know what kind of a person you're going out with.' I said, 'Stop this. Just stop it.' I said, 'Why can't you be like a human being and if you want to go out with me, ask me out like a person, like a man?' And he said he didn't like to do that. I think he was afraid of rejection, and so he said, 'All right. Will you go out with me?' I said no. And then I said – I thought, 'Oh, this will fix it' – I said, 'OK, I'll go out with you with my mother and father.'

JLC: [*laughter*]

JL: Jamie, this is the absolute truth.

JLC: *I believe you. I'm just –*

JL: And – and he said OK.

JLC: *And so where did you go out to dinner with Fred and Helen Morrison?*

JL: We went to the Sportsman's Lodge.

JLC: *Stop. You're saying now that Fred Morrison, Helen Morrison and Jeannette Helen Morrison went out to dinner to the Sportsman's Lodge –*

JL: – with Howard Hughes. And the three of them had a wonderful time, because he was their age.

JLC: *Right.*

JL: And I was bored to tears. I mean, it was fun because I saw Mom and Dad were having a good time.

JLC: *Did you neck with Howard Hughes?*

JL: Never.

JLC: *Never?*

JL: Never kissed him, never.

JLC: *Now you have to understand, I think you're a beautiful woman. I will always think of you as this beautiful woman. I see pictures of you, and I don't believe it's you. I know you're the most beautiful thing I've ever seen, and I still don't believe it's you, because I never knew you then. So here's this woman I'm going to call Jeannette Helen Morrison who's a fucking knockout. And knowing Hollywood the way I do, when a beautiful, young, single woman is in town, there is some attention paid.*

JL: Oh yeah.

JLC: *So did you enjoy that? Was it fun?*

JL: Sure, I had fun. I was also very lucky in that I never had to knock around Hollywood like a lot of young girls did.

JLC: *Right, to try to get their breaks. You know what? You and I are the same in that regard, meaning I had a contract with Universal and then a TV series – which luckily didn't go on very long but gave me some experience – and then boom!* Halloween *hit. I have said to this day, if* Halloween *hadn't been my first movie, and if it hadn't been this very successful low-budget horror movie which gave me some foothold within the film community, albeit the shitty end of it – horror movies – it doesn't matter . . .*

JL: It doesn't matter.

JLC: *My point is, I don't think I would have survived show business struggling.*

JL: I know I wouldn't.

JLC: *Well, that's where you and I are very similar.*

JL: Yeah.

JLC: *I never had the kind of ascension that you did; mine was much more gradual.*

JL: We didn't have to knock on doors.

JLC: *And because of that, we had a place within the industry, a foothold where we could stand and breathe. We didn't have to clamber – if I can use an image – up a mountain. We weren't struggling up the granite slope.*

JL: That's right.

JLC: *So here you are on this little foothold. Did you feel that being lucky is difficult?*

JL: Very difficult.

JLC: *Go on.*

JL: Because you never feel that you've earned it.

JLC: *This is something I have struggled with. I want to talk to you a little about it, because you have had a long, long, long, long career. I mean, I'm sitting right now in the den in your house, and all of the scripts of your movies are bound in leather, as they are in my house; they're directly behind you, so as I look at you there they are. They're bound in black with gold letter-ing. The first one is on the left,* The Romance of Rosy Ridge, *and the last one on the right –*

JL: Oh, I don't know if they're in order.

JLC: *You've gotten through how many years as an actress?*

JL: Fifty.

JLC: *Fifty years as an actress.*

JL: Well, I really haven't acted in the last ten, but it's fifty years since I was signed.

JLC: *And with that kind of underlying insecurity. Just talk about that.*

JL: Because I was discovered, because I didn't go through the struggle of knocking on doors, of doing auditions and every-thing, because I never went through all that, I always felt I was just so lucky. So I worked very hard. I really wanted to do my best because this industry had given me so much, and I was really grateful.

JLC: *But when somebody has struggled, really clawed their way up, worked really, really hard and finally lands it – you know, knocks one out of the ball park and becomes a big star, and they walk around with great confidence – I don't like people like that, and I don't think you do either.*

JL: Well, it depends on how they walk around. Let me see if I can explain it to you. I react the way I react because that's who I am. Other people have arrived by a different road, and I can't say that that road is better or worse in terms of their behaviour. I mean, I can't say that their behaviour is wrong or right, I can only say that it's different. Maybe the difference is that Jeannette Helen Morrison is who I am. That's the reality. Janet Leigh is who I am working, and that's my profession. I think that possibly trouble happens with some of our stars who do claw their way up; once they get there, it's almost as if they feel that the profession becomes the reality of their life, and to me it didn't – for me, the reality was my life. Does that make any sense?

JLC: *It makes sense to me.*

JL: But if people do that, that's the way life has made them, or that's where they are in their life.

JLC: *But it's also what people really want to believe. There's one thing that you and I battle from. I once talked to you about it. You got an award from a film organization, and I presented it to you and gave a speech; in it I recalled a comment from a member of the crew where I was working. He said to me 'Your mother is the only person in Hollywood who nobody has anything bad to say about.' And I remember what you said to me: 'But I hope they have something good to say about me too.' So I was actually going to ask you: do you think you're a good actor?*

JL: Yeah, I do.

JLC: *Do you think you're a great actor?*

JL: Define 'great'.

JLC: *You just answered the question. It's a stupid question, by the way. Who we are and how we think of ourselves – you know, I struggle with it myself a little. So out of all the work you've done, what do you think was the hardest for you to do?*

JL: *The Manchurian Candidate.*

JLC: *Why?*

JL: Because in *The Manchurian Candidate* my character is plonked down in the middle of the picture. John Frankenheimer and I had lunch before the scene; we talked about it, and what he said – which I had already realized, but he verbalized it – was that everyone else, like Laurence Harvey and Frank Sinatra, had had twenty minutes to establish their identity and where they were going in the film. The audience was interested, they'd already been grabbed. He said to me, 'You have twenty seconds to grab the audience, because they don't know who you are: are you a red herring? are you for real? are you crazy? are you planted? are you what?' I had twenty seconds to grab the audience, the others had twenty minutes. So that's the hardest I've ever had. You know, I don't think anyone could have done a better job than I have in most of my pictures. I mean, they would have done it a different way, but I don't think they could have done it better in terms of my approach.

JLC: *You and I don't talk much about this stuff.*

JL: No.

JLC: *I think most people think Hollywood families all sit around and talk about movies and acting . . .*

JL: See, there's something else that people forget. For instance, talking about you, they said, 'Thank God she got out of the horror things,' and I always said, 'Hey, those horror things were right for the time that she came in, for her age, and for getting experience.' I said, 'I'm glad she got them. One, it was a job, and two, it was a very successful exposure.' And it was the same back then – they always say, 'Thank God you graduated from those *ingénue* parts, the cute little thing next door roles,' and I said, 'Well, let me ask you another question. At eighteen, did you want me to play Mrs Miniver?' You play what your age

The Manchurian Candidate: Janet Leigh with Frank Sinatra.

is. If you're eighteen, you play eighteen. There aren't a lot of deep roles at eighteen. They're light; you're the *ingénue*, the love interest, and there's not a lot of drama. The roles change as you mature as a person and as an actress. I think the best example is you can't play Mrs Miniver at eighteen and you can't play Gigi at forty.

JLC: *I'm not very good with chronology, but you met Tony and got married – and I look at Demi Moore and Bruce Willis right now, and the way they navigate their success, their family, their dual careers – you know, her escalation above his career at some point, his escalation above hers at some point – and I think they do well at it. They're the only real power couple – except Tom Cruise and Nicole Kidman – who would be in the same league as you and Tony were when you were at the height of your fame, the two of you making movies, making movies together, having children and raising them. Do you remember that?*

Jamie Lee Curtis in *Halloween*.

JL: Oh, sure. It was a very heady time.

JLC: *Describe 'heady'.*

JL: We were on top of the world: extremely successful, happy, we mixed with the élite of Hollywood.

JLC: *Is it true Tony asked you out for a first date as Cary Grant?*

JL: Yeah. On the telephone.

JLC: *But then you figured it out?*

JL: I had read in one of the trades that week about how Tony Curtis did a great imitation of Cary Grant. I had met Cary Grant, but there was no reason for him to call and ask me out – at least, none that I could think of.

JLC: *The phone rang at your house?*

JL: Yes, at my house, and I was taken aback at the beginning because it just didn't make any sense, but then I remembered the article and that's when I knew it was Tony.

JLC: *He resurrected some old family footage, some old Super 8 movies, and it's interesting to watch because you can actually* chart where you guys are as a couple, how the relationship progressed from the beginning to the separation. So from being Jeannette Morrison, you were now a movie star married to another movie star who began as Bernard Schwartz. Jeannette Helen Morrison and Bernard Schwartz.

JL: Right.

JLC: Then you had a very public divorce, and somewhere in the middle of that your dad killed himself. I just can't imagine how you managed it. Did you work? Were you able to work through that?

JL: One of the things that I think was a big block for your father and myself in our marriage was that when he achieved the heights that he did, it was almost like he didn't want to know about Bernie Schwartz any more. He became Tony Curtis, and I think what started to bother me was that I married Bernie Schwartz and we weren't approaching things the same way as we had before.

JLC: I actually recommended to him – the marketing genius daughter he had raised – that he do a book where on the front of it was Bernie Schwartz by Tony Curtis, and literally half-way through you flipped the book over and the back cover became the front cover of Tony Curtis by Bernie Schwartz. At the point where he became Tony Curtis, you literally stopped one book, flipped it over and printed it as if it was another book. I do think that's appropriate, because there is that very clear separation with him. Let's go back to your career. Psycho is the movie that you will be remembered for. That's just how it is.

JL: Well, listen, there's nothing wrong with that.

JLC: As your child, even I would describe you as the woman who got killed in the shower. I'm not going to delve into Psycho stories, because you've just written a very good, conscientious overview of the making of the movie; interviewed all of the surviving members of the crew and cast, and really produced the definitive book. But what I will delve into a little is: you were a star of great proportion at that time, a big star, and yet

Psycho: Janet Leigh with Hitchcock – the shower scene.

*you took a part where you were killed off in the first twenty
minutes of the movie.*

JL: No, it was just under forty per cent of the movie.

JLC: *Oh. So how did this movie come about? That story I don't
know. Did Hitchcock call you?*

JL: No. He sent me the novel by Robert Bloch. They didn't have
a script. And he said in the note, 'Please consider the role of

Psycho: Janet Leigh warming up John Gavin.

Mary' – it was Mary in the novel. He said that there would obviously be many changes from the novel, but read it just so that you know the intent. And I read it, and immediately called MCA and said yes.

JLC: *Just right away.*

JL: Oh, number one, to work with Mr Hitchcock, and two, it just grabbed me.

JLC: *Tell me the story of the bed scene with John Gavin, and what Hitchcock said to you. It didn't look as if Mr Gavin and you were as sexually aroused as you should be in the scene, and Mr Hitchcock actually pulled you aside and said –*

JL: 'Could you sort of see to it that he warms up?'

JLC: *You don't have to be coy here, Mommy. What did he want you to do?*

JL: I have a feeling he wanted me to touch him.

JLC: *Actually touch him?*

JL: In that area.

JLC: *In that region.*

JL: Yeah.

JLC: *OK.*

JL: I mean – you know – or maybe accidentally.

JLC: *Right, I've heard stories about Hitchcock where he says: you start here on this line . . .*

JL: That's right.

JLC: *. . . and on this line you move to there.*

JL: That's exactly right.

JLC: *He'd tell you this and then you would rehearse? You would never just go into a room and say: Here's what I'd like to do?*

JL: No, never. His camera was absolute.

JLC: *In every scene?*

JL: Every.

JLC: *There was not a moment when you'd go up to him and say: I shouldn't go there, I should go here?*

JL: Nope, there was not a moment.

JLC: *That's pretty wild, because nowadays there seems to be a lot more collaboration.*

JL: Well, that's because Hitchcock's camera told the story. Hitchcock's camera was the most important thing in his mind; before the picture ever started, he knew how to get the most suspense economically – and I don't mean just in terms of finance. I mean economically in terms of film and storytelling. I truly had great love for this man. I just worshipped his talent and his sense of humour.

JLC: *You worked with another great director, Orson Welles. On* Touch of Evil. *It's an amazing accomplishment for a young director.*

JL: Yeah.

JLC: *There must have been some sort of buzz about him. I mean, at that point in his life.*

JL: At that point he was out of favour because he was his own worst enemy. He had no discipline. He really disregarded

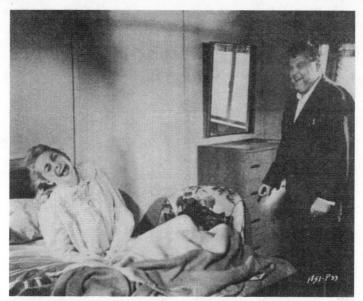

Touch of Evil: Janet Leigh with Orson Welles.

budgets and authority. When he was riding high it was impossible. He was like a wild stallion who you couldn't put the bridle on.

JLC: *Had you ever met him before he cast you?*

JL: Yes. Your father and I met him in London at a gala at which we performed. There's a photo of Orson and your father and myself. He's showing us a magic trick – which is funny because your father and I had once done *Houdini*. But anyway, Charlton Heston was the one who suggested Orson as the director, and fought for him. He just felt that – that Orson's weird sense of dramatics would suit the film.

JLC: *Was he right?*

JL: Oh, of course he was right.

JLC: *Was it based on a book? Was it an original screenplay?*

JL: It was originally 'Badge of Evil'. I don't know whether it was a book or not. I don't really know, I hadn't heard of it before. So, anyway, the studio acquiesced and said, all right,

Touch of Evil: Janet Leigh with Charlton Heston – the opening shot.

but, boy, he better tow the line in terms of budget. They were very budget-orientated – you know – forget the creativity.

JLC: *They must have been thrilled with the shot . . .*

JL: The opening shot?

JLC: *Yeah.*

JL: Well, what thrilled them was that Orson was so smart. I mean, what thrilled them was the scene after the explosion when they go to this guy's apartment and all these police are there. The reporters are there, and they're looking at everything – and they had it scheduled for four days. This is where they plant the evidence.

JLC: *Right.*

JL: And Orson shot it in one day. There were all these people in these tiny quarters and he had to get the close-ups and then over-the-shoulders and then in the bathroom when you see the empty box and then you see the box with the dynamite in it, so you know that it's been planted. The whole thing was scheduled for four days and he moved his camera, catching the action where it needed to be caught. He shot it in one day. And the studio is saying: Oh, my God. He's come back.

JLC: *The maestro.*

JL: The maestro has come back. Look, he's three days ahead of schedule.

JLC: *Right.*

JL: And we did not go over schedule. They were relieved. We went down to shoot nights in Venice, California, and that's when this opening shot was done. It took all night. An incredible shot. Again they were eating out of his hands; so what happened after that was that we shot the rest of the picture, mostly night shooting in Venice. Some of those scenes weren't even in the script. I mean, the thing in the motel when Mercedes McCambridge . . .

JLC: *'I want to watch. I want to watch.' That fabulous voice.*

JL/JLC [*together*]: *I want to watch.*

JLC: *A lesbian biker. How bizarre.*

JL: Half of this stuff wasn't in the script. And so it was fun. You'd come to work and you'd never know who was going to be on the set or what was going to happen.

JLC: *Now, I want to go into the other story that I know nobody knows about.*

JL: Cut to the chase.

JLC: *You had a broken arm from the beginning of shooting?*

JL: Absolutely.

JLC: *OK. You had been signed to do this movie. He called you up. He called your agent. How did he . . .*

JL: No. He sent me a telegram. One night we came home from dinner and then there was a telegram there. 'Janet, I'm so thrilled you're going to be in my movie, can't wait to work with you,' signed Orson. I had never heard of it. I didn't know what was happening. I called my agent, and he said: God, the negotiations aren't finished yet. He wasn't supposed to contact you like that. I don't care, negotiations – smotiations – I want to work with Orson Welles. So, OK, I was set to do it. Now, in the interim I shot a TV movie, *Carriage from Britain*, and in that movie a burglar comes in and tries to steal my English pram, which I valued with my life for my baby. Anyway, I come down the stairs, jump on the intruder's back, and fight him. Well, in the rehearsal, we twirl around and he trips and falls. I fall on a step, and he falls on top. And it broke my arm.

JLC: *And you knew it right away.*

JL: I wasn't sure. I couldn't move it. At first I hit my head, and I was kind of out for a minute, and when my arm ached they X-rayed it and I had broken my arm, but I didn't set it, I just took some pain pills; I didn't move it. And I still had work to do on the TV show. So I finished that shoot and then had it set, but I had it set at a ninety-degree angle so that it wasn't so obvious. I put a coat on it, and I went to see Orson. He said, I heard you broke your arm. I said, well, I did. And I showed him. He said, oh, no problem. So I played the whole picture with a broken arm.

JLC: *And you hid it?*

JL: I hid it. Then what we did was in the scenes where we couldn't hide it, they sawed the cast open and we'd take it off just before we'd shoot so the arm was there, like in the nightie. Then after the shot, we'd put the cast back on and tape it.

JLC: *Right. Now people are going to go back and look at this movie and just see sort of this inert right arm.*

JL: Well, you know, you don't notice it.

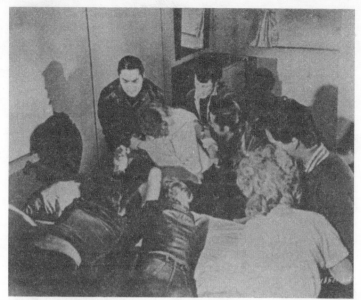

Touch of Evil: the seminal lesbian scene.

JLC: *Believe me, Mother, if you start looking for it . . .*
Now, tell me something about Mercedes McCambridge,
because I think she's just so fabulous, so weird.
JL: Yes.
JLC: *So she was playing this lesbian biker, but obviously that*
sort of lesbianism wasn't particularly thought of in the movies
very much. I'm sure the ratings commission was still in existence.
JL: Of course. But it's not spelled out that she's a lesbian.
JLC: *'I want to watch.'*
JL: It could mean that she just . . .
JLC: *'I want to watch them beat you up.' I think it's funny that*
you are emerging with this seminal lesbian scene and Tony's in
Spartacus *with the seminal homosexual influence.*
JL: Oh, right, with Olivier.
JLC: *I just think it's fascinating. It was very dangerous water to*
tread in the fifties.

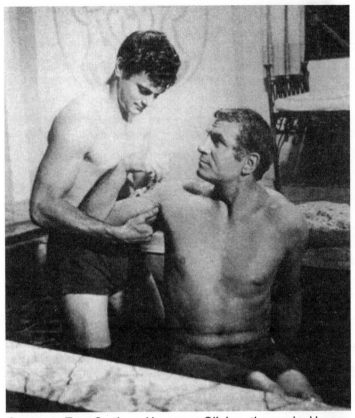
Spartacus: Tony Curtis and Laurence Olivier – the seminal homo-sexual scene.

JL: Right. But on the other hand, it doesn't say she's a lesbian, whereas with Olivier it was much more overt and they cut that scene.

JLC: *I know, but they've put it back in. Did you know that Tony had to revoice it?*

JL: Yes, I did.

JLC: *And they got Tony Hopkins –*

JL: To do Olivier.

JLC: *And Tony said that he fell right back into the scene. It was as if he'd never left it. He could just pick it up.*

JL: I'm sure that's the case because I remember when he shot it – he was so pleased with that scene because it was such a fun scene to play. I remember how excited he was. You know, creatively, it was just a big thing.

JLC: *Going back to* Touch of Evil – *any other things you can think of?*

JL: Um – you know – Marlene's part – if it was there at all – was minuscule. It just kept getting more and more and more – um – which was fascinating. You'd really go to work and not know what was developing.

JLC: *When Orson Welles is by the river at the end, he looks so big.*

JL: Oh, yes. He was padded. Subsequently, Orson became as heavy as he was in *Touch of Evil*, but at that time he was padded.

JLC: *Oh.*

JL: He wore pillows and things in his jowls like Marlon Brando did in *The Godfather*, because he wasn't that big. I recently heard that AMC advertised that they were going to show *Touch of Evil* with the original cut – which was Orson's cut. Orson did his cut, but the studio didn't understand the picture. They just never understood it; I mean, they were really into *Francis the Talking Mule*.

JLC: *Chuck Heston the talking Mexican.*

JL: Yes. Ted Mull, who was the head of the studio at that time was not one of our brain trusts; I mean, he was a nice man, but he did not understand *Touch of Evil*. He made Chuck and me do retakes – dull, linking retakes that for him helped explain the story.

JLC: *It would be interesting if they ever did a laser disc of* Touch of Evil, *for you to do a narration saying which things were added.*

JL: Anyway, we both didn't want to do the retakes. We tried to argue with him that they were losing what was the intrinsic, what was really different about the picture. But, of course, by S.A.G. rules we were forced to do them. But I understand, and I don't know if it's true, that AMC were going to show the original, full picture.

JLC: *Director's cuts are more and more popular now.*

JL: Though sometimes the studio is right because very often a director will become too subjective to have an objective view of their picture.

JLC: *Although* Psycho *is the movie that everyone talks about – and I like it – it's not the work of yours that means the most to me. There's* Boardwalk; *a lot of people will never have seen it. A lovely performance.*

JL: I thought that the character I did in a made-for-TV movie called *Mirror, Mirror* was very good.

JLC: *Do you know what? There's a moment in it when she goes back to a place and looks in the mirror in that room. I was actually there the day you shot it. I remember it very well. Do you ever look back on your movies? Do you watch them?*

JL: If I'm on the exercise machine, and I turn on the TV and there's one on, I'll watch it.

JLC: *Tony loves to watch them.*

JL: But I don't. It's not that I'm not proud of what I did or anything, it's just that I don't dwell on it. There are phases in your life, there are directions that are taken, and I think that to try to go back to one of the other phases is standing still, or even retrogressing, not moving forward, and I think moving forward is healthy.

JLC: *And so have you gone back to Merced?*

JL: No, I've never gone back to Merced. I've gone back to Stockton quite a few times.

JLC: *You have old friends there.*

JL: My friends are the girls who were the bridesmaids and the matron of honour at my first wedding to Stan.

JLC: *Knowing you the way I do, I think that the most interesting thing is that your best friend is the woman who was with*

Touch of Evil: a padded Welles with Marlene Dietrich.

you at the transition point between Jeannette Helen Morrison and Janet Leigh. She may have even given you Janet Leigh, and that's Lillian Sidney, the woman you called Miss Burns earlier.

JL: Right. She was married at the time to director George Sidney.

JLC: *She was the drama coach of the studio. And she was your first friend.*

JL: Yes. You know, I want to go back on something, and I think that to be perfectly honest, I should have gone a step further with you. When we talked about how I always felt I didn't deserve success, there's another reason there.

JLC: *Which is?*

JL: Which is that when I was very young, when I was fourteen, I ran off and eloped. And I was obviously made to feel that I was really a terrible person, a worthless person, a bad, bad, bad person. And I was. I mean, I did something very wrong. And I think that the effect of that, the reaction to that, is a major

major reason – as well as the other reasons – why I never felt that I deserved it.

JLC: *Because you felt from the beginning that –*

JL: That I was bad.

JLC: *What's most interesting to me, Mom – and the reason why I admire your honesty – is because we can all look back on our accomplishments, but not always to the underpinning of those accomplishments; the foundation of who we are as people is so affected by our early experiences. For you to say that to me today, that experience when you were fourteen years old, running off because you were lusty, because you had passion. You wanted to be with this person. It was not the social norm to have sex at fourteen. And you ran off and got married, which was the acceptable thing to do, so that you could legitimately have sex.*

JL: And I didn't want to leave the town because we had moved twice.

JLC: *And here I sit looking at this woman. You've made millions of dollars in your life, you have won awards, you have worked with the best people there are in Hollywood, and still Jeannette Morrison exists. I don't need to say any more. That's how this talk started. I won't delve any more. Your husband Bob Brandt's home now. This is perfect. But I just want you to know that I have always known that about you. It's why somehow I've referred to you as Jeannette Helen Morrison all our lives together, and I refer to you as Janet Leigh sometimes, and now you can go and be Janet Brandt.*

JL: Now I'm going to be Janet Brandt.

JLC: *And I love you.*

JL: I love you, sweetheart.

James Stewart with Frank Capra.

4 Learning Your Craft

James Stewart talks to Gregory Solman

Introduction

This close to the millennium, it seems safe to pronounce James Stewart one of the greatest film actors of the century. In fairness, it's been safe for quite some time now. Some would argue a pre-war trilogy as the start of the lanky stride that would gracefully ford five decades of film-making: *Mr Smith Goes to Washington* (1939), *The Shop Around the Corner* and *The Philadelphia Story* (1940). Others catch up with him later, after the bluebirds return to Dover, looking as comfortable as conceivable while straddling the distant mountains of Ford's classicism and Hitchcock's modernism. He was always, it seems, a step ahead.

The subject of directors – among other diverse pleasures – is the focus of this talk with Jimmy Stewart, one of the last any film critic might enjoy. Since the passing of Gloria, his wife of forty-five years, in 1994, Mr Stewart withdrew from all public and most private activity to mourn. But we visit him here on one of his good days. His responses have a summary, rather than revelatory, character. Like many a man struggling with his memories – he turns eighty-eight on 20 May 1995 – he tells some of his most familiar stories in, frankly, familiar ways. In editing these comments, I've often tried to preserve his patois, trading warm familiarity for breezy reading. Notwithstanding, the substance of his answers reveals the truth of his character.

Compiling his seventy-eight film credits here feels unnecessary, if not a subtle form of ingratitude. This seems rather the place for a sentimental anniversary celebration. So, a half century later, a re-citation: As a bomber pilot and squadron commander in the US Army Air Force, his was not simply the morale-boosting tour of many stars. He flew nineteen missions from England's airfields to Bremen, Frankfurt and Berlin. He earned his Distinguished Flying Cross with two Oak Leaf Clusters leading a squadron to aircraft factories in Brunswick. He was awarded the Croix de Guerre with Palm and the Distinguished Service Medal. He left active duty a colonel, fifty years ago, and retired a brigadier general, the highest ranking officer in Hollywood history.

And, as tempting as it might be, in Golden Anniversary glow, Mr Stewart still declines to discuss the war. It's been his unwavering position, even before losing his eldest son in Vietnam. But before being joined by the dean of Hollywood press agents, John Strauss (his publicist since 1958), a modest plaque from a B-24 group in his Beverly Hills office provides a small opening. I dust off the old joke about his aircraft back then, the Liberator, a flying bomb rack so ungainly looking it was derogated as having been made from the crates B-17s came packed in. As he tinkers with my notebook computer, the first he's ever seen, I start to tell him how nice they are for working in planes, then reconsider. I suddenly remember that Mr Stewart knows enough about working in planes for one life.

In *The Man Who Shot Liberty Valance*, Stewart's Eastern-bred Western hero is solemnly advised by a journalist, 'When the legend becomes fact, print the legend.' Here's a little of both.

GREGORY SOLMAN: *If there are actor's directors, I'd argue you're what might be called a director's actor. Do you buy that?*
JAMES STEWART: I don't know how to answer that exactly, because I have such respect for the motion-picture director. And I've been fortunate enough to work with some of the best around. It's hard to say, but it seems that directors are the basic thing of the film, and everything goes out from them. I suppose

that this started during the big studio system, because each studio had its boss – who was the head of the studio – then there were departments, and heads of departments were in charge, and [then] this thing happened with directors. This is when it was really, really competitive.

GS: *When you were under contract, were you forced to work with directors with whom you really didn't want to work?*

JS: If I didn't want to work with them, that had nothing to do with it. Nowadays an actor will sit home and read scripts until he finds one he likes, he gets on to his agent, and goes. In those days, you went to work at eight o'clock in the morning and got finished at six at night. You worked six days a week. And worked all day. You did little parts in big pictures, and big parts in little pictures. Or [you were] doing tests with people they were considering to sign under contract. Or you were in the gym taking exercises – you were required to do a certain amount of that every day. Or down in Texas plugging a picture that you weren't even in.

GS: *At the behest of the publicity department?*

JS: Yes, the publicity department would write a speech for you, usually at the opening of the picture. You came out first and made the speech, every Saturday matinée, and once or twice during the week. You may have never seen the picture. But you worked all the time. As I say, as far as picking parts, a fellow would come up to you, hand you a script, and say, 'You play the part of George. Go down to wardrobe and get fitted out for what you'll wear.' And, 'We start Tuesday.' And that's all. You'd never seen the script before.

GS: *I sense that you like the work ethic that Hollywood used to have.*

JS: I have a better vision of it now, looking back at it. But I realized how important it was – and how much better it was for everyone than it is now – after the studio system was gone. Because you learned your craft by working at it. And you worked all the time. And now you don't have that; you don't have that advantage, that tremendous advantage, for your development, for what you're learning . . . you're learning about film acting. It is an entirely different ball-game.

GS: *I hope you'll take this as a compliment when I say that I think that you're the last great silent-movie star who never made a silent movie. There are sequences in* Vertigo, *for instance, that could stand as silent films.*

JS: Well, that's something that I learned during this time, growing up. And this didn't come right away.

GS: *When you say growing up, do you mean during the 1930s?*

JS: Well, I got out here [Hollywood] in 1935, and had a seven-year contract with MGM. I was here until 1942, then four years in the war. My contract with MGM ran out while I was in the war. MGM offered to sign me again, but Lew Wasserman, my agent – Jules Styne had one of the biggest agencies in town, and Lew Wasserman was his assistant – advised me not to sign. And he told me years later that there was a feeling, long before it happened, that the studio system was not going to survive.

GS: *Not going to survive the war . . .*

JS: Yes.

GS: *So there's a clean break for you because of your participation in the war. Were you more of a free agent? Were there directors you had wanted to work with, but couldn't because of contractual obligations?*

JS: It was the other way around. One of the many good fortunes I had was the chance to work with the Capras and John Fords and Premingers.

GS: *And you worked with King Vidor and Walter Lang. And I note with some interest you worked for Cecil B. De Mille. What was that like? This was 1952, but he goes back to another era.*

JS: Just great. I was making a picture in London . . .

GS: *No Highway in the Sky?*

JS: Yes. And I read in the paper that they were going to make a picture about the Barnum & Bailey and Ringling Brothers' Circus, and C. B. De Mille was going to do it, and Chuck Heston

The Greatest Show on Earth: James Stewart
and Gloria Grahame

had the main part in it. And I'd never met Mr De Mille. And I sat down and wrote him a letter. I said that all my life I'd wanted to play a clown, the part of a clown, and I had such admiration for the circus, a lot of it having to do with the clown, especially Emmett Kelly. Remember him? 'I was just wondering if in the casting of your picture you would consider me as a clown.' And a week later I had a telegram from De Mille saying, 'You're in the picture.' And I didn't know that then, but he rewrote the whole thing. I was not only a clown, but the reason I never took my clown make-up off was that I was wanted by the police, which never came out until the last scene in the picture.

GS: *You didn't expect to be a clown-fugitive, did you?*

JS: No. And Emmett Kelly was just great with me. He'd say, 'When we go into this, I'm going to make a speech to the audience, and I'm going like this, and when I hit you, you fall on your ass.' And this is sort of the way it went. And I enjoyed every minute of it.

GS: *At this point, you are in your mid-forties, and De Mille is getting pretty old [seventy-one years].*

JS: He didn't seem very old.

GS: *But did his method seem different to you? By then you'd worked with very modern directors.*

JS: No, but you can imagine the problems he had in getting the circus on the screen, getting a story, a very definite story about Betty Hutton's problems and everything. But what I noticed, and what I've come to see as one of the great things about motion pictures, is that De Mille was a visual person. The important things to him was getting the essence and the meaning of the scene up on to the screen visually. I think John Ford said it better than anybody. I remember him saying, when he was mad about something, 'If you can't get [the] story that you're making up there on the screen visually, without relying on the spoken word, you're not using the motion picture correctly.' And this says it a little better, but Hitchcock was the same way, and Frank Capra, though you don't think of him this way . . . visually!

GS: *If you compare the visual style of* The Man Who Shot Liberty Valance *[1962]* with something like Mr Smith Goes to Washington *[1939], you could say that you are being used more interestingly visually in the earlier Capra film than the later Ford film.* Liberty Valance *is a dialogue-intensive project.*

JS: Yes, but think of the other Ford pictures. *Two Rode Together*, with Dick Widmark. Nobody said much.

GS: *Well, that's a brilliant example of Ford's visual style, I would agree. I read comments you've made about colouriza-tion and I felt that your analysis of the image is astute and sophisticated. And I don't want to say I was surprised by that, since you've worked with so many great visual directors, but many actors don't pay any attention to visual space.*

Two Rode Together: discussions with John Ford.

JS: But this is one of the things that has changed in motion pictures: they depend more on the spoken word. You see television do it, of course. You see a person here, and another here, and they're talking and it's cut, cut, cut, cut. And you use the spoken word. And you are misusing the medium, because it's not supposed to be for that. The stage is for the spoken word. When you think about how long the motion picture existed without the spoken word, and what an audience it got and maintained without the spoken word, and then suddenly . . . whether it was an accident or whether is was actually meant to be like that. Al Jolson's picture was a musical, so the spoken word was really singing, so it was eased in to the audience.

GS: *Your point here is that it wasn't necessarily a conveyor of narrative at the beginning.*

JS: I think that so many people at that time thought it was a great advance in the art of film-making, to add the spoken word, and it's not necessarily true.

GS: *How would Hitchcock work on long silent sequences, or, for instance, in* Rope, *which was almost like the theatre in that there were scenes as long as fifteen minutes with no cuts.*

JS: In *Rope*, all we did was talk, and there was no cut.

GS: *Here's an example of where learning from the theatre paid off. How would Hitchcock rehearse something like that?*

JS: Number one, Hitchcock would not rehearse at all. No rehearsals for dialogue. He was most interested in what was he was getting from the scene, visually. And Bob Burks, his cameraman for all the time he was out here, knew exactly what he was getting. And Hitchcock had this place, which was quite near the camera, and he'd say, 'Bob come here,' and Bob would stand right by him. He'd say, 'Bob, I want this [*gesturing with his hands*] like that.' And it was just amazing how he would get it. I never saw Hitchcock look through the camera. (I don't think he could get up high enough to look through the camera.) Bob would say,

Rope: Hitchcock with Farley Granger, James Stewart and John Dall.

'Ready.' Then Hitchcock would say, 'All right. Actors.' This would be a fifteen-minute scene or a ten-minute scene, with four, five, six actors, and he would say, 'All right, now all you actors get in and move around, and don't run into the furniture, and let's see how you can make this thing run.' And we all knew how to do that, because we found out that's the way things went. *Rope* was shot so that there were no cuts, ever, in it. This is the only time Hitch made one like it. This wasn't the only one he was going to do. He was going to do one with that wonderful Swedish actress.

GS: *Ingrid Bergman?*

JS: Ingrid. Anyway, he was going to make a picture in London with her, using this technique, and halfway through the thing he called her and put it off.

GS: *Interesting – I think there's a reference to* Notorious *in* Rope.

JS: About halfway though *Rope*, he called Ingrid and said, 'Forget about doing this thing. This is the last time I'm ever going to do this.' It's the last time anybody did.*

GS: *Who would block scenes? Who would have worked in a different mentality?*

JS: Well, the ones I worked with had this same feeling, and the same method of not only letting the actors know what they wanted up there on the screen, but letting the actors pretty much figure things out for themselves and sit back. Going back to Hitchcock and dialogue: I forget what picture it was ... Anyway, there were five of us in the scene, and it was quite a long scene, with several moves with the camera. And Bob Burks finally came over to Hitch and said, 'The camera's ready.' He said, 'All right, actors, get on set,' and he said, 'Are you ready?' then, 'Roll 'em.' So we went through the whole thing, and Hitchcock said, 'That's fine. Bob, come over here.' And the poor

*In fact, Hitchcock did continue his experiments with the illusion of continuous camera movement and real-time continuity with *Under Capricorn*, starring Ingrid Bergman.

script girl came over and said, 'Mr Hitchcock, please, I have to show you this. In this page, Stewart says only half the lines but the half that he says, he says backwards.' And Hitchcock said, 'Well, it all *looked* fine, print it.' That's sort of the way he was.

GS: *In another words, he was saying, 'I don't have to worry about your interpretation.' Did that change as you became a more famous actor, or did you have that kind of respect at the beginning of your career?*

JS: No, I never – until way, way – almost at the finish of my career – I never had the feeling that the directors gave me this thing and said, 'Let him alone. He can figure it out.' Never. Capra, no. None of them. Preminger, certainly not. With Preminger, you did it the way he wanted it.

GS: *Tell me about Otto Preminger. It sounds like he was more dictatorial on set.*

JS: Right. Which was fine; he was dictatorial, but the things he wanted, and the things he was plugging were right. As far as movement of camera, the way you felt in doing the scene, he had his way of doing things. For instance, *Anatomy of a Murder* was a true story. We were doing it up in Ishpeming, Michigan, and every scene was in the exact same spot that the actual murder or event took place, including the courtroom – and a lot of the extras were in the courtroom at the time of the original trial.

GS: *In that sense it was one of the first crime recreations. Did you prefer working with a director like Preminger with whom you didn't have arguments about the role? Were there directors with whom you did have arguments about the emotion that should be conveyed or how to read the script?*

JS: Most of the time they weren't arguments, they were just asking questions: could I try it this way, instead of another. Tony Mann was a good example; I made, what, twelve or thirteen pictures, with him?

GS: *Well, a lot.* The Man from Laramie, Strategic Air Command, The Far Country, *which is a wonderful picture*, The Glenn Miller Story, Thunder Bay. *It's a lot of pictures with one director. At this point, who's asking for whom? You have a big streak with Anthony Mann and another with Ford. Is this part of an agreement?*

JS: No. Anthony Mann had the visual thing. *Winchester '73* . . . You know, when they first started doing dramas on radio, it was thought they'd discourage people, that they'd listen to radio instead of coming to the movies. I know in my home town (Indiana, Pennsylvania) there was one movie theatre and, at one point, when radio really started going, it closed down Monday, Tuesday and Wednesday, because it was Jack Benny and George Burns those nights . . . This was something that just occurred to me. I was talking about *Winchester '73* . . . The studios said: 'Well, I guess radio is here to stay, so we might as well get along with it.' And they suddenly found out that they were not only able to advertise their movies on radio, but that it was good advertising and it brought in good audiences. And I was on several times. The studio sent the movie script for *Winchester '73* over to the Lux Radio Theater, and they sent it back to the studio and said, 'We can't use this, nobody says anything!' . . . Those were interesting days.

GS: *And theatre was bigger then, too. When you started out, did you think you'd be typecast as a heavy or a leading man?*

JS: I hadn't the faintest idea. As I say, they would just come to you and say here's the thing, you play the part of so and so, and you start Tuesday. The first week I got there, they showed me where the dressing room was, and took me around to wardrobe and make-up, and showed me where you had your lunch, and somebody handed me a script called *The Murder Man*, [with] Spencer Tracy.

GS: *That was in 1935.*

JS: Yep. And he was just great to me. God, he was such a wonderful help. Not in the way of: 'Now this is going to be very difficult for you,' but he would say things like, 'Do you say much in this thing?' I'd read over my lines, and he'd say, 'Well, say it like that, that sounds fine.' That's the way he'd give

Anatomy of a Murder: Otto Preminger directing James Stewart and Ben Gazarra.

advice – as encouragement, not in giving me ideas as to how to behave myself.

GS: *Was he considered an elder statesman at that point?*

JS: No. At that point, no one was considered . . . well, maybe Garbo. Garbo wouldn't come to the commissary; she had her meals in her room. Joan Crawford, too; she had her meals in her room. But the rest of them all ate at the commissary. They had a

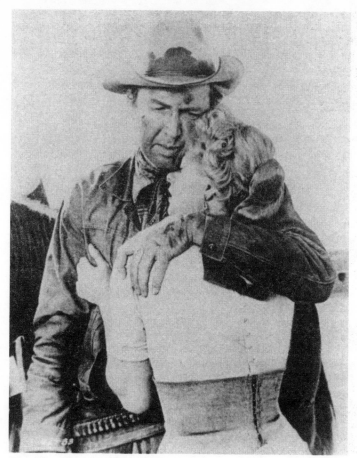

The Man from Laramie: James Stewart and Cathy O'Donnell.

big dining room – it's maybe still there – and everyone, including all the big shots, was there, and they'd visit the sets every so often, and there was a friendship, a sort of a mutual interest between so many people. I remember a couple of weeks ago they were doing something about Judy Garland and they showed a couple of scenes from big musicals she'd done. And I remembered [having seen] them. Because when they did the big scenes, on a big stage, they'd tell everybody – everybody that would be working on the lot – 'Go over and look at it, but be back in ten minutes.' And we'd all go over and watch it. That was the kind of thing that was done for young people, people just getting started, just to show what kind of business you were in, to show you different things besides acting in a serious play . . . like singing with hundreds of chorus girls all around; giving you knowledge in the best possible way, by showing it.

GS: *Did you enjoy one period of your acting career more than another?*

JS: I think probably I did enjoy this period. This was a more exciting time because I was getting started in the business and, as I say, the studios were competitive, but they also depended on one another. The first part I did where I got some notices from the New York critics, they'd loaned me to Universal for a picture with Margaret Sullavan called *Next Time We Love*. This went on to do very well, and they brought me back [to MGM]. And I stayed there for a while, but they loaned me a lot of times, and everyone did this. It was a community of individual companies that depended on one another, as if it was a big family. We worked six days a week, then on Saturday night, it would seem like everybody in town would meet at the Trocadero. It's not there any more, but it was up on Sunset Boulevard.

GS: *You humbly accepted any role they gave you. What do you suppose would have happened if you'd have felt differently about the roles?*

JS: That's just not the way things took place in those days. You didn't say, 'I'll take this,' take it home, and then say, 'This is the worst thing I've ever read,' and mope around. Never. You'd say, 'This is what they want me to do, they gave it to me, and I'm going to do the best I can with it.'

GS: *Who then would you rely upon to make sure that your career path was correct for you? Was that Lew Wasserman?*

JS: No, in those days they never did that.

GS: *Was it the studio head?*

Next Time We Love: James Stewart with Margaret Sullavan.

JS: No. As a matter of fact, the guy I always used to go to was the casting director at MGM, Billy Grady. Even before he became the casting director. Billy Grady was the guy at MGM (and all the studios did this) who would go to Broadway, he would see all the plays and pick out young actors that MGM could use. He picked me out and I made a screen test there, on Broadway.

GS: *This is 1933?*

JS: No, 1934. And he came back here and I didn't hear anything. Hank Fonda and I were rooming together. People don't realize that in 1931, '32, '33, '34, – that was the rock bottom of the Great Depression – that was the time when business on Broadway, in the theatre, was bigger that it has ever been, before or since.

GS: *A fair time for cinema, too, with* King Kong *and all.*

JS: Bigger than it has ever been. And I suppose it had something to do with people wanting to escape. They'd go see a story on the screen before they'd have to go back to the family and wonder where the next meal was going to come from. I remember Hank and I always used to talk about it, how lucky we were to be acting on the Broadway stage at that particular time, because we went from one play to the other. An awful lot of them weren't successful, [but] we went from one play to the other, never unemployed.

GS: *Theatre was a cheap night of entertainment, but not compared with the motion pictures. I imagine they were, what, 25 cents?*

JS: Well, at 10 a.m., at the big Paramount Theater in Times Square, 25 cents.

GS: *When you were working with Hitchcock, later, the system had changed from what you'd grown into. Was there any difference in choice of roles?*

JS: No. The studios and casting people may have picked out roles that they thought I could do better than others, but I guess I was too busy acting, doing one part then a different part and – the same thing I was talking about – learning my craft by working at it. When I became independent after the war, then it was pretty much a matter of choosing my own roles, but by this time Jules Styne had turned a lot of the stuff over to Lew Wasserman; Leland Hayward, who I got to know very well, worked for Lew Wasserman, and he got to be very good at picking parts and talking to people at the different studios about parts for me. So the whole Styne/Wasserman set-up was a tremendous help to me in those days.

GS: *It's odd to hear you say that, because you were at the top, but still being deferential to other people's opinions of scripts. You didn't even have your choice of genres; you know, 'I don't want to be in a Western, or a suspencer.' But the pictures you did after the war were so interesting.* Rear Window, *for instance, is amazingly advanced, very modern.*

JS: That was the thing with Hitchcock. I think *Rope* had a lot to do with my getting that part.

Vertigo: James Stewart with Kim Novak.

GS: *That was the first film you'd done with him?*
JS: Then *Vertigo*, I think, then *The Man Who Knew Too Much*.
GS: *Tell me about what happened on the set of* Rear Window?
JS: Well, everything went smoothly. We were all so crazy about Grace Kelly. Everybody just sat around and waited for her to come in in the morning, so we could just look at her. She was so kind to everybody, so considerate, just great, and so beautiful. And Thelma Ritter was wonderful. And Bob Burks, the cameraman. The thing is, no one had ever done a picture exactly like this. The idea of me not moving out of a chair for the whole picture, because I had a cast; never moving until Raymond Burr comes in and throws me out the window, and I break the other leg . . .
GS: *That was every man's fantasy, having Grace Kelly nurse you back to health.*
JS: I remember one particular scene. I was here, in this cast, and across the way was Raymond, and the girl that Raymond Burr

Rear Window: James Stewart with Grace Kelly and Hitchcock.

was after was down here. And in one of the important scenes, Hitchcock wanted me here, so I could get all this, because I had to witness the events through the camera and the long lens. That's the way I found out that something screwy was going on. Now, Hitchcock got behind me, and said, 'Now, Bob, I want to get Raymond Burr and the girl in their apartment, as the action's going on, but I want Stewart and the camera to be in focus, and to be part of the picture.' And to do this, camera-wise, is tough, because you have to cut the lens down to some small thing, f/22 or something, to get the distance [the depth of focus], and this takes more light . . .

GS: *And you're supposed to be hiding in the shadows, too.*

JS: Yeah. But we just needed more light. So they brought all the lights at Paramount that weren't being used. So Burks is here with his light meter. He says, 'We're not near. We haven't got enough light.' And Hitchcock says, 'Well, if Paramount doesn't have any, try MGM.' So they went over to MGM and had to take some time to make connections, but they got some – I don't know how many, but they were these big lights – and some from Columbia. The lights were so [*gestures large*]. He turned them on and Bob said, 'Well, that does it. We're home.' And he almost hadn't finished saying that when the fire sprinklers went off. And it started raining. I'm not saying trickling down. You could hardly see through the rain! And Hitchcock turned to Bob, 'Well, see if somebody can turn off the water. And, in the meantime, could somebody bring me an umbrella?' And he went over, sat down in his chair and somebody handed him an umbrella. And he sat there until they got the thing fixed.

GS: *Was John Ford a droll man in that way?*

JS: Oh, yes. I have great admiration for John Ford.

GS: *Were there pictures of his that you like in particular?*

JS: I like *Two Rode Together.*

GS: *Wonderful film . . .*

JS: And I just liked the idea of *Liberty Valance* . . . Ford just amazed me, the way he got things done, the way he was absolutely dead-set on getting it up there, visually. And at one point, when . . . Was this on *Liberty Valance*? What else . . . What other pictures did I make with him?

GS: Cheyenne Autumn . . . How the West Was Won . . . Two Rode Together . . .

JS: I guess this was *The Man Who Shot Liberty Valance.* Well, we were in a big room, and I forget what was going on, but there was a coloured actor, I forget his name [Woody Strode]. Everybody had a different costume and everything. And Ford came up to me and pointed out that the black fellow had a new costume on. And Ford said, 'How do you think he looks? Do you think he looks all right?' And why I said this, I don't know, but I said, 'He looks a little Uncle Remus-y.' And Ford just looked at me. And he turned to one of his assistants and said, 'Blow a whistle.' And he blew a whistle, and Ford said, 'Everybody get around.' And they got everybody, including the electricians – everyone. And Ford said, 'I just wanted to get

The Man Who Shot Liberty Valance: James Stewart with John Wayne and Woody Strode.

everyone around so that I could let you know the rather unfortunate condition that exists: in this company we have a racist . . .' and he pointed to me. And he said, 'Treat him the way you should treat a racist.' And everybody pointed. Ten minutes later, Duke Wayne came up to me, and said, 'Well, I thought you were going to get away without him getting to you at all, but he finally got you right in the ass, didn't he?' I just remembered that.

GS: *Did you play jokes on Ford?*

JS: [*aghast*] Oh, no, no . . . I had a Western hat that I wore in all my Westerns, and he went to see me with my big Western costume on. And I came in with the hat on, and he said, 'Well, everything's fine, but where'd you get that hat?' And I said, 'This is the hat I've worn in all of my Westerns.' He said 'Well, it's terrible. I'll get you a hat.' And I finally got to keep it through Duke Wayne. He helped me. He got to him, and Ford let me wear my hat.

GS: *You had to go through Duke Wayne? What about your power as an actor?*

JS: Nothing.

GS: *I feel that even in your films of the late 1930s you are far in advance of acting styles. There's a level of realism to your performances, even in a film like* Harvey. *Though it has its basis in a play, you never seem stagey.*

JS: *Harvey* was quite an experience, because I got into it pretty much by accident. Because it played all through the war; Frank Fay had been in it for two years and I'd come out here and found out that my contract hadn't been renewed and everything. So I went back to see my family in Pennsylvania, then went to New York. And everybody said you've got to go and see *Harvey*. Between the acts, Brock Pemberton, who was the producer, came in, and asked, 'How do you like it?' And I said, 'I think it's one of the most wonderful things I've ever seen.' And he said, 'Well, why don't you play it?' And I said, 'Look, any time you want me, I'll do it.' I thought he was kidding, of course. Well, in a month I was back in New York playing it, and playing it with the same cast that had been with Frank Fay. And – a newspaper man told me this, I didn't make these figures myself – the critics gave me the worst reviews that they had for years, absolutely the worst.

GS: *Was that because you had, perhaps, changed the character from how Fay had done it?*

JS: [*stony-voiced*] I never asked them why. So Pemberton came back to me and said, 'Well, I'm sorry about this. We're almost sold out for the next two and half weeks you're playing it, so can you try to get more into the character or something?' I did, because I loved the thing so, and the audiences seemed to get more and more interested in it. And I played to full houses for the rest of the time. And Pemberton said thanks.

I went back [to Hollywood] and the next year he called me and said, 'I just want to tell you, Frank liked that vacation he had last year so much that he wants another one. And I was wondering, I know that the critics are going to have a different feeling entirely, but would you come back and play it for three weeks?' I was about to start a picture, and so I got Lew Wasserman to delay it and I went back. And Pemberton came in on the opening night and said, 'I've invited every one of the critics, every one of them. They're back there.' And the place was full. And in the meantime, I'd been sort of working on the thing, and I did it and it seemed to go fine . . . The next morning, the reviews were worse than the first time! And Pemberton says, 'Thank you very much. I'm sorry about the critics, but you've kept the play in good shape and everything.' So when Mary Chase sold it to the movies, she gave me a good write-up. That's the way I got in the movie.

And in the movies, it was harder for me, too. I never thought I got the same feeling I got in the play, because on the stage you

Harvey: James Stewart with the invisible giant rabbit.

have the audience to react. And the audience almost follows the rabbit when he leaves you. A fascinating thing. Because you work hard enough on it to get them convinced that you have this rabbit. I'd convinced them. But there was always a Saturday matinée. And 'they' were always there. And I could see why, because their mother would say to the kid, 'I'm going to take you down to see this play. This is the play about a man whose best friend is a big white rabbit named Harvey.' So I could see them. There were usually two or three different ones. It got so that I could watch them, and I could see them moving more from one side to another, maybe talking to their mother. And it almost never failed. Every Saturday, one of them, either a small kid like this, or a little above, right in a big important scene, the kid would shout, 'Where's the rabbit?' And the audience would absolutely fall apart, and, of course, I could have just said lines for the rest of the play.

GS: *Just like a circus shill.*

JS: But the movie opened pretty well, it played for a while, but during the last four or five years, it was amazing! I had a whole new set of fan letters from it, lots of them from thirteen-year-olds. It's amazing, and it speaks very well for the play itself.

GS: *When you worked with Lubitsch, from a European tradition, did you get a distinction in your mind between how European directors worked versus Americans?*

JS: I didn't attempt to analyse it at all. He had a little accent, but not enough to bother. He, more than Ford, more than Hitchcock, would explain, but not exactly, what he wanted. He would say, 'Now, in this story, I think it would be wonderful if you could bring out so and so at this point . . . Maybe if you could try and fool around with it, if you could bring this out.' And Maggie Sullavan – who I'd known and met when she was back in New York and I was getting started; an excellent gal and wonderful actress – she understood. I enjoyed doing that movie so much, and Lubitsch made it so clear to us not only what he wanted, but what was there in the script for us to get up there on the screen.

GS: *And he would come around the back way to the emotion?*

JS: Without saying, 'Now I want you to do this.' He would say, 'I think . . .' Also, he would speak in terms of the characters. He would say, 'Now remember, she has been in this part of the store, so I believe that when you come up and have this confrontation with her that you, having been there and watching, you would know . . . Don't you think that?' That type of directing . . .

GS: *I heard there was a scene you had to do over and over again.*

JS: It was a scene with Margaret Sullavan in that movie. I did it fifty times. And it was a very short scene, it lasted two minutes; I had just come in, she was waiting there at the table for me, and people were walking outside the restaurant. I had this thing to tell her, she would start the scene, and I would start telling her about this and I would get it all screwed up! And Lubitsch would say, 'All right, do it again.' And I'd do it a couple of more times, and then I'd get it all right, and I'd look at him and he'd say, 'That was terrible.' So we went on like that . . .

GS: *Do you remember exactly what scene we're talking about?*

JS: It wasn't an important scene in the picture. I was telling her that I was going to meet her there, but I was delayed for some reason, I forget why. It was a little complicated, telling her why, but it wasn't an important thing. And, as I say, I got through it several times, and the times I got through it, Lubitsch said, 'That's terrible, try and do it right this time.' And off we'd go again.

GS: *I imagine Lubitsch wanted something very precise. Did you ask him what he was looking for?*

JS: No. By this time, all I wanted to do was go home. But he was very good about it, and Maggie, so was she, bless her heart. But fifty times . . . Forty-seven, I think.

GS: *Did this ever happen with Hitchcock?*

JS: I just don't remember Hitch asking to do it again. I just don't remember . . . I may have.

GS: *When did you feel best as an actor? When did a director make you feel most comfortable?*

JS: I felt that way about Capra. I felt that when he said it was OK, that it was all right, and he wasn't sort of giving up and saying,

The Shop Around the Corner: the café scene.

'Well, let it go.' Frank Capra, one time, in the filibuster scene in *Mr Smith* ... I'd been doing it for four days, I had maybe another day left. And at the end, about five o'clock, Capra said, 'All right, that's enough for the day,' and as I came down, Frank said, 'I know you are supposed to be losing your voice, but your whisper doesn't sound like a real whisper to me. It just sounds like [*in a husky voice*] you're doing this and anybody can do that; that's nothing.' And he said, 'I'll see you tomorrow morning.' But it worried me. I stopped at an eye, ear, nose and throat man, a doctor that I knew, and by good chance he was still in his office. I came in and said, 'Is there any way that you could give me a sore throat?' He said. 'Wow. That's remarkable. For forty-five years I've been studying, and working, and making every effort that I could to keep people from getting a sore throat, and you come in here ... They've told me you actors are crazy, but you come in here and want me to give you a sore throat? I'll give you the sorest throat that anyone one ever had!' He said, 'Come here.'

Mr Smith Goes to Washington: the filibuster scene.

And he took a bottle with a squirter in it and said, 'Put back your head.' And he put three drops in and said, 'Now swallow,' and I did, and he said, 'Now say something.' I did, and he said, 'Well, you wanted me to give you a sore throat: there's a sore throat. How long does this have to last?' I said, 'Well, I've got one more day, that will mean maybe four or five hours that I have to talk this way.' He said, 'Well, this won't last more than an hour. Where are you making the picture?' I told him: 'Columbia.' He said, 'When do you start?' I said, 'Eight o' clock.' And he said, 'I'll be there.' Well, I don't know what happened to his practice . . .

GS: *You can imagine, a doctor being invited to watch Jimmy Stewart make a film . . .*

JS: He was there until four o'clock that afternoon. And I know Frank knew about it. He stayed in a little box dressing room I had on the set. But I know Frank saw him and I know Frank found out, but he never said anything to me.

GS: *Did he say that your voice was better, at least?*

JS: No. He just didn't say anything about it. He said, 'That's fine.'

GS: *I hear you had a run in with Lionel Barrymore on the set of* It's a Wonderful Life.

JS: I kept saying, 'I don't know whether this is right because I've been at the war for four years.' And he yelled at me, and pointed his finger at me, and said, 'How dare you say that about acting,' and everything. And he scared the shit out of me. But he helped.

GS: *I've noticed in the* Sight and Sound *poll of critics and directors, how well regarded* Vertigo *still is. Are there any of your films that you feel are under-appreciated?*

JS: No. I pretty much agree. Some of them went around for a couple of months and have never been heard from since. And I pretty much agree with it.

GS: *They were simply programmers?*

JS: It was just part of my work. I didn't start out to make a lousy picture.

GS: *Films like* Vertigo *and* It's a Wonderful Life *have gone up in critical reputation. Are there any films you are surprised did as well as they did?*

JS: I suppose *The Stratton Story* did better than I thought it would.

GS: *Did you always feel you were going in the right direction?*

JS: I didn't think about it that way. I just did it, day to day . . .

GS: *Did your work habits change over the years?*

JS: I think that probably the way I worked, the way I did scenes, changed from time to time, but it changed in a way I didn't notice.

GS: *And your methodology?*

JS: I've always had that.

GS: *My time is up. It's been a delight.*

JS: Well, I've enjoyed it. You got me talking about things I haven't thought about for a long time.

5 Being True to the Character

Frances McDormand talks to Willem Dafoe

I first saw Frances McDormand in *Blood Simple* – an eye-opening film and a 'where did they get that woman?' performance. Next I saw her in *Raising Arizona* (a film I had been eager to see, since I had badly wanted the Nicolas Cage role). Finally, I met her on the set of *Mississippi Burning*, where she played a battered Southern housewife and I played an FBI investigator. For her performance, she was nominated for an Academy Award.

In *Mississippi*, Fran struck me as down-to-earth, direct and funny. Very serious and great at what she does, but I swear sometimes when I'd be with her I'd almost forget that we were actors. That's why it was strange to do this interview: I feel we have talked each other's ears off many times since we've met, yet we never talked about performing.

I'm a Coen Brothers fan. I've seen all of their films – of which Fran has done four or five – and I've seen many of her other films, each one wildly different from the rest. Among them: Sam Raimi's *Darkman*, Ken Loach's *Hidden Agenda*, Robert Altman's *Short Cuts*, and John Boorman's *Beyond Rangoon*. Strong directors and not a formula picture in the lot.

On stage, Fran has played Masha in *Three Sisters*, appeared in *The Sisters Rosenzweig* at the Lincoln Center, *The Swan* at The Public Theater, and was nominated for a Tony Award for her performance as Stella in *A Streetcar Named Desire*.

We began this interview over lunch at a noisy restaurant, and I was nervous the whole time about whether the tape was picking up the conversation. We eventually went to her and Joel Coen's place – but then her infant son Pedro woke up from a nap and we just couldn't continue. Fran went away to LA for a week of publicity, and when she returned we talked over the phone about her role as Detective Marge Gunderson in the Coen Brothers' *Fargo*.

WILLEM DAFOE: *Your character is pregnant in* Fargo. *How did you arrive at this? Did Joel and Ethan [Coen] talk with you while they were writing the script?*

FRANCES MCDORMAND: No, they never do. I mean, I'm around when they're writing all the time, but they don't talk to me. I'm not a writer, I wouldn't presume to say anything. Now when it comes to casting, and choices as an actor, then I'll say a lot, whether they want to hear it or not. But Joel and I talked about the script after I read it, and really there were only two things: one, that they incorporated the morning sickness thing, and two, the Mike Yanagita thing. They told me they wanted to develop Marge's character in a different context, other than with her husband or with the murder case. Any character development – that's good. So when they come up with this Mike Yanagita scene – I didn't really get it until I saw the finished movie.

WD: *What did you think your job was in that scene?*

FM: Steve [Park], who was playing Mike Yanagita – I wanted to show how uncomfortable Marge was when he broke down. She is a cop, she can handle a lot of stuff, but when it comes to public displays of emotion, she was very uncomfortable. She had to leave. I liked that, it showed she is fallible. And also that, just because she's pregnant, she's not this mother image. That was the last thing I wanted. If she was too sweet and understanding with Mike Yanagita, then it was going to become this whole 'mama' thing. That would have been too easy. And I wasn't interested in playing a 'mother-nature' type either.

WD: *When they give you a script, what's the first thing you do with it? Is there a working pattern that you tend to cling to? Do you go to external details of the character? Do you look for a model?*

Frances McDormand.

Willem Dafoe (photograph by Glenn Rigberg).

As Marge Gunderson in *Fargo*.

FM: I don't do a lot of research. And I never have, in film or in theatre. I do all my work in rehearsal. Granted, it hasn't always succeeded. How do you know in a month of rehearsal exactly what's going to work? I don't sit at home and learn lines, although I have learned to go back to the script a lot more than I used to. One of the problems I had when I was younger was that I had no idea what the arc of the character was, I had no idea how the character's story told the story of the play. I was just going scene to scene to scene. If I was lucky, it came out OK through the rehearsals. But then I started working in film, and everything would be shot out of sequence. I had to have a much better idea of how it was plotted.

WD: *It's funny, my impulse is just the opposite. You can't know how it's going to be plotted, it has yet to be edited, so in fact, you've just got to be present, and intuitively find a way to play each scene.*

FM: Definitely. To me, it doesn't make any difference how much I know, or how much I've thought about it in my head. When it comes to playing emotionally tough scenes, I'm not going to sit at home and think, OK, this is where the tension builds, because it all depends on exactly where you are when you're doing it. The whole emotional-recall thing can be very good for another actor, but it doesn't work for me. For me, it's all about emotional catharsis. All I have to do is stand right in the middle of a group of people pulling cables, doing the lights – I just stand there, and the isolation of being alone in the middle of a group of people can get me to a vulnerable place. For the majority of the human race, joy or pain or emotion gets put in a very safe place. That's the healing process. But actors don't let the scar tissue completely heal over, and since it never completely heals, it's not about manipulating a memory or an emotion as much as it is about not having to dig too far – not having to pick off the scab as much. You don't have to spend all your acting time making it bleed. It's just there, you're carrying it around.

WD: *Do you choose a project because of the role or the director . . .?*

FM: With *Fargo*, I hadn't read the script or prepared for an audition. I got the part because I've worked with the Coen Brothers, they've known my work for twelve years. They were offering me a challenge. It's interesting, because I'm not sure how I would have felt about that character if I had just read the script. I took it for granted with them. I wanted to work with Joel and Ethan.

WD: *It's a great role. But she's one of those characters who doesn't go through a transformation.*

FM: She is what she is. In that scene with Mike Yanagita, she realized he was lying. That's the biggest thing she has to accept, because at the end when she talks about greed and not understanding why these guys did what they did, that's just Marge's general condition. It would have been interesting to see what would have happened if other actresses had read the script and wanted to audition. I never heard about who else they were considering, or who else was fighting for the role. I don't know how many people would have wanted to do Marge.

WD: *Are you conscious of that competition normally?*

FM: I'm often interested in the casting process because it puts what you do in perspective.

WD: *In performing for film, how much technique do you think there is? It's easy to recognize in theatre, but in film, it's so much about trying to catch these intuitive moments. And what you do in film is so mediated. Do you think it's really about being present and being receptive?*

FM: It changes. Working with Joel and Ethan is a lot more like theatre than other films I've done. Their movies are theatrical. They're very stylized, in a way that a company of actors has to be. The screenplay's like a play script. You're not trying to fix the holes in the script with improvisation or character development. It's given to you, it's there.

WD: *Do you get a clear idea of their world before you shoot?*

FM: When you read the screenplay and then you see the movie, there's no alteration of the original idea. Joel and Ethan start making it when they write it. They don't write screenplays for somebody else to direct and somebody else to edit. From the minute they get the idea, they're talking about the dialogue, writing the script, thinking about camera movements and locations. Everything starts at the same time. It's a really good example of feeling the difference, because for a long time, I was flying by the seat of my pants.

WD: *In what respect?*

FM: I never had any training in film. I studied the classics, but never had any work on camera.

WD: *Had you worked much in theatre before your first movie?*

FM: No, *Blood Simple* was my second job out of Yale Graduate School. The first was a play I did right before that, in Trinidad. The Jamaican poet Derek Walcott had just received a MacArthur grant, and took some money to produce a play with Trinidadian actors and two American actors. Some nights we didn't perform because nobody showed up, but it was great to be down there. And it was interesting because he was a poet first and a playwright second. When he did rewrites on the play, he would come in with a poem first. And we'd say, 'Well, Derek, it's not very realistic to start speaking in poetry.' He'd say, 'I'm going to work on that,' and it would gradually become dialogue – the poem, then the syntax. In *Blood Simple* the only choice I made was not to be theatrical. I never moved my face, and my mouth's always open like I'm terrified – I was a lot of the time. I just did whatever they told me to do, which was perfect for the character, but it's not like I made that decision as a character choice. It was from not knowing what to do.

WD: *What's changed?*

FM: Exactly. What's changed? Well, it depends on who's doing the film.

WD: *When you start something, what are your expectations or obligations? What do you find pleasurable in your approach to a project? Is there any pattern?*

FM: Yes, it's character work, although I didn't choose *Beyond Rangoon* because of the character I played. It was the classic supporting role: she had no other life other than the support she gave to Patricia Arquette's lead character. But I got to work with Boorman, whose movies I love, and I got to go to

Malaysia. But I choose characters in theatre and film that I know are going get me somewhere as an actor.

WD: *You mean challenge you?*

FM: Yes, that will take me to the next place. If I waited for those characters only, I would still be playing battered Southern women with less than a high school education. But I go back to the theatre, I do Irina in *Three Sisters* and I also do Masha. I bust my butt. They kill me, they knock me flat. I see how I let my theatre muscles atrophy. I get them built back up and then I go – see, the timing is really specific. For three months I was working on stage, doing Stella in *A Streetcar Named Desire*, then I got to do that kind of character on film, and I had to clamp down the volume and play on screen. It was great. I really found out what the different muscles were. You don't work with the bottom of the feet in movies. It's focusing it all on your face, and your ears, listening. For example, in *Mississippi Burning* I didn't do research. All I did was listen to Gene [Hackman]. He had an amazing capacity for not giving away any part of himself [in read-throughs]. But the minute we got on the set, little blinds on his eyes flipped up and everything was available. It was mesmerizing. He's really believable, and it was like a basic acting lesson. I think that's the thing I do most in film, I listen. Which is hard if you don't believe the person talking to you. But if you truly listen to the other characters, then something happens to your face. Enough happens to your face, and you don't have to project in any way, you can just let it happen. What was different with *Fargo* was that we never saw the rushes with an audience. The first time I saw the film with an audience, my jaw was shaking because I was so tense. I was amazed, I'd never done a character that caused such hilarity. And it's not like I was playing her as comedic, but the audience laughed, not only at her, but constantly.

WD: *Did you feel pressure to be 'funny' when you were shooting it?*

As Abby in *Blood Simple.*

FM: There were times on the set when I would crack myself up, or the crew would crack up, but I thought it was just because Marge was that kind of familiar character. And we'd all be like, 'Oh God, Marge is eating again.' But I realized that the old standard drama school thing about comedy is accurate: if you're true to your character and make that character believable, and you're true to their behaviour, then whatever situation you're in, the comedy will be revealed. On stage, when I've tried to do comedy, I've always overshot it by trying to be too honest. For instance, when I played Pheni in *Sisters Rosenzweig*. This character is at a turning point in her life, a really hard point. I always overshot my character because she was unhappy. She had these speeches about refugees and war-torn countries. Now how can you make that funny? I couldn't. No matter how true I was to her behaviour, I couldn't find the comedy that was inherent in the character. But with Marge, it was not like there was an audience to help figure out the timing of the comedy. Like you said, it's going to happen in the editing process. If Joel cuts from the right or the left of the frame, it's going to make the joke or it's not going to make the joke. So there was no point in thinking that Marge was a comedic character.

WD: *How much has your work changed as a result of natural growth, and how much has it changed by the experience of*

Mississippi Burning: with Gene Hackman . . .

. . . and Brad Dourif.

encountering certain things that have made you see yourself differently, or made you realize what was possible or what wasn't possible? It's always interesting for me to ask myself what there is that people won't let me do, that I want to do. Is there such a thing for you?

FM: Oh definitely. That's the whole athletic side of being an actor. The stronger you get and the more powerful you feel, then you know what the next challenge is. You don't plateau. It's a seeking profession, not a complacent profession. There has to be a search involved.

WD: *But there are all kinds of sucker punches along the way. Like the idea of doing a diversity of roles. That's one thing I find: actors often want to play everything.*

FM: Yes, definitely. Joel's taught me some big lessons about that. Countless times he's had to go through the audition process with me, and you know what that process is to an actor. And even though it still fucks me up sometimes, I really believe now that I'm not in control. There is a nice little tag line he gave me once: The only control actors really have is saying No. You have no other control, no matter how big a movie star you are. No is about as far as you're ever going to get, which is pretty damn powerful. And also that you cannot play everything. It doesn't matter how good an actor you are, it can be as stupid as you're too tall or you're too short.

(We interrupted the interview here and took it up a week later over the phone.)

WD: *This is cool, I feel like a spy tapping the phone* [laughter]. *So let's just launch right into it. Fargo is a reality-based crime drama. Does your character actually exist, did you ever meet her?*

FM: No, I did not meet her. From what Joel and Ethan told me, she does exist. But I did work with Officer Nancy at the St Paul Police Department, who was pregnant, and she took me to the shooting range.

WD: *Oh cool. How'd you do?*

FM: I did pretty darn good [*laughter*]. It was great to talk to her, because she was on the vice squad and was still working on the street, going into crack houses and stuff, seven months pregnant. She couldn't afford to stop, she's a single mom. So it was good talking to her, finding out what the guys she worked with thought about her. They didn't really seem to be prejudiced in any way. But yeah, I never met the woman the character is based on.

WD: *Marge on paper didn't look as colourful as she ended up being. What gave you the inkling that playing her was going to be fun? Did this have anything to do with your being from the Midwest – or did you think that if your life had been different, this could have been you?*

FM: No, if it had been anybody else's script but Joel and Ethan's, I would have said, 'Great script,' but I wouldn't have necessarily been drawn to Marge. She's not the kind of woman I thought I wanted to play. But in this case, I didn't think about it at all, because I wanted to work with them again. I figured they had a good reason for wanting me to play Marge. It wasn't until I started working on her that I realized how much fun she'd be.

WD: *You said the casting process puts what you do in perspective. What do you mean?*

FM: It clicks on the part of my brain that's always reserved for acting problems. Whether I get the job or not, I start working on a character – it's the process of reading the script, becoming attracted to the character, auditioning, proving that I can do it. So whether I get the job or not, I've still been given a shot at it.

WD: *Ethan and Joel know you, but do you see a tendency in other film-makers to label you?*

FM: Yes.

WD: *Probably has most to do with what they've seen you in last.*

FM: Yes.

WD: *What do you do in that process you just described to shatter their preconceptions?*

FM: It's always flattering to be offered a part, because you think, 'Oh they've seen my work, they think I'm good.' But I will always read. I'm able to show a lot more in an audition situation if I do read than if I just chat with somebody. Especially if it's a character part. Actors shoot themselves in the foot if they're trying to do something different and they refuse to read for a director.

WD: *When they get to a certain level, they don't want to deal with the anxiety and rejection of auditioning, don't you think?*

FM: Yeah, I think so. The rejection is never fun. But I've also found that recently – maybe because playing Marge was leaving something behind, leaving the vulnerable 'victim' roles behind – I've been having trouble showing the characters' vulnerability. I'm feelin' a little confident these days [*laughter*] – you know? They know I can do the classic vulnerable role because I've done it so much. So then I try to show something different, and the feedback I get is, 'Well, she just doesn't seem to be comfortable with the vulnerability of the character.' It's like, 'Oh my God, I'm trying to show you I can do other things.' I'm actually more anxious about the chatting than the audition. I feel if I get a chance to read I can prove myself.

WD: *Do you have a preference between doing comedy or drama? When you go to the movie, and you see it all said and done, do you get more satisfaction out of hearing people laugh in the audience? Or having people be moved to tears?*

FM: There's no preference. What was great about working on Marge was that I was never obligated to some emotional catharsis. The working process was satisfying because I got to explore other things. I've been in other comedies, but this is the first time I've ever sat in an audience and felt that there's this large group of people who come from different places and who get to laugh at the same thing. That was really satisfying. But I think probably my strength is drama.

WD: *Sometimes in drama you feel like you got to beat yourself up a little bit. It must be nice to have your Minnesota cop who plugs along without too much trouble.*

FM: Oh, definitely. It's also great from a feminist perspective to be able to play somebody like that. I don't think all the

Fargo: 'The men in her life are defined by her.'

characters I've played have been victims, but there's been a certain requirement of vulnerability to tell the story of whatever lead character I'm supporting. And usually the character I'm supporting is a man. But in *Fargo* the only story I was telling was Marge's. The audience feels really connected to her, and emotionally involved with her, but she never has to bring them into that by showing her own emotional vulnerability. That was really exciting.

WD: *She's also not defined by her relationship to a man.*

FM: The men in her life are defined by her. And in a seemingly conventional marriage, they're both doing exactly what they want to do, and taking care of what needs to be done. There's an equality there.

WD: *How do you think* Fargo's *going to do in the Midwest? Do you think people are going to recognize Marge? Or do you think they're going to think it's too heightened?*

FM: It really remains to be seen. We shot the film in Grand Forks, North Dakota, which is close to the border of Canada; a small community, not a lot of exposure to big-city life or whatever. Steve Buscemi, who played Mr Pink in *Reservoir Dogs*, is in *Fargo*, and people were yelling at him from across the street, 'Hey, Mr Pink!' They were buying him meals in the diner . . . Clearly, their imaginations were captured by a movie like *Reservoir Dogs*. And because Marge is built around so many iconic characters from television series – *Cagney and Lacey*, *Columbo*, all those things that are really familiar to an audience through television – I think there's enough there. The one thing that will throw them is the whole true story thing. But then again, *America's Most Wanted* gets big ratings. The movie taps into American culture in a way that just might hook a smaller town audience. But it really remains to be seen. There is a certain, not satire or parody, but it is a heightened reality. And then there's the Minnesota accent which is a score to the story as well as the music.

WD: *I've lived in New York for twenty years, but since I come from Wisconsin, the accent was an absolute hook into the* movie. My sisters sound like that. It gave the film a specific place, set it very specifically in my life, so that I wanted to come along for the ride.

FM: If you've never been there, or spent time there, it seems foreign – you haven't heard the Minnesota/Wisconsin accent used that way in a movie.

WD: *What did you mean when you referred to the scene in* Fargo *and said, 'the Mike Yanagita thing'?*

FM: Mike Yanagita breaks down at the end of that scene, and Marge can't handle this emotional display in public. She's very uncomfortable and wants to be out of the situation. But also, dramaturgically, it is very emotional. And the audience in fact feels bad for Mike Yanagita, they're moved. Which does not happen that often in a Joel and Ethan movie. You don't get these emotional, cathartic moments. But the fact is, you find out very soon after that it's a complete lie. So they put the cathartic moment in, but they still have to pull it out. What they do let ride is the end of the movie, with Marge and Norm. It's very sweet and tender. And they let it go, they don't pull out with a joke on that one.

WD: *People, when they speak to artists, talk about intent. But as an actor, we're often serving someone else's construct. To what degree do you find that frustrating, and to what degree do you find that liberating? I know there's always collaboration, but basically, in the imagining, in the being, in the pretending, you are directed – someone else frames you. You don't make the frame.*

FM: Yeah, actors are in a service industry. I mean, I've directed a couple of things in the theatre.

WD: *Are you going to direct some more?*

FM: I'd like to, yeah. In the theatre, definitely.

WD: *Not film.*

FM: No. Because . . .

WD: *Because you're very close with a very good director.*

FM: Right, yeah. I don't think I can tell a story with movies, as a director.

WD: *Do you feel the need?*

FM: No, I don't. But in the theatre, I do. I've lived there longer, and I've lived there more. I feel like I know what I have to offer in the theatre as a director. But it does get frustrating in film, because I don't necessarily want to work with a director who's known to be 'good with actors'. Sometimes that phrase puts me off. I would rather work with a director who knows how to make a movie.

WD: *I'm right with you.*

FM: I don't mind if they have a respect for the craft of acting. I like that, that's good, that means they'll let me do my job. But I would much rather they know what lens to use, how they're going to edit it – have that in their head. Because then everything I bring to it, whether it gets cut or not, is going to be able to be used.

WD: *I know exactly what you mean. Well said.*

FM: In the theatre I like to do new plays, to explore new languages and new styles that haven't really been set yet. I like doing classical theatre with directors that need to do the play. The first time I did *Three Sisters*, I did it with Liviu Ciulei who was sixty-five years old at the time. He hadn't done that play yet, though he had done a lot of other Chekhov, because he wanted to wait until he was old enough. The second time I did it was with Emily Mann when she was in her late thirties. It was a completely different production. She needed to do it, but for a different reason. They both needed to do the play. And so whatever journey I went on as an actor, however I served their production, it was for a really good reason. Whereas I was in another play that was very hard to do, and a bitch of a role to create, and in the end I realized the production wasn't successful because the director had chosen it for other reasons than having to realize that play in his own terms. So then it becomes like, Who are you going to serve? Who's the best boss?

WD: *What are you thinking about doing next?*

FM: Ever since we talked, that was the one question that I've gone back to over and over in talking to friends . . . you asked me that question, and I went blank [*laughter*]. And it was the first time in fifteen years that ever happened.

WD: *Well, that's probably good.*

FM: I think it's really good. I'm waiting to be surprised. I'm really content to wait until I know exactly what's right. It's not a career move. It's not like I'm waiting for the leading role in a blockbuster Hollywood movie, or the lead in some play on Broadway.

WD: *It's just your life.*

FM: It's got to be something that I can commit to in the same way. That's what's so fucking hard about working with Joel and Ethan. It's so satisfying, it's so complete, it's really hard not to judge whatever you do after in the same way. Same thing after doing *Three Sisters*. I usually have some idea as an actor of what I want to try. It's either something in complete contrast to what I've done most recently, or it's a movie versus a play, or a play versus a movie. But right now I have no idea. The one constant now is that I've got something really fun to do when I'm at home [*laughter*].

WD: *Yeah.*

FM: Whereas before, I'd say yes every time they'd call me to do a reading because it was work, it was exercise. Now it's like, Do I want to go do a reading? I think maybe I'd rather go to the Circus Gym today.

This interview originally appeared in BOMB *magazine, Spring 1996, issue No. 55.* BOMB *is published quarterly by New Art Publications, 9th Floor, 594 Broadway, New York, New York 10012, USA.*

6 Lee Marvin

by John Boorman

The profound unease we feel in identifying with an evil character in a movie is the recognition that we may be capable of such evil. Conversely, identifying with a hero elevates us, leads us to believe ourselves capable of sacrifice, honour and courage. So many actors when required to play bad guys cannot resist some coded plea to the audience for sympathy. My dear friend Lee Marvin never did, which is why his villains were so shocking. Lee knew from his war experiences the depth of our capacity for cruelty and evil. He had committed such deeds, had plumbed the depths and was prepared to recount what he had seen down there. What characterized his performances was an unflinching truth that was sometimes almost unbearable. He knew this stuff was hard to take. Also he had to live in the world, the Hollywood world. Just as alcohol offered him an escape from unbearable reality, so his other acting persona, the bumbling drunk, released him from his obligations to truth-telling. The two manifestations are perfectly paired in *Cat Ballou*, where he played the dual roles of deadly killer and hopeless drunk.

Point Blank became an inner portrait of Lee Marvin, a set of variations on his relationship with violence. We continued this journey into his psyche in *Hell in the Pacific*, which took him back into the Pacific War that he had fought (I always liked the contradiction in that phrase, Pacific War, and wish I had been allowed to use it as the film's title). It was to be a redemptive experience for him, finding his way towards an accommodation with Toshiro Mifune, the enemy. Yet it was an outcome he devoutly desired, rather than deeply felt.

Lee Marvin in *Hell in the Pacific.*

Marvin was driven by the American *Zeitgeist*, so, although he came to love Mifune, he still wanted to kill him, which is how I should have ended the film. Lee's widow Pam is, at my insistent promptings, writing his biography. On my desk are her latest chapters. A fascinating picture emerges. He was a young boy when he witnessed and perpetrated the atrocities of war. His wounds never healed. They left him raw, and all life was salt that rubbed into them. Here is a brief extract from Pam's book, an account of his wounding in his own words:

Phase 1
Saipan, Mariana Islands, June 1944

Fourth Day – Called up to replace K Company of 3rd Battalion, 24th Marines, as they had received heavy fire and casualties and had fallen back to their original cover. The assault platoon, 1st Plt., and 4th Plt. of I Co., 3rd Bt., 24th Marines would jump off from the same position, only in flanking positions, 1st to the left, 4th to the right. All positions are looking north. Meanwhile the 2nd and 3rd Platoons would push straight forward. At the signal we moved out. Mike Cairns and I were the 'point' of the assault platoon. Moving at a slow walk, we bore to the left and forward. There was nothing to be seen, the ground cover was thin and high, high brush with an occasional tree. The terrain was flat and slightly dish-shaped. All was quiet. We had just passed an abandoned thatched hut approaching a slight mound with three palm trees on it about thirty yards in front of us when suddenly there was a shot and a loud slap to the immediate left of me. It was Mike and he was down. He said a quiet 'Oh,' and then, 'Corpsman,' just as quietly. There was blood on his dungaree blouse. I went down to him and tore open his jacket, and there, just one inch below his left nipple, was a small dark hole. The blood was pink and bubbly, a lung shot. I tried to put my finger in the hole, but it would not fit. His eyes were closed and he said 'Corpsman' twice more in a whisper and was dead.

The high-sounding Jap machine-gun and rifle fire, then I heard Mac's voice, our platoon leader, shouting for all BAR men to stand

and fire magazine. Mike's BAR was next to me. I picked it up and put twenty rounds into the brush at the base of the palm trees, but didn't see anything. Mac was shouting for me to pull over to the right and join the rest of the platoon. There was no way that I could get Mike's ammunition belt off him as it had shoulder straps, so I pulled the trigger group off his BAR and threw it away and, grabbing my MI, headed off low and fast where I thought the rest of the platoon were.

All was chaotic, shouting voices, the heavy sound of our weapons and the high, shrill, fast sound of theirs. I still could not see the Japs! They were close, for I could feel the blast of their weapons. Then I could see the 1st Platoon, they were all down, some firing forward, some on their backs and sides. 'Oh my God! They got us!' As I was running, the twigs and small branches were flying through the air as their machine guns were cutting everything down. I figured I had better get down too. And just in time. All the brush around me knee-high just disappeared. I looked forward and my leg flew to one side. I couldn't feel anything. 'This is getting bad.' Looking down my side, I saw that the heel had been shot off. Looking up again to see where it had come from, there was another crack and my face was numb and eyes full of dirt. It had a set-up of rhythm. I knew. Burying my face in the ground and gritting my teeth in anticipation, SLAPPP!!! The impact caused a reflex that lifted me off the ground. I lay still for a long time. I knew that I was hit. I shouted, 'I'm hit!', and a voice nearby said, very calmly, 'Shut up – we're all hit.' I was slowly tensing my various muscles. By the process of elimination, I figured it was somewhere below the chest. By then, Schidt and Pedagrew crawled up and told me I was hit in the ass and proceeded to dump some sulfa in the wound and said they would try to get me out of there and to follow them.

I disassembled my MI; my cartridge belt had already been cut off, so we began to crawl to the right. I could not believe the number of dead marines. I would recognize certain personal touches of equipment my friends had and there they were, lifeless. We got over to the 2nd Platoon area and they were as bad off as us. We started back towards our line. Now most of the fire was Jap. Where were our mortars and tanks? All at once we were stopped by an opening, completely with no cover, a fire lane about 20 feet wide. There was no way to get through there crawling. Schidt said, 'If we can get you up, can you run?' They did get me up and shoved me out into the cover on the other side, then crawled to a large-trunked tree, about 4 feet thick. Rose was sitting there with his back to the fire. He asked me if I wanted a cigarette and gave me one; he also offered me water. On returning the canteen to him, he leaned out a bit to put it away in its cover on his cartridge belt. He was hit immediately and fell over on me and died without a word. I could not get him off me. Then somebody stepped on my wound. I shouted. Fortunately, they were stretcher-bearers. Then Callelo was brought in; he had been hit in the head and was screaming that he could not see. They loaded him on the stretcher and at the same time they got hit again, killing one of the bearers. He was out of his head now. They got him out of there fast. I shouted, 'What about me?' They said I was next.

What frightened me now was that I would be lying face down on the stretcher about 1½ feet above the ground. Just the height their machine guns were usually set at. There was nothing I could do. I had to get out. The bearers were running as fast as they could, the fire was all around, then one of the front bearers went down, only a stumble, they got me back to Battalion aid, still under heavy fire. At Battalion, a guy, stripped to the waist with two nambu pistols stuck in his belt, asked me if I needed plasma but I didn't know. He gave me a surrette of morphine and had me put behind a long stack of 81mm mortar HE shells. They were still in their clover leaves and I could hear the strays hitting them. All at once I noticed Schidt squatting by me and he was asking me for my .45 automatic, which I had in my shoulder holster. I had to give it to him, he had gotten me out of there. I told him it was my father's pistol and not to lose it. He thanked me and took off.

Just then somebody in the distance started shouting, 'Counter-attack, counter-attack,' and the panic of trying to get the wounded out of there began. I didn't even have my .45 any more. And by now my leg was totally useless. Then a terrific explosion, a big ammo dump about 100 yards away had gone up and I could see people floating through the air. A lot of confusion and I found myself in a stretcher jeep, two of us and two ambulatory, but we were going the wrong way, back to the fire fight. I shouted at the driver a number of times and finally he swung around and headed for the beach. I don't remember too much of the trip; we were about three or four miles in on the fourth day.

When the haze cleared, a corpsman was filling out a tag and attaching it to me with its wire. Then he took a red crayon and made a mark on my forehead saying that he had given me morphine. There was a lot of heavy stuff going off around us. I was under a torn canvas fly on the beach: equipment was stacked everywhere and it was getting dark. I asked him if there was any chance of getting off tonight and he said, 'No!' My heart sank. The Japs had the beach zeroed in and were pounding it. We would never make it through the night. Above all the noise, a voice from the water shouted, 'Anybody going out?' The corpsman hollered, 'How much room you got?'

The next time I awoke, I was listening to a diesel-engine throb. I knew we were passing ships but didn't much care. I was face down on a stretcher and was aware of much light, then a pair of shiny black shoes with white trousers. A lot of shouting, then I was in a bright companionway painted yellow with Glenn Miller's 'Moonlight Serenade' playing from somewhere. A nurse in white was reading my tag and asking if I wanted some ice water or ice-cream. I didn't know what to say. Some man's voice said, 'GU' and they took me away. Still on the stretcher, I was next to a low bunk with a thick mattress and white sheets on it. A voice asked if I could climb on to the bed. I said I'd get the sheets dirty, and the voice said, 'That's OK, we got more.' They cut the dog tag off my shoe and put it in my hand. I asked them not to take my helmet, and please turn off the lights. 'Don't worry.' In and out of focus for a while, then I heard it: from the island, the fire-fight was still going on. My company, what was left of it, was still there and I was safe on a hospital ship. Ice-cream, water, clean sheets, Glenn Miller, nurses. I was a coward! And cried.

Phase 2
Oahu, Hawaiian Territory, November 1944

Out on the south-west beaches of this beautiful island they had it all set up for us. Plenty of beer, good chow and even things like inner-tubes so that we could play in the surf if the fancy caught us. There was no schedule, except for eating and lights-out. A real rest camp. We were told that we would probably be here for three or four weeks, so enjoy it. After this, the doctors would examine us again and it would be back to duty or Stateside. There was a general uneasiness among all the men.

I had a lot of time to think about things, starting with the hospital ship, *Solace*, then three months at fleet 108 on Guadalcanal, Espirito Santos, New Caledonia, and finally Navy no. 10 at Aiea Heights. I had long ago arrived at the decision that I could not go back.

The days drifted by. But I was starting to have a recurring half-dream and half-fantasy. As 'taps' would sound each night, we would climb into our bunks and pull the mosquito netting down. There were eight of us to a paramedical tent with the sides rolled up as the nights were so balmy. Each evening, as I was drifting off to sleep, I would see figures slipping from one palm tree to the next. Very quietly and with caution, coming towards me. They were Japs! I would sit bolt up and stare at them and they would disappear. I would look around in the tent – all seemed secure – and peer under my bunk. My MI was there, but we had no ammo. We were in a rest camp in a rear area. It was 3,000 miles to the action, but we had slipped in on them at night. Why couldn't they do the same thing? By now I was fully awake and realized how foolish I had been, so I would change the subject of my thinking and fall off to sleep.

I got very comfortable with this fantasy, even anticipating it as I would go to bed. After all, how secure can a guy be? 'I will wake up and they will all disappear.' Then one night as I sat up to look at them, the loudest siren I have ever heard turned on. What?! Then the 90mms started up. It sounded as if the air-raid siren and the anti-aircraft guns were right in my tent. I leapt out of bed grabbing my rifle at the same time, landing on my knees on the plywood floor. There was a lot of shouting and screaming, lights were flashing and the 90s kept blasting away. I had my rifle clutched in my hands, but no ammunition! Caught again – I tried to stand up but my legs would not respond. Just immobile panic. I stayed like this for I don't know how long and then things began to slow down. The guns ceased firing and the siren wound down. I could see and hear men running and shouting, 'It's all right – it's all right – just a test – just a test.' The lights went on in the camp and in our tent. We were all in strange positions and just looked at each other. I don't think much was said. Slowly, we all crawled back into our cots and the lights went out again. I don't know. I don't know.

A lot of that experience found its way into *Point Blank*. Lee was hypersensitive to everything going on around him. He could walk into a room of people and feel all the pain. His mind was still on combat alert. Drink desensitized him, but he always carried America's guilt in his heart. He felt America was doomed because it was founded on the genocide of the Indian nations. He believed, therefore, that America could only express itself through violence. America was war, and he was a conscripted warrior. My camera held Lee at arm's length in *Point Blank*. It framed him in stark compositions. He was beyond human help, beyond redemption. The audience could feel compassion for his isolation, for a condemned man, but at a distance. A man, a nation, in violent and hopeless pursuit of their destiny.

7 Jodie Foster talks to Mike Figgis

MIKE FIGGIS: *How would you describe what you do?*

JODIE FOSTER: God, I never know how to describe it. I don't think I do a different job as a director than I do as an actress, or as a producer. For me it's all about creating this reality out of nothing – so that an audience member can sit inside of it and be completely surrounded, and forget who he is and where he came from, and only be with the people on screen.

MF: *But why would we do that? How can we rationalize doing that?*

JF: You know, for me, going to see movies is a primal thing – maybe because I've been seeing films since before I can remember, and it's always been a part of my life. But it's something that I need to do. I'll be on location, having a great time all week – and then I have to go see a movie on the weekend, so that I can cry. It can be the stupidest movie in the world – just so that I can cry for a good solid hour and a half. I can release myself emotionally as a spectator in an audience in a way that I can't do in my own life, I think.

MF: *Do you think that's any different from the function of theatre a hundred years ago?*

JF: Unfortunately, theatre just hasn't fulfilled the same thing in my life.

MF: *Because cinema is better at it?*

JF: I think the experience of going to a movie is so completely different from sitting in a theatre – and maybe you have to have a suit on, and you're sitting next to somebody that you don't really know very well, but you have to be nice to –

MF: *But movie-going can be like that too.*

JF: I think you have the experience of being alone, watching a movie. You can dress any way you want, it doesn't cost fifty dollars. And you feel much more at one with those faces on the screen. You forget where you are.

MF: *Yes, but that's a technical thing. The sound is bigger, it's more real.*

JF: Definitely. And because of that, it can touch more people in a much more elementary way than theatre does. Theatre somehow goes to your head first – it sort of gets translated through the senses, and then eventually gets to your emotions. And, for me, film works the other way around. It starts from your gut first, and goes out the other way.

MF: *I did theatre for fifteen years. And I saw a lot of European theatre, and ninety-eight per cent of what you said I agree with. But the two per cent that I can remember – they were possibly greater experiences for me than film-going experiences.*

JF: With theatre I think it has to be a *great* play, a great experience. Maybe it's once every year or two years that you sit down and you pay the fifty dollars and you actually see something that you hadn't expected, that took you to another place. That's happened to me a few times in my life.

MF: *I've never had an experience like that in the fifty-dollar venues. But I've had great experiences in small rooms, where there's no proscenium arch, and an actor can speak naturally, without projection. It's usually been a bunch of mad Polish people, and it's been extraordinary. But free of theatrical convention. And I agree, intellectually you're thrown on to the writing in a certain way. Whereas in cinema, when it's good . . . Let's talk about cinema – is it good right now?*

JF: Well, there's always been many tiers. There's the conventional Hollywood stuff that lots of people go see, which is a little contrived – you've seen it before and there is an audience for it. Then there are other layers, there always will be – it just depends on how many people want to go see the smaller, more unique films.

MF: *The balance between those various 'layers' – how do you think it compares now with how it was, say, twenty years ago?*

JF: It feels like there are too many movies being made, in all arenas – the independents as well as the grander studio films that are more expensive. I certainly can't keep up with it. And, unfortunately, the moment that you have that much quantity, your quality goes way down. You can only make so many great films – it takes hard work and a lot of inspiration, and you just can't have that inspiration twenty times a year.

MF: *So we're talking about a market that is saturated on all levels – arthouse movies, mainstream movies. Do you ever feel there's a danger that if ten great films happened to come out at the same time –*

JF: Would anybody notice? I don't know. The 'entertainment industry' now has a much wider sense – the news has become entertainment, we have so many more different outlets, everywhere we look there's Pay-Per-View ... I think audiences' expectations of films have changed a lot too.

MF: *A century ago, theatre was such a special thing – a kind of community activity, a ritual of social behaviour. I have the sense now that the entertainment industry which we're involved in is so big that it's out of proportion to the cultural need for it. And that worries me. Let's accept that we both love cinema, and we demonstrate that by staying in the game and making films. But do you think cinema is over-valued now?*

JF: Actually, I think it's the opposite problem, which is that there's so much of it coming at us constantly – it's like a food that you get one hundred and fifty times a day. Even if you liked it at the beginning of the day, by the end of the day you've seen enough of it to not really have that much respect for it. And everywhere you go, you can always see another film.

MF: *What about the rituals that the community has come up with for revering film – the Oscars, the Golden Globes, the critics' awards?*

JF: Unfortunately, there's so many of those accolades – once again, always propelled financially by what's best for the studios or the film-makers. The more award shows you have, the less special they become. The more movies you have, the less special the experience of going to the movies is. The great thing about the seventies was that the actors you liked most only liked to work once every two years – because they felt that they couldn't give their all more than that. It became almost like a fashion. So you really looked forward to seeing a Robert De Niro movie or a Dustin Hoffman film or an Al Pacino movie. I mean, now you have five Robert De Niro movies a year.

MF: *I went to one last night – it's opening this Friday. The budget's your usual fifty-plus. And for the studio in question, everything will be riding on this Robert De Niro movie this weekend.*

JF: The great thing about the seventies, which I really think is our golden age in America for films, is that they were so interested, all of those actors, in making movies for the right reasons – in having a true and emotional reason for making them. Budget size didn't really matter. It was the content of the story that mattered the most, and that's why those films are so good – why they still stand out.

MF: *What's spoiling it? Money? Is it because Hollywood is such a blatantly capitalistic organization? Or is that naive? Has it always been that way?*

JF: I guess it always has. But then it hasn't always been a global marketplace as much as it is now. I get this weird feeling that Hollywood has kind of gone the way of religion. There's the local priest that you know is passionate, and is doing it for the right reasons. And then there's that guy on TV at three o'clock in the morning, creating these great performances and milking everybody for their dough. When you think of what 'religion' means, the local priest is the guy you think of. But I'm starting to feel that when America thinks of who an actor is, they think of this greedy guy who makes way too much money, making films that are emotionless and kind of substandard. And it sort of ruins it for everybody else.

MF: *What can we do about that?*

JF: Oh gosh, I think you just have to hope that you make movies for the right reasons, and that some day you'll become fashionable again. It's like miniskirts.

MF: *I want to talk to you about the difference between actors and actresses, the way they're treated and the way they're paid.*

You always figure on the earnings lists as an actress who commands a certain income. How hard is that for you? Are you aware that you have to maintain a certain market value?

JF: Well, sure, I think about it a lot. I try to be a good businessperson. You want to keep working. And the idea is to be as valuable as possible, but to also make the best movies that you can think of. Once I got a lot of accolades for making movies that I cared about, I thought, 'Well, why change my strategy? Why don't I just keep doing this? This seems to be the right path.'

MF: *Did you have a plan? Were you lucky?*

JF: Well, I had a plan and I was also lucky. Also I'd been doing it for a lot longer than most people my age. I guess, because I started when I was three years old, I got to have a long time to come up with a plan. I wasn't one of those young actors who graduates from college and says, 'Now I've got to get up there and make as many movies as I can.' For me it was much more about wanting to be involved in films that I could be proud of. It didn't matter whether I was acting or directing or writing –

MF: *As long as it was one of those three or four.*

JF: Well, no – I have fantasies of being a caterer on a film, or a technician. It's a really active fantasy of mine, because I just love being on movie sets. I like the night shoots where you talk to everybody and you complain about the food. I like the rapport between people. I like being on location and having this common goal. But I don't always like the responsibility of being the top banana on the movie. So sometimes I would love to do a movie where I was a second assistant camera person – loading the magazines, cleaning the lenses, saying, 'Hey, what's this movie about anyway? Anybody read the script?'

MF: *'Does anybody know what they're doing?' . . . Do you understand how a film works? Technically?*

JF: Yeah, I think I understand that better than I understand the other aspects of it.

MF: *And is that just through being around and watching? Or did you actively say, 'I want to know how that camera works'?*

JF: The technical stuff is what I was obsessed with when I was a kid.

MF: *Really?*

JF: The acting didn't really interest me at all. But that's what I was paid to do, so that's what I did. I spent a lot of time asking questions. I think most child actors feel that way – they want to concretize the experience, because acting seems so nebulous and strange.

MF: *Do you care more about acting now than you did then?*

JF: I guess I do. Back then, I think I had a remnant of my mom's feelings. She would say to me, 'Acting's not a very important thing. When you grow up you'll probably be a doctor or a lawyer.' She was preparing me for failure, for the fact that usually at fourteen or fifteen most child actors' careers are over. She didn't want me to be lost. And she knew that I was interested in school and other things, and wanted me to go on that way. So I think I immediately got this idea that actors were dumb, and that it was a dissatisfying life and not something you did as a grown-up.

MF: *Do you think a lot of people think acting is silly?*

JF: A lot of male actors secretly feel very demeaned by it – because they feel like it's a girl's job.

MF: *That's the Mickey Rourke Club, isn't it?*

JF: Yeah – it's thinking about emotions, talking about emotions . . .

MF: *And preening yourself and looking pretty and caring about your appearance.*

JF: That's right. You go in with the guarantee that in some ways you'll be exploited for your looks. That's much harder on male actors than it is on the women. Frankly, it's part of women's culture – to know that their face and their body are part of who they are, their appearance has everything to do with their relationships with the world. And I think guys aren't really used to that.

MF: *Yes – 'I know I look good but I'm not really comfortable with this, okay?' A lot of younger male actors seem to have that kind of bearing and attitude.*

JF: Yes, it's funny. Sometimes, when I try to cast young men between the ages of eighteen and twenty-five, I find it very difficult – because every guy that walks in has the stubble and the trench coat and the tough look. I'll be looking for somebody who's light and full of joy, and naive but accepting of that – somebody who enjoys being young. But you find young male actors want to be brooding and act like they take the world terribly seriously. That's part of being young emotionally.

MF: *How did you find making the transition from being a child actor to being an adult actor?*

JF: It was a rough time. I think I had it luckier than most because I went away to college, so there was a whole period where people didn't really see me. And when I came back, it was with a movie that was very, very different from what I was seen in previously. But psychologically – coming back to the film business and saying, 'Okay, now I have to try and get a job', and I have to go out with all these young actors, and when somebody says 'Turn around', you turn around – that whole casting scene, which I had never really been aware of as a young actor . . . I mean, I like testing for roles now, because I like to know that I can play the part and I'd like the director to know that I'm the right person for the part. And the best way to do that is to get in a room and read. But when I was nineteen or twenty it really wasn't about ability, it was about image – once again.

MF: *Did you just observe that? Or was it ever graphically pointed out to you?*

JF: Oh, it was definitely pointed out to me. There were a lot of parts that I knew I wasn't pretty enough for, or I wasn't their version of 'sexy' enough for. *The Accused* is a good example. I really wanted that part –

MF: *Why?*

JF: I was drawn to it for a number of reasons – mostly unconscious, of course. I thought it was a role that I could sink my teeth into – a woman who was completely unlike me, but like people I had known in my life . . . So, I think the producers had a foregone conclusion about me, that I wasn't 'sexy enough'. And that means, 'Who do you want to rape? Do you want to rape somebody that looks like this? Or somebody that looks like that?' There's really something kind of creepy about that. Of course, rape is about power, it's not necessarily about how somebody looks. And the producers were making a movie about the worst-case scenario – somebody who was tough and also questionable.

MF: *I'm going to jump in a lot because you're raising so many issues. Were you aware of the feminist issues that would occur to women who saw the film?*

JF: Oh yes, absolutely. That was my last year in college, I was very aware of those issues. And that's why I wanted to tackle the movie – because I thought that its point of view was really the correct point of view. I remember there was a screen test and I really wanted to be involved, but the producers said that I couldn't take part in it, because they felt that I wasn't attractive enough.

MF: *They literally said that?*

JF: I think they said something like, 'Well, isn't she really overweight?' And an agent said to me, 'Just show up in this guy's office, show him you're attractive and you're not overweight, and then we can go get you the screen test.' So I did it. I felt kind of like a shmuck, but I figured, 'Whatever – because once I get the part, then I'll be able to show people it was for all the right reasons.'

MF: *It's this thing of there being two levels of acting, always – one just to get the gig, then the gig itself.*

JF: I guess that's true. So then I did a screen test and the producers hated it. They said, 'She's not vulnerable enough, there's something very tough about her body language and the way she smokes' – all that kind of stuff. So the director came to me and said, 'Look, I really want you. Why don't you come in and read for them again and play it a certain way? And then, when we do the movie, you can have your way back.' Which is exactly what I did. I think the second test that I gave was the worst performance I've ever given in my entire life. And they loved it, and they hired me.

MF: *If I can ask, what did you do that you thought they wanted that was so horrible?*

JF: Well, I think it wasn't so much that it was horrible – it made it safe for them. I think they liked the idea of a victim who has a little weakness, rather than the idea that any of us could be victims at any time. I really wanted to make that point – that it was about somebody who was unlucky enough to be in the wrong place at the wrong time.

MF: *When the film finally came out . . .*

JF: Everybody, producers included, gave me a big kiss and said, 'What a great job you did.' That's why I don't bear any regrets or grudges about this kind of thing. It's always a big leap of faith to cast somebody or to hire somebody as a director; you're always putting your throat on the line.

MF: *You were specifically playing a rape victim. I seem to see a lot of films about women in vulnerable situations where they are victims.*

JF: It's a terrible thing. At least half of the scripts that I read, the women's stories, their lives are never central. They're always the mother or the sister of the person in peril, so that the male actor can show his heroism.

MF: *So then I want to know why this happens – because it's not always been that way. I mean, nineteenth-century European literature is not that way. Brilliant characterizations of women exist there. In films, too. It seems to be a fairly recent phenomenon whereby women have really taken a dip in the storytelling.*

JF: I'd like to say things are changing in the right direction. I think that for a long time people believed that women's stories weren't inherently interesting to the public. Or that the public, in some ways, was male, and they couldn't relate to a woman as the central character – the hero – of a movie.

MF: *And younger women also wanted to see men, so they won both ways.*

JF: That's right.

MF: *Who was making these decisions?*

JF: I don't know. The only thing that I know about the film industry is that it's very averse to risk, until the day when somebody bucks the system and comes up with an idea that other people haven't thought of. And then pretty soon everybody else is copying that, and that becomes the convention. When you have millions of dollars on the line, you want to put your bet on the easiest risk. And so far the easiest risk has always been male, white, rich adventures. Immediately, when you go to minorities, women or anti-heroes, you find yourself in the independent realm, quickly.

MF: *So what makes you think it's getting better – other than optimism?*

JF: Oh, well, I'm sure optimism has a lot to do . . . But I think Hollywood is becoming much more conscious about their effect on the world.

MF: *Because of economics, the global market? Or because of goodness?*

JF: I think they're reading their own press. I think Hollywood really wants to do better. They'd love to be able to figure out how to be more liberal – how to bring blacks and Hispanics and Native Americans into the process. I always say this, it's the last bastion – but there are so few women directors, especially union DGA directors. And the reason is because directing is psychologically just a very different realm. When you're a producer and you're giving a first-time director his shot – a guy walks in the room and you say, 'I don't know anything about you, I don't know if you're going to be my worst nightmare or my best dream. But for some reason I feel akin to you, I like you, and here's five million dollars.' People don't do that with women. They'd rather do that with a white guy.

MF: *There's nothing much to be done about that, is there?*

JF: Well, no – except that the more pioneer women who are lucky enough to get the opportunity to make films, the more it changes. It just happens slowly.

MF: *But there's no reason, other than that, why women couldn't direct as well and as often as men, is there?*

JF: I don't think there's any reason except that – for all sorts of subtle reasons – there are fewer opportunities for women in the film business.

MF: *What resistance have you had?*

JF: Oh, I'm lucky, I've had very little resistance because I came in as an actor. A lot of the women who have had opportunities to direct came in as something else – a script supervisor, a producer, a writer. In my case it made a lot of sense for them to bank on me for my first movie because I acted in it for a quarter of my fee, and I brought in other talent at a minimal fee. So they already had a movie that financially was without risk.

MF: *And you worked it out – that was the way to go?*

JF: Right. Also I came in with, say, twenty years of experience with guys. Eric Pleskow was running Orion at the time – he had already made three movies with me. He knew I'm the kind of person who gets there at eight o'clock in the morning and does what they say they're going to do and brings everything in on time. And so I became, in some ways, the prodigal daughter. I guess I got in through paternalism.

MF: *To take a slightly different tack – do you think if more women came in with a different attitude, there would be more female directors?*

JF: No, I don't. In order for the establishment to accept you, they have to know you. I think that if they don't come into contact with women, then they don't have any reason to give them any opportunities. When I was making movies, aged seven or eight, I didn't see another woman on the set. Occasionally there would be a make-up woman, a script supervisor. Otherwise, they were all guys – except for the woman who was playing my mother.

MF: *You're not a believer in conspiracies?*

JF: No, not really.

MF: *So there's a rational explanation – it's economics, or a social thing?*

JF: Yes – almost every decision that's made in Hollywood today is driven by money.

MF: *Let me put it a different way. Hollywood has this heady blend of hedonism and money, and sex as a commodity. That seems to be a very volatile mix, a mix that can corrupt. And often there is a kind of a smell of the decadent about the place, in certain pockets.*

JF: Well, like anywhere else in the world, there's a little bit of everything. Yes, I think there's a side of Hollywood that's extremely decadent. There's a lot of money, a lot of temptation, the power structure is all about who's hot today – so it breeds that kind of backbiting.

MF: *But now it's also organized itself so well. It's harder to get away with stuff now, because there's too many gossip channels and so on, that pounce all the time. Innuendo becomes fact very, very quickly. You must have felt somehow pressured by some of that.*

JF: It's an incredibly small town. The world is changing and information has become entertainment. Now the news is supposed to be as entertaining as going to the cinema. So the news has to have a logo and funny graphics, and a soundtrack and all that stuff. I bet you, if you sat down and plugged somebody in, you'd find out that people are receiving entertainment fifty per cent of their day, whether they were watching television or walking down the street looking up at billboards, or listening to the radio. The thing about this onslaught of entertainment is that, of course, it takes more blood now to really make people shiver, it takes bigger explosions, it takes more scandal, it absolutely has to be incest and fratricide to get people really going.

MF: *Do you go to the cinema? To public shows?*

JF: Yes. I usually can't handle the screenings. I'd rather go see a movie in a regular theatre than to have to put on make-up and be photographed. I just never feel like doing that.

MF: *How often do you go?*

JF: Well, since my son was born, I haven't been for months. But usually I try to go at least once or twice a week.

MF: *Of the films you see, what percentage would be in a foreign language?*

JF: Well, unfortunately, in America we don't have enough foreign films to go see them very often. When I was younger I would say it was probably fifty-fifty. But now I see mostly American movies. You have to keep up, and there are so many coming out.

MF: *I'm in a dumb question mode for a moment – but how important to you is the whole phenomenon of the Oscars?*

JF: Well, objectively you know they're not important, because we all know who votes for the Oscars. But having won a couple of them – it's a big moment. Somebody yells your name and you go to the podium and it's like a dream. It's the dream that anybody in the film industry has.

MF: *I agree with you, by the way, and I was immensely disappointed when my name wasn't called. Why is it so important?*

JF: Oh, everybody wants to win. And they want that to be acknowledged by billions of people.

MF: *Would you rather win an Oscar or the acting prize at Cannes?*

JF: I'd rather win an Oscar. You kiddin' me?

MF: *Let me put it another way – would you rather be nominated for an Oscar, or win the first prize for acting at Cannes?*

JF: Oh, I'd rather win the prize at Cannes.

MF: *Why? Is winning more important?*

JF: Winning is just a bigger moment. I would be lying if I was to say, 'Oh, winning doesn't really matter.' It's just a big damn deal. I still get really heated about the Oscars, no matter how much I know about the industry. Every year I turn it on, I order the Chinese food in, and the person wins who I don't believe should have won. And I storm around and have a twenty-minute tirade about why they shouldn't have won. I don't know why I care about it so much. I'm sure it's just because it's some tradition of acceptance.

MF: *But also you are a part of this community, you know the people well. In London, the Sunday newspapers write about British actors 'taking Hollywood by storm', as if Hollywood is some kind of real place. But it's an industry. So I see why you get upset about who won.*

JF: Very often the *New York Times* runs these pieces on Hollywood, and you know that the people who write them live in New York. They really don't know anything about the industry. And they write about these phenomena sweeping Hollywood, as if there was some golden book that everybody could open up and say, 'Oh yes, British actors this year – we all agree, don't we? All the studios agree, we've all got together and come up with this idea.' It just doesn't work that way.

MF: *Internationally, 'Hollywood' seems to mean whatever people want it to. But the more you think about it – you are just a group of people who live in Los Angeles and make films, aren't you?*

JF: That's right. Having grown up in Los Angeles – in Hollywood, in the film business – I get really mad at people who see Hollywood as this sort of powerful icon that just makes Steven Spielberg movies and nothing else. But I also get really mad at people who over-revere it. It is a combination of those two things, but it's not just one.

MF: *I came here quite late, about ten years ago. I already had a career. And then I had a hard time on one movie, I came back from it, and I became a bit of a hero, and people would talk about the system as being like a conspiracy that I'd taken on. I said, 'No, no, I had a fight with Ray Stark and I lost. It wasn't that complicated.' But the studio system is spoken about as being almost like the Gestapo or the SS in full flood.*

JF: I've never had a problem with a studio, never had one of those vendettas. The closest I've ever come was to hate one producer, who I vow to hate for the rest of my life – that kind of thing. But other than that, I've just never had any of those sob stories. Partly because I think, to survive here, you need to be polite . . . I kind of believe that you get back what you give. This sounds like somebody's grandmother, like a Hallmark card. But it's really worked for me. Eventually, in this town, this industry, there comes a moment when you're not on top. You're at the bottom going, 'Gee, could you help me out? Could you maybe send me a movie that would be good for me? Could you give me this supporting part?' And you're going to have to depend on your relationships with a lot of people, as to whether they put out their hand and help you back up again. I've seen it happen over and over again, where my career has gone like this – and then these father figures have said to me, 'You know, Jodie, I knew you when you were five, when you were ten. You're a good girl, you were always on time, you've always done what you said you were going to do. Here, let me help you out.' And I know that if I'd been an asshole, they would have said, 'Yeah – stay there and rot.' But I thoroughly anticipate that that will happen again.

MF: *I asked a talent manager about this. 'How do you come to terms with working sometimes with a person whom you know to be not a very good or sociable or pleasant individual?' Because we do see actors behaving appallingly. Within a year, they become very big and high-priced, and they seem to fall apart. Have you observed the phneomenon?*

JF: Yes, but it can be true of producers and directors as well as actors.

MF: *Oh, sure.*

JF: Yes – that's where I feel like there's this emotionally adolescent character amongst actors. They don't think long-term, they think short-term.

MF: *Do you feel sorry for them when it happens?*

JF: No, I just feel like in ten years they'll turn around and realize what they've done. I have to thank my mom. When I was five or six, she had all these things, about being absolutely on time for what it was on the call sheet; revering the director as the visionary of the movie. 'You're here to do a job, you're here to serve your director. Obviously you're supposed to give your opinions, but finally it's his film.' All of those lessons, I wish I could turn around and give them to young actors as well. But I don't know a lot of actors. I don't know why, I just don't.

MF: *You don't look for those friendships within the business?*

JF: Not with actors. I have a lot of friends who are technicians, but not actors.

MF: *You almost made the sign of the cross there. What's the deal with actors?*

JF: I don't know if it's an old wound of mine, or some throwback to my upbringing. Or maybe it's just a personality difference. In general I don't have a lot in common with them.

MF: *Do you not trust them?*

JF: I think they're flaky. It's like being out on a date with a guy, and for three hours he talks about himself – that's like going out with an actor. They're very self-absorbed – as I am. But I guess I look for people who are a little different from myself. Off-screen, actors are very bad listeners, I find.

MF: *I find that directing is like being a shrink a lot of the time. I've walked on to film sets with my life in tatters, but I've had to go into nurse mode and say, 'Oh, God, your boyfriend didn't ring? That's awful – that bastard.' Without feeling bad about it. And then at the end of the day I suddenly felt, 'Nobody asked me how I was.' And I felt miserable.*

JF: You have to like that relationship. I don't mind it, professionally. But I don't tend to have actor friends – except for Mel Gibson, who is different from any other actor I know.

MF: *Why Mel?*

JF: He's the funniest guy in the world – just a barrel of laughs. But there's something very private about him. I suppose there's a kinship we have, because he's a likeable guy, and feels this need to be liked. And he's very polite, he shakes hands, and he sends flowers and thank-you notes and all of that. But there is a darker side to him, a seething side – because he's such a good boy on the outside. Which is something I think I feel as well. I have to be good – that's why I'm so exhausted at the end of the day. You have to please other people's visions for a good twelve hours.

MF: *You mean not just on the take, but around the take.*

JF: Yes. The cameraman wants me there, the lighting guy wants me there, the director wants this out of me. And you have to continually try to manicure yourself. So that you please everybody, but you also stay central to what you were trying to say. And that's just much more exhausting than anything else – much more so than directing.

MF: *What about directing?*

JF: I love it. I like the stress of directing. I enjoy making decisions. Saying 'A', 'B', 'Yes', 'No', 'Full crane' . . .

MF: *Did you love the fact that when you came to directing you already knew so much about it?*

JF: But I wasn't sure that I did.

MF: *How was the first day?*

JF: Oh, it was a nightmare. It was one of those days when it poured down rain, like a monsoon. We were meant to be doing exteriors, because for interiors I would have to act, and I had tried to make sure that on the first day of shooting I wouldn't have to be acting. But immediately we go to interiors, and I have to act. And there's no air-conditioning, it's one of those humid months, so I'm dripping sweat with curlers in my hair and half my clothes on while I'm looking through the eyepiece . . .

MF: *Did you have to agree to act in it in order to get it made?*

JF: Yes. It wouldn't have been my choice otherwise. At the time you don't think you're sacrificing anything. You get everything done, you wear all the different hats, you have no time at all, not even to think about the next shot – especially as a woman, because you have make-up and hair, so that pretty much eats up any down time you have. You're the only person who says which shots to print. And how do you know which ones are better? You don't. You have the video monitor but, frankly, I don't think you can rely on that at all. So what you find is that you continually short-change yourself – because you're the one you think doesn't need any attention. Mel found this as well – that he was continually making sacrifices for everyone else, and then he got to the end of the day and he didn't like his perform-ance, or didn't have the time for his performance. Once you get into the cutting room, you realize you don't ever want to act and direct at the same time.

MF: *Would you consider doing it again?*

JF: I'd consider doing a small part, or a character that was in half the movie, but not the whole film.

MF: *A couple of short questions: pieces of music that have touched you?*

JF: Oh boy . . . You mean, like songs?

MF: *Anything you like that involves music – a soundtrack, whatever.*

JF: You know, the Joni Mitchell *Blue* album I still play over and over again.

MF: *Me too. I think it's one of the best albums ever made.*

JF: *Let's Get It On* – I play it over and over again. Well, those two popped right out, didn't they?

MF: *That would do me. Some literature?*

JF: *Song of Solomon*, Toni Morrison. I wrote my senior essay on it when I was in college, and it's kind of followed me as the years have gone on. Raymond Carver short stories. A book I read that's out of print called *The Crying Heart Tattoo* – it's really romantic.

8 Missing Sandy Dennis

by Viggo Mortensen

There are always moments, sometimes entire scenes and characters, that are cut out of a movie. For anyone who takes an active interest in the story they are helping to tell, whatever their capacity in a production, there is bound to be a degree of mental and emotional adjustment that has to be made between reading the proposed shooting script and viewing the finished work. Often, what is lost – what has been altered or discarded along the way as a result of rewriting, rescheduling, editing, dubbing, or scoring – can play as important a role in shaping one's overall perception of the movie as anything that actually ends up on the screen. Even when one understands and agrees with decisions to change significantly what has been written or shot, the spirit of what was attempted not only lingers in one's memory of the process, but can also colour one's judgement of how well-accomplished the movie finally is. Like it or not, for most of the people involved, their job is completed by others in the windowless rooms of editing bays and sound stages. At times this can be very frustrating. The trick is to find a way of continuing to care about one's contribution and yet be able to walk away when the job is done with a minimum of second-guessing and regret. It can take a long time and many movies to achieve that kind of balance. I know that, as an actor, I am still struggling with this.

Someone who was capable of giving herself completely to a performance and yet still managed to move on immediately, only glancing back at her work with unsentimental objectivity, was Sandy Dennis. Indeed she may have struggled for years to become as self-possessed and pragmatic about her acting as she was when I first met her in 1982, though it is hard for me to imagine that she ever had much trouble in restricting the visible drama of her life exclusively to her performances. Having won critical, as well as a degree of popular success early on, including Tony awards for *A Thousand Clowns* (1961) and *Any Wednesday* (1962), and an Oscar for *Who's Afraid of Virginia Woolf?* (1966), she none the less had a fair amount of trouble getting good roles and making a living throughout her career.

During the last twenty years of her life, though respected by many for her stage work and occasionally given a movie role in which she could shine (such as *The Out-Of-Towners* [1970], *The Four Seasons* [1981], *Come Back to the Five and Dime, Jimmy Dean, Jimmy Dean* [1982], *Another Woman* [1988] and *The Indian Runner* [1991]), she found herself largely marginalized by critics and by those with the power to hire. This was particularly true within the movie industry, where she was generally dismissed – when remembered at all – as a quirky has-been, a benign but overly complicated and totally unbankable actress. She did not complain about this, other than – very rarely – to wonder out loud how she was going to make ends meet and care for the many stray cats and dogs she had taken in over the years. She did not dwell on the past and never claimed to be the victim of injustice, personal or professional, though a case could easily be made for that being so. She was essentially a modest woman with a great gift, one which she enjoyed sharing, as both an actress and a teacher of actors. A professional artist in the best sense.

In 1990, it was my good fortune to work on what would prove to be her last movie. She played the role of the mother to David Morse's 'Joe' and my 'Frank' in Sean Penn's directorial debut, *The Indian Runner*. Charles Bronson played our father, and the cast also included Patricia Arquette, Valeria Golino and Dennis Hopper. When I first met with Sean Penn and his producer, Don Phillips, to discuss the possibility of my playing Frank, one of the first questions I asked them was who, if anyone, they had in mind to play the mother. When Sean answered that he did not want to consider anyone other than Sandy Dennis for the part, I couldn't have been happier, or more in agreement. Aside from my feelings for her as a friend, I believed she would be a great asset to the movie and would inspire us all to do our best. This proved to be true.

As it turned out, however, most of what she did was cut out of the movie. This was not due to any shortcoming on her part. On the contrary, she was brilliant throughout. The bulk of her role was in one eight-page scene in which Frank is taken by Joe to visit their parents for the first time since returning from a three-year tour in Vietnam. Frank is ill-at-ease from the start, and we gather that his relationship with his parents is not a very good one. Joe tries to keep the peace, as is his wont, but Frank rejects their hospitality and attempts at small-talk, insults them and eventually storms out of the house. This is particularly devastating to his ailing mother, who dies not long after. On viewing the assembled footage back in Los Angeles, it was decided that the story would work better if Frank refused to visit his mother and father and, in fact, never saw them again. A subsequent scene was shot in January 1991 to support this plot change.

I agree with the decision; dramatically the movie works better without the home-coming scene. It is perhaps more cruel and a greater source of guilt for Frank that he chose not to see his mother before she died. What I do miss, however, is seeing Sandy's performance in the scene, and having others see it too. She was working on a level far above the rest of us. The concentration and vulnerability that she invested in the scene were remarkable. Heart-breaking. The fact that most of us knew that she was dying of ovarian cancer as she showed us the emotional disintegration of the character made the experience all the more poignant.

I will always remember the three days we spent working on that ambitious scene: the sense of family, the pride in acting with her, the undercurrent of loss. She left Omaha and her native Nebraska, returning to New York the day after completing her job with us. That was the last time I saw her.

Sandy Dennis and Viggo Mortensen in the scene that was cut in *The Indian Runner* (photo by Michael Tighe).

For Sandy Dennis

I

In an Omaha steakhouse full of indian summer
sunday dinner feasting families you modestly
celebrated what you knew would be the closest
thing to a goodbye glimpse of home by eating
and drinking as if willing the red-robed walls to
fall on our table without a thought for the candle
flame that would surely get sucked out as the
particle board and plywood left the door frames
and windowsills behind and rushed to the floor
with a last gasp of generations of paint and
wallpaper glue swirling into your lungs.

2

No movie can show your eyes as they looked
after completing one last scene playing our
mother, when you limped outside worn out and
uncomplaining to squeeze onto the flimsy,
rusted seat of a child's swingset for a photo
opportunity. Your shaky hands gripped the
chains and I felt your back tense with the strain
of holding onto the unbearably ripe fruit of a
half-stomach, but you allowed your swollen feet –
at last freed of those horrible sandals – to trail
back and forth through the cool September
grass of the unmowed backyard.

3

You're packed and ready to go early the next
morning, sitting on the well-made bed in a fresh
dress and humming slightly out of breath with
the radio, done hours ago with fighting off
dreams.

4

You've pulled apart the heavy hotel drapes to let
in the sun, and exclaim that there isn't a cloud in
all that blue as if you'd never seen such a sky.

5

I carry your suitcase downstairs and we embrace
in the driveway. I worry that I'm holding you too
tight, and start to let go. Refusing to let me take
you to the airport, you kiss me on the cheek and
get in the taxi.

Sandy Dennis in the 1960s (photo by Vytas Valaitis).

Animation

9 Animation and Dynamation

Ray Harryhausen talks to Adrian Wootton

Ray Harryhausen with two of his creations.

Introduction

Ray Harryhausen is undoubtedly the greatest artist in stop-motion animation alive today. In a career that spans over forty years of cinema, his name has become a by-word for innovation, excitement and entertainment in the world of special effects and film fantasy. Born in 1920 in Los Angeles, Harryhausen was fascinated by model animation from an early age and inspired by seeing *King Kong* at Sid Grauman's theatre, at the age of thirteen, he began to develop animation as a serious hobby. He was also lucky enough at this stage of his life to meet King

Kong's creator, Willis O'Brien, who provided him with good advice and became his first and greatest mentor.

After training at Los Angeles City College and then USC in painting, drama, sculpture, anatomy and photography, he managed to obtain employment with the European animator George Pal on his seminal *Puppetoons* series, in 1940. After gaining two years of valuable experience, he was drafted into the army and worked for three and a half years in the Special Services Division of the Frank Capra film unit as an assistant cameraman. Also at this time, he did model animation for the Special Services Division animation department, contributing to the SNAFU cartoons. In the post-war period, Harryhausen reunited with Willis O'Brien and was taken on as an animator to O'Brien's ambitious fantasy film *Mighty Joe Young*. Simultaneously, Harryhausen experimented with the short film format and produced a series of his own, *Mother Goose Fairy Tales*.

While attempting to complete what proved to be the final fairy tale in his short film series, he was offered the opportunity to work on another feature film, *The Beast from Twenty Thousand Fathoms*, and in 1953 moved for ever more into feature-film work. Immediately following *The Beast from Twenty Thousand Fathoms*, Harryhausen was introduced to a young producer, Charles Schneer, and formed a productive partnership which then lasted for over thirty years of successful movie-making. Harryhausen and Schneer produced a whole series of films during the height of the science-fiction boom of the 1950s, including *It Came from Beneath the Sea*, *Earth versus the Flying Saucers* and 1957's *Twenty Million Miles to Earth*.

All of these low-budget black-and-white films were enlivened by Harryhausen's developing artistry and innovation within the field of stop-motion animation. It was also during this period that Harryhausen pioneered his new form of stop-motion animation – dynamation – which became a feature of all his subsequent work. From this point onwards, Harryhausen's work was consistently singled out for special critical acclaim, elevating many low-budget movies which would not otherwise have been notable.

At the end of the 1950s, Ray Harryhausen and Charles Schneer made a distinct break away from science fiction into the fertile world of fantasy, fairy tale and myth, with his groundbreaking and highly acclaimed *Seventh Voyage of Sinbad* in 1958. *Seventh Voyage of Sinbad* also was Harryhausen's first opportunity to experiment with colour film and its success was such that it led to a series of highly popular *Sinbad* movies culminating in *Sinbad and the Eye of the Tiger* in 1977.

The late 1950s/early 1960s also saw Harryhausen and Schneer decide to move their production base from Hollywood to London, where they could exploit the technical expertise of British studios and crews, while also being able to utilize a range of exotic European locations, particularly in Spain.

In 1963, Ray Harryhausen produced arguably his most famous and successful film, *Jason and the Argonauts*, which

Jason and the Argonauts.

has remained a perennial classic for children and adults for over thirty years. *Jason and the Argonauts* is also regarded by Harryhausen himself as his most complete film, incorporating as it does much of his most seamless and yet outstanding stop-motion animation in many memorable sequences, not least of which is the famous fight between Jason and the supernatural skeletons of the dead.

During the 1960s, Harryhausen also contributed to notable films such as *The First Men on the Moon* in 1964 and *One Million Years BC* in 1966.

Harryhausen finally brought the curtain down on his film career in 1982 with his and Charles Schneer's Greek mythological epic, *Clash of the Titans*. In 1991, at the sixty-fourth Academy awards, Harryhausen was justly, if somewhat belatedly, recognized for his abilities by being awarded the Gordon E. Sawyer Award for Technical Achievement.

Ray Harryhausen, now residing between London and Spain, lives in comfortable if not quiet retirement. Ray has made regular appearances at the National Film Theatre and the Museum of the Moving Image, to talk to new generations of film fans and students about his ground-breaking career, and his work is permanently celebrated in the Museum of the Moving Image. In addition, he also gives generously of his time to numerous festivals and conventions worldwide.

Harryhausen is an intelligent, unassuming and extremely amiable man, and the following interview was conducted in a long session at his house, where I was entertained by his great good humour. I would also like to thank Ray Harryhausen for giving up his valuable time and also for his subsequent substantial editorial revision of the final interview script that follows.

ADRIAN WOOTTON: *Let's go right back and perhaps you could explain where this unusual interest in animation came from?*
RAY HARRYHAUSEN: It came from a big motion-picture gorilla called *King Kong*, back in 1933. I was thirteen years old at the

time. Nothing like the contents of the film had ever been put on the screen before. When I was four years old, I vaguely remember a film called *The Lost World* in which prehistoric animals were portrayed on the screen, but I was far too young to really question how the picture was made.

King Kong.

Before *Kong* surfaced on the silver screen, there were several other so-called gorilla pictures such as *White Pongo* and *Ingagi*, where men in obvious gorilla suits would carry screaming young maidens off into the jungles. I knew for sure *Kong* was not made in this way. Besides the great ape, there were the many dinosaurs that were portrayed so realistically that I could not get them out of my mind. Max Steiner's dynamic scoring of the production was another contributing factor to what I would call a 'mind-blowing experience'. All this was projected on to a giant-size screen at the Grauman's Chinese cinema on Hollywood Boulevard. It certainly is not the same exciting experience if one sees *Kong* for the first time on a small TV screen.

Preceding the screening of the film was a very elaborate live stage show, with native dancing and scantily clothed maidens flying through the air on trapezes. This was a typical Sid Grauman prologue for the first opening of a new spectacular motion picture. Unfortunately, showmanship such as this no longer exists.

It was a year or two before I was able to discover how the film had actually been made. A big part of the fanatical attraction of the picture was that I could not figure out how the dinosaurs and gorilla were made to appear so real, and yet unreal. *Look* magazine finally had a two-page spread revealing all of the secrets and glories of stop-frame animation. This and other exposé articles stimulated my interest in photography and the making of motion pictures.

During my early school years, I had a hobby of making small dioramas in clay depicting the prehistoric mammals found in our local Rancho la-Brea Tar Pits. Through the use of stop-motion animation I would be able to make my dioramas move and look alive. While still in high school, I enrolled at USC night classes where they had just started some courses in film editing, art direction and photography under the guidance of Lou Physioc. This was a great blessing to my desire to know more about film-making. I borrowed a friend's 16mm camera and started a long process of experimenting in my father's garage. After much time, and trial and error, my rather unusual hobby grew into a profession.

AW: *So how did you get to meet and eventually work with the technical creator of* King Kong, *Willis O'Brien?*

RH: I remember vividly being in a social studies class in high school. Across the room, I saw a girl sitting reading a big book which had large illustrations from the picture *King Kong*. During recess, I introduced myself and told the young lady about my fanatical interest in *Kong*, as well as my experiments with dinosaurs. At that time, there was very little interest or knowledge about dimensional animation. I seemed to be the only enthusiast who knew anything about it.

I found out her father had worked with Willis O'Brien at the RKO Studios. She suggested I call O'Brien at the MGM Studios, where he and Merian Cooper were working on the preparation of a spectacular production called *War Eagles*. Unfortunately, the picture was never completed because of the war.

It took all of my courage and nerve to give Mr O'Brien a phone call. He and Merian Cooper had been my mentors for years. After finally getting through to him and telling him of my great interest in his work, he kindly invited me to his office at MGM. It was a dream come true. I loaded some of my models into a suitcase, hoping to proudly show him the results of my early experiments. The three rooms of his office were covered with drawings and oil paintings for the new production. My mouth was down to my navel trying to absorb it all. At the time, he had three artists working with him, making all the necessary preliminary sketches before production could take place. He finally asked me to show him some of my experiments. The first model I brought out of the suitcase was my pride and joy: a stegosaurus. O'Brien looked at it for a few minutes then said, 'Unfortunately, the legs of your dinosaur look like sausages. There is no character in them. You must study anatomy and learn where the muscles connect to the bones.' Before I could take umbrage at the remark, I suddenly realized he was right. Needless to say, the study of anatomy became my priority for months to come.

AW: *Well, from there we fast forward through your early experiments and training at college to your first proper professional job in 1940 with another legendary animator, George Pal, on his* Puppetoons.

RH: Mr Pal had just come over from Europe to produce a series of short subjects for Paramount Pictures called *Puppetoons*.

They were basically animated wooden puppets. Their construction necessitated them being very stylized, almost cubist in design. It would take twenty-five separate figures, carved in wood, to take one step. The principle was to have separate puppets for each frame of film. Each puppet was minutely advanced from the previous one. Needless to say, this took many hours of construction.

I had seen an article in the paper about Mr Pal starting up a studio on McCadden and Santa Monica Boulevard in Hollywood. I took some of the experimental film I had shot for a 16mm production of *Evolution*, to show George Pal what I could do. He seemed impressed and consequently I was one of the first animators he hired for his *Puppetoon* series.

AW: *How many of those did you do with him?*

RH: I animated about twelve of his early films. We did about six short subjects, each seven minutes long, in a twelve-month period. They were all carefully synchronized to music. André Kostelanetz and David Racksin scored some of the early subjects.

AW: *So, obviously that must have been quite a formative experience.*

RH: In a way, yes, it was. If nothing else, it taught me patience and discipline. It was really not the type of animation I wanted to do. Being somewhat pre-animated on paper, it left very little creative opportunity during the photography period. With the O'Brien technique of using single-jointed figures, there was more chance for creativity while actually animating. With Pal's puppets, one had to use a cue sheet which pre-dictated the movement of the figures. There is a big difference between the two concepts when one is actually involved in the animation process. Even so, I did enjoy working with George; he was a delightful employer.

AW: *Then you went into the army, but you managed to keep on making movies. How did this happen?*

RH: When the war came along, I knew I would probably have to go into the army. In my naive way, I thought I would like to be a combat cameraman, not realizing that they were later shot like clay pigeons. Columbia Pictures and Eastman Kodak sponsored night courses in combat photography. I enrolled to learn more about the different phases of using specialized cameras. During my spare time, I had also made an animated short film on 16mm showing in dimensional animation how one could bridge a gorge during combat. This was done with simple miniature sets, using toy models of tanks and armoured cars. It was only about five minutes long. Quite by chance, I showed it to my head teacher at Eastman Kodak. He was quite impressed with it and asked if he could show it to Frank Capra, who had just started the Special Service Division at the old Fox Studios on Western and Sunset Avenues. After a few weeks, I was transferred to the Special Service Division, where Captain Capra was to make the famous *Why We Fight* and *Army Navy Screen Magazines* for the US troops. By the time I finished the course in photography at Kodak, I had been upgraded to a Technical Sergeant, third class. During my stay in Special Services, my main job was to be an assistant cameraman to Joe Vanentine and Joseph Biroc. I also assisted in the cartoon department headed by Ted Giesel, who went under the pen name of Dr Seuss. He was in charge of preparing the government cartoon series called SNAFU. After the stories and characters were created, it was turned over to regular cartoon studios for execution. I have always felt that was three years of very worthwhile experience.

AW: *So then, obviously, you came out of the army and you were reunited in a way with Willis O'Brien in terms of* Mighty Joe Young.

RH: We had kept in touch throughout the three years of the war. During that time, O'Bie [Harryhausen's nickname for O'Brien] started to prepare another film at the RKO Studios called *Gwangi*. It was to be a cowboy and dinosaur epic which takes places in a remote part of Mexico. He spent almost a year helping to develop the script with the writer, making many

Mighty Joe Young.

continuity drawings. Unfortunately, once again, the production of the film was cancelled.

During the three-year period, in my spare time, I had shown O'Bie some of my more recent experiments. After getting out of the army, I had produced my own puppet series on 16mm film called *Mother Goose Stories*. All of this material helped me to become Willis O'Brien's assistant.

AW: *So what was it like to work on such a big feature production?*

RH: Working on *Joe Young* with O'Bie was a most wonderful experience. Once again, another dream come true. I assisted him in the long pre-production period of developing the script along with his pre-production drawings. At that time, we were never quite sure if the picture would ever reach the production stage. Finally, we got the go ahead from Merian Cooper. O'Brien set up his construction and animation facilities on the old silent stage at the Culver City Studios of David O. Selznick. We sometimes had as many as forty-seven people working on the miniature and animation stage.

My sole job was to do the animation. O'Brien's time was consumed by overseeing all the various details of new set-ups and glass paintings. Most of the jungle effects were created by painting the scenery on three large planes of plate glass, with the animation table sandwiched between the foreground and middle plane. The construction of the animation models were in the capable hands of Marcel Delgado, who had worked with O'Brien on *King Kong*.

I really enjoyed the luxury of having to worry only about the movement of the gorilla and nothing else. I think that some of my best animation came from this way of working as I was able to concentrate fully on what the gorilla should do during a scene. The script and drawings gave only a broad pattern of what the scene was all about.

AW: *But if we could go back to your work on the 16mm* Fairy Tales, *some of which you were making simultaneously with* Mighty Joe Young. *That was a very different kind of working method.*

RH: Yes, it was. With the *Fairy Tales*, I did practically everything myself from designing the figures, building the sets and models, doing the photography, etc. It was also necessary for me to finance them myself. Occasionally, my father would help in his spare time and my mother would dress the characters in proper costumes. My main costs were the sound-recording periods and film processing. Unfortunately, I found out the films would not pay off for a very long time. When the money finally came in, they proved to be very profitable and popular in school Visual Education programmes. They are still in circulation in schools and churches all over the US. In an earlier period, I had visualized doing seventeen or twenty of these eight-minute shorts for TV, but after I got halfway through the fifth one, *The Tortoise and the Hare*, the opportunity to do *The Beast from Twenty Thousand Fathoms* came along. It was much more profitable to be a monster man than a fairy-tale man.

Fairy Tales.

AW: *As far as* The Beast from Twenty Thousand Fathoms *goes, was this an opportunity to put into practice what you had learned earlier, but in a simpler, less costly way?*

RH: Yes, it was. *The Beast from Twenty Thousand Fathoms* had a very low budget. It was almost ridiculous to think such elaborate subject matter could be made so cheaply. The completed picture, including the special effects, cost only about $200,000. The only way I could rationalize my personal sacrifices was to tell myself this was an opportunity to show what I could do on my own. Of course, the producers took advantage of my first solo effort, but I did not mind as I desperately wanted to see the film made with effective special effects.

At this stage, I devised the so-called Dynamation process. It was a relatively inexpensive way of intimately combining live-action actors with animated creatures and miniature backgrounds. The backgrounds and live action were photographed first, then, through a miniature rear-projection process, I would split the screen with black foreground matter for the insertion

The Beast from Twenty Thousand Fathoms.

of the animated model or miniature. Throughout my whole career, I made use of this basic technique.

AW: *So, in that sense, necessity was the mother of innovation.*

RH: That is certainly true. I had to design all of the effects scenes myself as I was the only one who knew what could be achieved within our budget limitations. Fortunately, we had Eugene Lourié to control the set construction and production costs. He was later given the job of directing the live-action portions as well – all in the name of budget restrictions. We both tried very hard to keep the cost-cutting from showing too much. A regular studio could never make a film for the money the *Beast* cost.

AW: *What is quite interesting is that in terms of your early science-fiction work, all the critical material that I've read says that the scripts and acting are not very good, but Harryhausen's animation is great!*

RH: Some critics have even said that 'Harryhausen should have animated the actors as well'. I was most flattered.

AW: *What's more serious, though, is that at the height of the 1950s science-fiction boom you were producing innovatory animation, but no one else took it up at all. What happened?*

RH: Most studios did not know what to make of stop-motion animation. It seemed to be something they could not control. Universal Pictures put a large amount of money into a film called *Land Unknown* where, to cut costs, they put men in dinosaur suits. Most embarrassing. They looked like refugees from a costume ball. In the 1941 *One Million Years BC*, they glued fins on the backs of alligators and lizards, hoping they would pass as dinosaurs. Again, there was a man in an allosaurus suit which was so bad and unconvincing, they had to shoot through foreground bushes so you would not see the creature very clearly. Other companies tried animatronics and rod puppets. No one wanted to know about stop-motion.

AW: *Why do you think that was?*

RH: Well, partly because *Mighty Joe Young*, on the books, cost over $2 million. Actually, it cost only $1,800,000. We were the only picture shooting at the studio when Howard Hughes bought RKO and the Culver City Studio. All of the Heads of Departments' overheads were dumped on our picture, even though they had nothing to do with the project. Word got around that our animation was very expensive and that it had gotten out of hand with the accounting departments. Producers do not like to depend on one person (the animator); they still clung to the traditional studio set-up where they can get rid of you if they want to hire somebody else. Dimensional animation is so specialized that it has to be done in a certain way, otherwise it wouldn't function properly. Even O'Bie, after having won the Academy Award for Special Effects on *Mighty Joe*, did not have producers knocking on his door.

AW: *But in your case* The Beast from Twenty Thousand Fathoms *was successful.*

RH: It was made by an independent company and sold outright to Warner Bros. who made millions on it. The only changes that were made was that they rescored the music. The original score was quite undemanding. When Warners became involved, for one happy moment I thought maybe Max Steiner would write the new music. Unfortunately, this did not take place. David Buttolph wrote the new score. However, having said all that, even though it was quite a big success, I was not fighting off job offers.

AW: *Nevertheless, you did keep on making films and moved towards independent production. I am presuming that much of this was as a result of developing such a close relationship with the producer Charles Schneer. Could you fill in the detail of how that partnership was created?*

RH: It was through an army friend of mine who worked for Sam Katzman at Columbia Pictures. He called me up one day and said that he knew of a young producer who worked at Columbia who wanted to make a film about a giant octopus pulling down San Francisco's Golden Gate Bridge. This sounded most intriguing. At the time, I was working on one of my Fairy Tales, *The Tortoise and the Hare*. The 16mm picture was about halfway finished. Still, I thought I had better investigate. I had a chat with Charles, who really seemed interested in making a good sci-fi story. That was the nucleus of *It Came from Beneath the Sea*. A week or so later, I made some quick sketches and then worked with a screenwriter. Once again, the picture was made for very little money. This was followed by *The Earth versus the Flying Saucers*. For the third picture we made, Charles went out on his own and formed Morningside Pictures with a release through Columbia Pictures.

AW: *Was that* Twenty Million Miles to Earth?

RH: Yes, it was. Charles and I had a good working relationship. He had a respect for me and my work, and I realized he could keep the budget under control and not let it run wild the way so many pictures had done before. We kept making pictures because we made them for a price at which Columbia knew they could make a profit.

AW: *Also, interestingly enough at this time, you made a film,* The Animal World, *produced by Irwin Allen, who later went on to become the king of 1960s sci-fi television. How did that come about?*

RH: I did *The Animal World* with him because he'd heard about my 16mm animation experiments. He did not want to spend too much money on the project and asked to use some of my footage from *Evolution.* It was blown up to 35mm in the optical printer and looked quite good, but unfortunately some of my scenes were shot 16 frames a second so when it was run at 24 frames, it made the dinosaurs move too rapidly. Irwin Allen then hired O'Brien to lay out the prehistoric sequence and hired me to do some limited animation. I was delighted to have the opportunity once again to work with Willis O'Brien. We were only six weeks on the project, which was all table-top miniatures and painted backgrounds. At times we would use two cameras on one set-up to get double the amount of footage.

AW: *In terms of carrying on with your working relationship with Schneer, did you then begin to establish with him a kind of consistent collaborative team of people that you worked with, or did they change from picture to picture?*

RH: We seldom used the same people, although we had a British cameraman, Wilkie Cooper, on many films. He worked out beautifully on *The Seventh Voyage of Sinbad* when we turned to colour. He was such a talented photographer, very quick and nothing seemed to frustrate him. While making *The Seventh Voyage* we had more problems than you can imagine, many of which he surmounted beautifully. We were one of the first companies from America to shoot on location in the Spanish wilderness.

AW: *You mentioned turning to colour at this time. Could you talk specifically about the challenges this created for you?*

RH: The main challenge was to do an effective colour feature film on a very low budget. Colour takes time. With black and white, you can match the foreground and the miniatures to a rear-projection screen by eye, many times, without making tests. When you go into colour, you have to send your test footage to the laboratory and wait until the next day to see the rushes. The human eye does not register the same colour and quality of light that is being matched to a rear-projection screen. Many times the colour may look good, but when the film comes back the next day it appears completely out of balance. You have to make new tests to get it right. That was the reason I disliked colour, because I knew it was going to slow down the whole process of matching and getting the picture out on time.

AW: *In terms of the animation, was that something on which you had a small nucleus of people working with you?*

RH: No. I did most of it all myself. I designed and built many of our early models with the help of my father. He would machine the armatures for the models. On a few of our early pictures and *The Seventh Voyage*, I had the assistance of George Loftgren, who was a fine taxidermist and prop maker. During our colour period, I would have just one electrician to watch and repair the lamps. I would light and photograph all of the set-ups. The camera and projector worked automatically after they were once set up. This was a necessity, as animation requires a great deal of concentration and I did not want too many people around me. For *Clash of the Titans*, I had to have help with the animation as we got behind schedule because of some technical difficulties.

AW: *And am I right in thinking that you still remained almost the sole exponent of stop-motion during these glory years?*

RH: Yes, we were the only ones doing it continuously. There were several other films made using a similar process, but they never received a very good release. Various early fans such as Jim Danforth, Jon Berg and Dave Allen later became professionals. Rick Baker, before he turned directly to make-up and animatronics, was a great stop-motion enthusiast.

AW: *Can you now talk about your conscious move away from science fiction, in the late 1950s/early 1960s, to concentrate on mythology and Arabian fantasy.*

RH: That was very necessary because we kept making films about large creatures destroying cities. I destroyed Washington, New York, Los Angeles and San Francisco. How many times could you repeat that? I was looking for a new avenue for stop-motion and that is how the *Seventh Voyage of Sinbad* came about. Specifically, I had always wanted to do an animation with a skeleton. I knew it would be unbelievable in a modern setting and soon settled on *The Arabian Nights* for a basic storyline. Sinbad, being a fantasy character, could be believable if he fought with a living skeleton. In my spare time, I designed and rendered eight large charcoal drawings of what could be the highlights of the film. I took my drawings and step outline around to the various studios, but could not interest anyone in the project. I then put them in my files, labelling them 'possible

The Seventh Voyage of Sinbad.

film projects'. It was not until I had made several films with Charles Schneer that I dug them out again. We were looking for a new subject for the next picture. Charles got quite excited about the possibilities of the subject matter. I then redesigned the concepts so we could make it inexpensively. Originally, I wanted to do the production rather lavishly, like *The Thief of Baghdad*. I had to rethink everything in terms of what we could do on locations in Spain.

AW: *It seems that from this point on, your characters, your creatures, your animation was the founding part of the movie that then generated the script.*

RH: Yes, they contributed enormously in generating the shooting script. Most of our projects, being mainly a visual pantomime, usually started with drawings. For example, when we were doing *It Came from Beneath the Sea*, I made many drawings of the octopus in different situations which the writer then

It Came from Beneath the Sea.

incorporated into the script. As for our later films, the *Sinbad* stories are very fragmented; mythology is very fragmented. Some of them do not have a continuity, so we had to juggle some of the situations around. We would have many so-called 'sweat-box sessions' with Charles, the writer and myself, where we would pick the storyline to pieces and try to fill in any missing pieces. The writer then did a treatment or first draft based on many of the drawings and ideas that surfaced during our meetings. This was a technique I learned from O'Brien. This was partly the way *King Kong* was constructed. It did not just come out of Edgar Wallace's and Merian Cooper's minds. In fact, Wallace had very little to do with the final storyline. Many of the visual situations came from O'Brien's *Creation* story, which was the forerunner of *Kong*.

AW: *Then how do you progress?*

RH: After many more sessions and the script is finally completed, I then make about 350 to 400 simple pen-and-ink sketches of each cut in the effects sequences. They are simple sketches of each set-up. We have to know if this part of the picture has to be shot first and another part of the same set-up shot second. There may be even a third or fourth part to make up one cut. The shooting of them has to be synchronized for the make-up of the shooting and production schedule.

AW: *And how long would you say this process takes from start to finish?*

RH: It varies considerably. *The Beast* took about eight months. *The Seventh Voyage*, I believe, was about eight or nine months shooting of the animation after the production part was finished. We would normally shoot all the necessary background plates during production. The longest period was on *Clash of the Titans*. It took about sixteen months for the effects. It took so long because we had problems with irregular sprocket holes. The film we were getting wasn't punched properly for special-effects use. When it was double exposed, there would be an unwanted movement between the two or three exposures.

This was a big problem as my whole technique was based on covering up part of the screen, then winding the film back and exposing the other parts later. Eventually, people like ILM [Industrial Light and Magic] ended up punching their own sprocket holes in order to get more accuracy. Sometimes, they had six or seven passes on one piece of film in order to make up a shot.

AW: *You have talked about your relationship with the producer and the writers of your films – what about the directors who worked on your films?*

RH: Well, our films were not what you would call a director's picture in the European sense of the word. With some directors, I had friction because they thought I was stepping on their toes when I directed the parts of my scenes. I do not do it out of ego but out of necessity. I am the one who has to finally put all the pieces together.

AW: *In terms of problems, I have always thought that actors must have had quite a difficult time on your pictures, because they were often having to perform to an empty space where one*

Valley of the Gwangi: original drawing.

of your creatures would later be added into the film. How did you manage to involve them?

RH: That is one of the reasons I made large pre-production drawings to show the actors what they were finally going to see on the screen. The continuity drawings also gave them roughly what was going to be there. Sometimes, we had a cardboard cut-out. When we were shooting the Medusa sequence in *Clash*, we had an eight-foot cardboard cut-out of her. It was also used as a stand-in so that the actors would know what they were looking at and how high to look. Sometimes we had a monster stick.

AW: *The other major significant thing about your career is that in the late 1950s and early 1960s, you started working very much more internationally, particularly in Europe and, in fact, you have been based in London for the majority of your entire career. What led you to that kind of break away from Hollywood?*

RH: There were several reasons for that break. One reason, we were given a script called *The Three Worlds of Gulliver*. It

Valley of the Gwangi: the completed film.

was very necessary to be able to put on the screen big people and little people. This required the use of travelling mattes. Hollywood never specialized in travelling mattes; they always preferred the rear-projection process. We had heard about the Rank Laboratories yellow backing, sodium-light system of the travelling matte. It was vital to us because we used almost 400 travelling mattes to complete the film.

The second reason was that Hollywood is miles away from locations. You cannot keep using Malibu Beach and the Grand Canyon for lost islands and fantasy locations. Television was using up all of the most picturesque scenery around California, so Charles and I agreed to put our headquarters in London as it is only a few hours from Spain, Jordan or Italy. We later shot three films in Italy, five or six in Spain as well as Malta. It was necessary to have fresh locations for our films that had never been seen in America. It was very important for a fantasy film, to have exotic locations. It was, of course, more convenient to take a crew from England than to fly them over from Hollywood. Much less expensive.

AW: *How important were financial considerations such as the Eady Levy?**

RH: I can't remember the details, but it was very helpful in financing our pictures. I think it is a shame that they discarded the Eady Levy.

AW: *Can I ask you to reflect on the importance of composed music to your kind of film?*

RH: I first realized the importance of music when I saw *King Kong*, because Max Steiner's score was so original and fresh. This lead me to analysing the music score. Steiner was highly influenced by Tchaikovsky and all the wonderful classical

---

* The Eady Levy was a subsidy for British Film production levied on cinema tickets. Introduced in 1948, it was made a statutory measure in 1957 and provided funding for a variety of British-made cinema films until it was abolished in 1984.

composers such as Ravel and Debussy. Charles and I realized that our films, being mainly visual and fantasy, required something to heighten them and make them bigger than life. And music, the right kind of music, does exactly that.

AW: *To be more specific, can I ask about your creative relationship with composers who worked on your films and, in particular, the legendary Bernard Herrmann?*

RH: On our early black-and-white pictures, we were forced to use mostly canned music from other films, because of the cost factor. Being in colour, that changed with *The Seventh Voyage of Sinbad*. When Charles told me he knew Bernard Herrmann and was going to try to get him to score our film, I could not be more pleased. I was very much aware of Bernie's music because of his association with Orson Welles's *Mercury Theatre* which was on the radio every week. We were a little worried about showing him the early rough-cut of the picture. So many elements were missing. Bernie had the reputation of being very outspoken if he didn't like what he saw. Many of the shots didn't have monsters in them, just somebody holding a long pole. It was difficult to get an idea of what the picture was about. But I guess Bernie read the script and saw the drawings, and he agreed to score it because he thought he could do something interesting with it musically.

Many times we would have sessions where we would all agree that the music should start at a certain place and maybe end at a certain cut. There would occasionally be a difference of opinion, but we simply talked it out. It is highly necessary to choose a composer who has a track record and where you know in advance what he is capable of delivering, because the day when a 100-piece orchestra turns up and you hear the music for the first time, it can be a kind of shock! Of course, what Bernie delivered was more than suitable.

AW: Clash of the Titans *was the last movie that you made and I wanted to ask what was your main reason for retiring at that point?*

RH: Probably several different reasons, not just one. There were many that built up over the years. I felt I had spent enough of my time in a darkened room while everyone else on the film went off and made two or three pictures, when I was still working on one. Then, too, trying to keep up one's enthusiasm on a project that extends over so much time I found quite difficult. The amount of money that is involved in making films today suggests that you have to have a big crew, and I did not want to end up delegating things and just being an accountant and a planner. The type of pictures that the front office seem to want, and the elements they felt should be in the script, were not exactly my cup of tea.

Nick Park.

10 A Lot Can Happen in a Second

Nick Park talks to Kevin Macdonald

Introduction

In 1989 a young animator called Nick Park completed his first two short films: *Creature Comforts* and *A Grand Day Out*. In an unprecedented situation, both were nominated for BAFTA and Oscar awards, *A Grand Day Out* winning the former and *Creature Comforts* the latter. Since then, Park has produced two further half-hour films featuring Wallace and Gromit, the stars of *A Grand Day Out*, *The Wrong Trousers* and *A Close Shave*, both of which have attained remarkable international popularity. Few home-grown British stars have captured the public's heart quite like Wallace and Gromit since the hey-day of their fellow northerners Gracie Fields and George Formby.

Born in Preston, Lancashire, in 1958, Park has done more than anyone (except perhaps Tim Burton and Henry Selick, the makers of Disney's *The Nightmare before Christmas*) to reaffirm the enormous possibilities of 3D stop-frame animation in the minds both of financiers and the public. Technically, his work is executed with a skill and attention to detail which has astonished fellow animators. He lights and photographs his films as though they were live action features, thereby endowing them with a sense of reality, and even dignity, which belies the daft plots and high comedy of his unashamedly entertaining work.

Since leaving film school, Park has worked for Aardman Animation in Bristol. Founded in the early 1970s by the animators Peter Lord and David Sproxton, today, largely thanks to the company's success in the world of commercials (notably the

'Heat Electric' series based on Park's *Creature Comforts*),
Aardman occupies an impressively refurbished one-time banana-
ripening warehouse on the outskirts of Bristol, employing a full-
time staff of around twenty and a horde of freelances.

The main studio space is partitioned into several sections
(with animation, of course, there is no need for soundproof-
ing), each of which has a small set and an animator at work,
painstakingly repositioning his characters. A further room is
filled with model-makers who construct the beautiful and
meticulous three- or four-foot-long sets, all the miniature props
and models of the studio's stars; six-inch-high Wallace and
Gromits greet you on every surface.

I met a somewhat exhausted Nick Park at the Aardman
studio last year, midway through *A Close Shave*'s nine-month
shoot. He is a diffident, extremely modest man, who looks
younger than his thirty-seven years. His voice is very soft and
gently reveals his Lancashire origins.

KEVIN MACDONALD: *Were you interested in films as a child?*
NICK PARK: I've always loved cinema. I used to go every
Saturday morning with my two brothers and we'd go to see
everything – we weren't at all discerning. The first film I specifically remember was *The Man from UNCLE*, the film made
from the TV series, called *One of Our Spies is Missing*. Shortly
after that I saw *Snow White and the Seven Dwarfs*. I've never
really been a film buff who knows every fact about cinema,
who made what and who played who; my fascination with
films is much more general.
KM: *As you grew up, what kinds of films did you like best?*
NP: I've always loved science-fiction films – I also used to read
a lot of science fiction when I was younger, though I don't any
more. I also enjoyed monster films. My favourites were those
1950s American science-fiction-fantasy films like *Forbidden
Planet* and *The Day the Earth Stood Still*. I loved all that kind
of thing with cheap and cheerful effects, and also *The Time*

Machine, *The Day of the Triffids* and a lot of those British science-fiction films.

KM: *When did you first get interested in actually making films?*

NP: When I was about thirteen. My parents had bought an 8mm Bell and Howell camera when I was about seven or eight. It was a present to my mum from my dad, just for recording holidays and home life, that sort of thing. We children weren't allowed to touch it. I remember there was a button on it labelled 'animation' and I always wondered what it was for. My father being a photographer, and my mother a dressmaker, they always encouraged us to be creative. There were seven of us in the family and we were all interested in making things. At the age of ten or eleven I got very interested in drawing cartoons and, when I watched cartoons on the television, I always wondered how they were made. At the same time I was fascinated by science-fiction films which had animated dinosaurs and creatures, especially with the work of Ray Harryhausen.

KM: *Things like* One Million Years BC?

NP: Yes, and earlier stuff than his, like Willis O'Brien's *King Kong*, which I just loved. But I don't know exactly what got me thinking that I could do animation myself. I remember there was a competition on a cereal packet. You had to make a zoetrope, one of those spinning discs with lots of pictures on it which seem to move if you look from a particular point – it's a kind of primitive animation. The first prize was a projector and camera, and I used to dream of what I'd do if I won them. In the end I didn't even enter – though I made a zoetrope – but somehow this got me going and I used to imagine the films I would make with dinosaurs and things like that in them.

KM: *So when you were thirteen your parents finally allowed you to use the camera?*

NP: Yes, and I immediately started to do animation on it. Being a photographer, my dad knew the principles of animation – although he'd never done any – and he explained to me how to do it. So I had a go and made a film which took about a week to make. It was drawn animation. I started at the back of a sketch pad and drew pictures, then traced each one and filmed it. When I was finished, the film was sent off to Kodak to be developed and never came back. So my first film was completely lost! We tried to get it back, but nothing happened.

KM: *But you obviously weren't too discouraged . . .*

NP: No, throughout my childhood, after that, I made quite a lot of films, mainly animation. I didn't tell anyone; my friends and family knew, but I didn't tell people at school, for instance. I didn't really think it was something you could pursue as a career.

KM: *Did you stay at school for A levels?*

NP: Yes and I continued to do animation as a hobby. I remember my very first taste of fame: when I was fifteen my first film was shown on TV. I'd entered the European Young Film-Maker of the Year competition and the BBC showed part of my film along with the winners, even though I was only a runner-up. It was on the day I left school for sixth-form college and I couldn't believe it. I thought, 'I've made it!' It was drawn animation and I think it was actually one of the worst things that I ever made. I didn't have any money, but I got free films from my dad and I used that same old 8mm camera. I couldn't afford celluloid cells to draw on, so I used tracing paper; I just bought a roll of the stuff, chopped it up and punched holes in it with a paper puncher, made a register board and register pins out of nails, and shot the thing in the garden – in sunlight! I didn't have any means to do a soundtrack, so I used a David Bowie song and slowed it down. It sounded weird. The BBC used it and they sunc it up better than I ever did because I could only use a tape recorder playing at the same time, which usually went out of sync!

Then I did an art foundation course because I knew I wanted to do something artistic, but I didn't know exactly what. Then I went to Sheffield Art School and did a film course. My tutors discovered that I did animation and told me that I should specialize in it, which I did. Then I went on to the National Film

School in Beaconsfield in about 1980 and stayed there until 1983 – officially.

KM: *Officially?*

NP: Well, they used to turn a blind eye and people stayed on much longer, finishing off their graduation films.

KM: *Did you find that a valuable experience, being there?*

NP: Well, it was difficult. It was *the* place to be, but it was very difficult being there. I really appreciated certain aspects of it: the facilities and tuition are great, and there was something very stimulating and good for me as an animator to be surrounded by live-action film-makers. But it's a fairly drab place and, coming from an art-school background, I missed the visual stimulation. So much of film-making takes place either on location or in a studio for three weeks or six weeks or whatever, and the rest of the time it's in the editing room or on paper. So I found it a slightly sterile environment.

KM: *When did you start concentrating on model animation – at Sheffield?*

NP: At Sheffield I did various types. But I also had another passion which took up my time and that was to be a wildlife photographer or film-maker, because I'm keen on birds and wildlife. I gave that up slowly.

KM: *But that love of animals comes across in your films.*

NP: Oh does it? It is there underneath, I suppose. I did try doing some wildlife photography, but I found it difficult as a student; you need so much time for research and such good equipment. And, of course, I found I was getting results with animation.

KM: *What do you think led you into model animation in particular?*

NP: I think it's because I'd been brought up on a diet of children's 3D animation. I wanted to take what I'd seen and apply what I'd learned from film-making, in terms of lighting and using the camera, a lot more inventively. I wanted to do something different from the usual puppet animation which was made for children. I suppose I was more interested in the

Eastern European style: Starewicz,* Trnka,† Svankmajer.‡ It was only when I got to the NFTS that I became aware of all these figures and of what a range there was in the world of animation.

KM: *Did you make many films at the NFTS?*

NP: No. When I got there I spent the first year really doing exercises – which was a good thing. There was a rigorous series of crash courses in general film-making skills: editing, directing, writing, etc. I wish I'd spent more time on the writing and directing sides, but after the first year, because of the time animation takes, we all just got on with animation. When I was there the school was geared towards directing, and animation was just coming in. In fact, I was one of the first animators they had there.

KM: *A criticism one often hears of the film school is that all the other disciplines are treated as though they are just there to facilitate the directors.*

NP: Yes, that's right. Sometimes even animators got treated like that. The directors would say, 'All right, you can do the titles for my film.' Or they just wanted you to do their special effects! I always regard myself as a 'film-maker' rather than

* Ladislaw Starewicz (1892–1965) entered films in Moscow and initially directed live-action films and animated cartoons. However, the field in which he excelled was stop-motion animation in such films as *The Grasshopper and the Ant* (1912). After the Revolution he emigrated to France where his best known work was the feature-length puppet-animation film *The Tale of the Fox* (1928–41) which he made independently over a number of years.

† Jiri Trnka (1912–69) set up the animation unit at the Prague film studios in 1945 and is still considered the undisputed master of Czech puppet animation. His films include: *The Emperor's Nightingale* (1948), *Old Czech Legends* (1953) and *A Midsummer Night's Dream* (1959).

‡ Jan Svankmajer is best known outside his native Czechoslovakia for his macabre, often nightmarish blending of puppet (or, in his case, 'object') animation with live action in films such as *Alice* (1983), a retelling of Lewis Carroll's classic, and *Faust* (1993). His work has been a great influence on the British animators the Brothers Quay.

A Grand Day Out.

an 'animator', but it took a long time to prove that at the film school.

KM: *It must have been broadening to work with live-action film-makers, not just animators.*

NP: Yes, I think that's the most valuable thing I picked up, because so much animation does suffer from not being very good film-making. It's either too indulgent or doesn't stick to the point of the scene. I think what I love about 3D animation is that, in many ways – the movement of the camera, the lighting, etc. – it's very akin to live action.

KM: *Were you still at the NFTS when you started to make the first Wallace and Gromit film,* A Grand Day Out?

NP: Yes, in fact it was my graduation project. We had a lot of problems getting equipment together because the National hadn't dealt with model animation before, and it took a while to find the right camera. I was halfway through my third year before they got all the equipment I needed. So I overran and was there for another year and a half trying to finish it. Eventually I got offered a job here at Aardman and I was so short of money that I had to take it.

KM: *So you came here before you'd actually finished your graduation film?*

NP: Yes, and because the school wanted to see this film finished (because they'd invested in it), they agreed that I could continue working on it and they'd keep it funded, and Aardman agreed that I could work for them part time. The result was that it took a lot longer to finish than it should have because I was only part time on it.

KM: *You started* A Grand Day Out *in 1982 and finished it . . .?*

NP: In 1989! Six years! I never ever imagined that it would take so long. The first year went by and I had filmed one page of the script!

KM: *Did you ever feel like giving up?*

NP: Yes, often, but it was a work of such love; it really was everything that I wanted to do at the time and – I'm not boasting when I say this – I hadn't seen anything like it before and I just felt I had to do it.

KM: *One of the things which differentiates your films from those of many other animators is the complexity of the characterization. Can you tell me where the characters of Wallace and Gromit came from?*

NP: Well, when it came to writing the film I needed a couple of characters. I went back through old sketch books and I found these two characters: one was called Gromit and the other . . . didn't have a name actually – the name Wallace came afterwards. In fact, Gromit was originally the name for a cat in another story!

KM: *What about Wallace – he seems to be almost an Alan Bennett creation?*

NP: In a way he started off as a fairly stereotypical Northerner – in some of the early drawings I did, he actually wore a flat cap and braces! At the time, I didn't rationalize the influences which were going into the character, I didn't think, 'Oh, I'll base him on this or that person,' he just sort of evolved. It really came together when I recorded his voice. The automatic choice was Peter Sallis from *Last of the Summer Wine* and the character developed out of that voice. But it's funny, because in retrospect I can't help but think that the character of Wallace was based on my dad. Of course, they don't look alike, but they do have a lot in common. In fact, sometimes I see similarities to my family in all my characters. I think that I naturally draw upon my past for all sorts of references in the Wallace and Gromit films. I know that on *A Grand Day Out*, whenever I wanted to make an object in it I referred to something that I knew as a child, like the lamp that my granny had, which became Wallace's lamp, and things like that.

KM: *How would you describe Wallace's character?*

NP: Well, he's fairly extrovert, though he doesn't socialize much. You don't really see him with other people, do you? But I think that he is an extrovert: he's pretty much on the outside, he doesn't hold in his feelings. In fact, he's rather insensitive to other people, especially Gromit.

KM: *He has that characteristic we associate with Northerners of being very straightforward, direct.*

NP: Yes, but I've always tried to steer him away from the stereotype, even though in some ways he may look like one, with the green tank top, etc. . . . . He may have started as a stereotype, but I think he has developed a rounded character now.

KM: *A lot of the humour of the Wallace and Gromit films comes from the contrast between Wallace's very parochial, English appearance and the science fiction of the gadgets and inventions which he and Gromit invent. Do you think the stories are influenced by your early interest in science-fiction films?*

NP: It's hard to trace . . . but I think so, yes. I remember somebody at art school asking the tutor, 'What shall we paint, what subject matter should we direct our energy and attention towards?' And the answer was, 'Paint what *you like*.' I still think that is quite a good key. You've got to find something that means something to you, you've got to go by what automatically grabs you, and I think that's what happened there. It always takes me a long time to find something to make a film out of, but when I find it I know that it's right because the very idea excites me so much. People often send me stories and ideas, but there's always something about them that doesn't quite click with me. I've got to have a reason to be interested in it for so long.

KM: *Did you write* A Grand Day Out *on your own?*

NP: No, I wrote it with a guy called Steve Rushton, who I was sharing a flat with at the time. He was a much more prolific writer than I was and he wrote the basic plot. But halfway through making the film I decided it was too long and rewrote it myself. To go back to your earlier question about influences, I've just remembered something. After finishing *A Grand Day Out*, with all those rockets and inventions and what have you, it dawned on me that as a child – it was actually when we first got that cine-camera, because I know we've got film of this – my parents built a caravan from nothing. From just a pair of wheels, they built a box on it and decorated it inside with makeshift furniture and bunk beds and wallpaper. The whole thing was fitted and seven of us went on holiday, camping in Wales, in this thing. It just struck me that that's the rocket: a kind of home from home.

KM: *Inventions and contraptions.*

NP: Yes. And it strikes me that my childhood was filled with such things. My dad spent his time in the shed making things – in fact he still does – just making things. And I used to keep a box under my bed full of bits of old toys and things I'd found, bits of machines and what have you. I used to call it 'my box of useful things' and would talk with my brothers about how one day we'd be able to build a rocket or a time-machine if we kept all these bits and pieces. I always loved that, the mad scientist or inventor.

KM: *From what you were saying about rewriting the script halfway through making* A Grand Day Out, *it sounds as though it wasn't that tightly structured or pre-planned.*

NP: No, it wasn't. I always felt that that was what I lacked, because Steve wasn't a real script-writer; he was just somebody who liked to write short stories off his own bat, and I hadn't the knowledge either. I wish I'd learned more about script-writing and structure when I was at the film school. I was never a great one for discipline and although I did storyboard *A Grand Day Out*, I did it only as I went along. No, it wasn't as pre-planned as it should have been.

KM: *But you must have had the dialogue all written in advance?*

NP: Yes, we always animate to the soundtrack, and we had scripted and recorded all the dialogue in advance. You need to do that because you have to analyse the dialogue to get the lip sync right. So it was planned in that sense. But I always wish *A Grand Day Out* was a bit more structured in terms of plot. It's very linear. I remember that the first tutor I ever showed the script to said it was too whimsical.

KM: *Can you tell me why you chose to come to Aardman to work? Did they want you or did you want them?*

NP: I've been very fortunate in that I've never actually applied for a job. David Sproxton and Peter Lord, the founders of Aardman, came to the NFTS to speak and show their work, and I was able to show them some of mine. They showed a lot of interest and a month later they called me up and said, 'Do you fancy coming to work for us in the summer?' So for two years I worked here in my summer holidays and eventually, as I said, they offered me part-time work while making *A Grand Day Out*.

KM: *What were the first things you did for Aardman?*

NP: When I started, I worked on a little character called Morph. Do you remember him? He was a little Plasticine character created for a BBC kids' programme called *Take Hart*. At first I wasn't allowed to do Morph himself – I didn't have enough experience – but I worked on his little friends and making props. The studio wasn't really involved in commercials at the time. It was only when I came to work full time that they began to get into commercials more fully. Morph was their bread and butter. I don't think they got a lot from it financially, but it was an on-going thing. Anyway, in the period between my working for them as a student and coming to work here properly, they had made a complete series of short animated films for Channel Four, which was a follow-on from an earlier BBC series called *Conversation Pieces*, which were films based around recorded conversations. You might have seen *Late Edition* made by Peter Lord; it's set in a newspaper office?

KM: *Yes. Did Aardman invent that technique of animating real conversations?*

NP: I think they popularized it in this country, but it was something that John and Faith Hubley,* a couple of American animators, first did in the 1960s. They used the same idea of fly-on-the-wall recording which is then edited into a script and animated. I think they were the inspiration behind the BBC commissioning Aardman and various other animators – Derek Hayes, Bill Mather and Andy Walker – to do that first series. Aardman were just part of a series and then they got commissioned to do a full series for Channel Four on their own.

KM: *To me it seems there is something slightly paradoxical about spending months and months animating what is often quite banal, everyday conversation. Is that why you seem to have stopped doing them?*

NP: We have stopped doing them, but not for good, I hope. I love that whole thing about the banality of the conversation – that's the beauty of it. Somehow it really points up how people are. It highlights the inconsistencies, the quirkiness and bizarreness of the human situation, of how we work; it shows

---

* John Hubley (1914–77) started his animation career working for Disney on such films as *Snow White*, *Pinocchio* and *Fantasia*. In 1949, he created the Mr Magoo cartoon character based on his uncle. In the 1950s, he and his wife Faith set up their own company and produced numerous commercials and intelligent short animated films.

that we're not clear and that we say all sorts of peculiar things. I love the imperfection of the soundtrack. That's what makes the difference, isn't it? We found that we simply couldn't write this stuff, there is no way you could write it! We gradually experimented with the technique and I suppose my *Creature Comforts* and Peter Lord's *War Story*, which was done at the same time, stepped sideways out of the fly-on-the-wall recordings, in that they were actually vox-pop interviews. In fact, the technique became a comment on the documentary form, which is normally about as far removed from animation as you can get. You have the documentary soundtrack and then you have it animated and animation is so contrived – every frame is contrived – in a sense that every frame is a lie! Was it Picasso who said that art is the lie that tells the truth?

KM: *I've noticed that you have some credits as an animator on a few interesting projects which Aardman did in the late 1980s, like the Peter Gabriel* Sledgehammer *video and Peter Lord's* War Story, *but you don't seem to have any director's credits.*

Peter Gabriel's *Sledgehammer*.

NP: No, because for the first four years I was doing a month on and a month off, so I wasn't given anything highly responsible to do. In those days everything was directed by Peter and Dave, and I was still a newish employee. You've also got to remember that, at the time, advertising agencies or pop-video producers usually brought in an outside director because – except for Peter and Dave – we weren't known for our directing. It wasn't until *A Grand Day Out* and *Creature Comforts* that I really got a chance to direct.

KM: *Can you tell me a little about the Peter Gabriel video? Did you enjoy animating to music?*

NP: That was really good. It was a big break for us, in a way – a chance to try something different from the rather slick, naturalistic animation we were mostly doing.

KM: *I remember that I was amazed when I first saw it, partly, I suppose, because video technology wasn't as developed in those days and one wasn't used to seeing pop videos that were so visually inventive and exciting.*

NP: There were about five or six of us in the company at the time and we were all desperate to try out new ideas; in particular we were dying for some kind of opening into the pop-video side of things. But at the time, videos were very conventional, they were always set in a giant warehouse with a lot of smoke or on the top of a mountain somewhere; they wanted it to look exotic and as much like a feature film as possible. I don't think anybody had the money or the vision to commission animation. It took somebody with a sense of adventure like Peter Gabriel to take us on. I remember the brief which the director Steve Johnson gave us: he said that he wanted it to look like a fourteen-year-old had made it in their attic! So there was nothing precious about it, and because it had to be done so fast – we had six days to do it – we had to work almost twenty-four hours a day. It was ridiculous but great.

KM: *Aardman did only one section of the video; there were other companies involved.*

NP: There were three companies involved: Aardman, David Anderson who was an individual company at the time, and the Brothers Quay.*

KM: *Do you like the Quay brothers' work?*

NP: Yes, I admire it a lot. I haven't seen much of what they've done over the past five years or so, but I know they've been doing some commercials work recently, as well as their own films. I've always liked their work, but sometimes I've felt that it needed cutting down a bit. Perhaps that's because I've seen it only at festivals, where it often seems as though everything should be cut down!

KM: *Compared with your work it's a lot darker, with that Gothic, Eastern European influence that a lot of animators seem to relish. Why do you think so many animators are drawn to that macabre side of things?*

NP: I think there has always been a pressure to be that way. I think that Svankmajer and the Quays, for instance, are both brilliant, but they are working in a completely different field to us. I feel happier about accepting that now. I think coming from art school, you always feel that you ought to be a bit more serious; there's the attitude that entertainment is selling out to commercialism. I used to sense that pressure, but I feel a bit more relaxed about it now.

KM: *So is Aardman the Hollywood of British animation?*

NP: No, I don't think so! Hopefully we haven't sold out.

KM: *I meant in terms of 'entertainment' coming before 'art'.*

NP: Yes, I think that's important. It's hard for me to speak about because I don't want to sound as if I'm boasting. But I

---

* Stephen and Timothy Quay (1947–) are twin brothers who always work together. American-born, they work in England. Their stop-motion films are dense, bizarre and symbolic, and exhibit Eastern European, rather than Western, influences. Their shorts include: *The Unnameable Little Broom* (1985), *The Cabinet of Jan Svankmajer* (1984) and *Street of Crocodiles* (1986). They have recently completed their first feature-length live-action film, *Instituta Benjamenta*.

think if you go round festivals you do see that most animators are interested in the darker, more serious side. It's something that has constantly surprised me. But, of course, there are pressures both ways. I remember at film school, sometimes students would say to me, 'Why are animators always into slapstick comedy?' And I used to listen to that and think, yeah, there's no reason why, really. But having said that, it isn't really true of many of the animators I know. You'd think that animation would attract people with a sense of humour and fun, but it doesn't. On the whole, it's the other way round and so when you visit a festival, you find the audience is desperate for anything that's funny.

KM: *Is that because animators are striving to be taken seriously?*

NP: Of course, some of the more art-house stuff can also be humorous. Svankmajer is humorous, though dark and macabre at the same time . . . But even with him, sometimes you want to tell him to put a few custard pies in there! A few banana skins! You know, I often think that animation in Britain is somewhere between the Eastern European and the American. I know that, speaking for ourselves at Aardman, we've slowly become more aware of the audience. I think we still write or make things for ourselves, but we are aware of the audience. I think it's getting that balance. So many films you see in festivals are not made for audiences – I don't think – or at least they're not made for me! I'm not saying they should be made for me, but I'd like them to be aware that I've got to sit through it. I'm not saying everything should be Daffy Duck.

KM: *You talk very easily in general terms of 'we at Aardman'. Do you all have something in common? Is there a house style, or do all the directors have their own signature?*

NP: We certainly have something in common and I think that part of our problem is to stay diverse. In the past, a project has come in and we've all worked on it, whether it be a commercial or a video. Each individual project was different and often whoever was commissioning the commercial hired an outside

Creature Comforts.

director. But now that there are more animators and directors within the company becoming recognized for their own thing, the problem is that since *Creature Comforts* my style has dominated: the wide mouth and the eyes close together, all that. There's no resentment or anything, but I think we have become a bit typecast. Quite often we'll be commissioned to do a commercial, one of the other directors will be directing it, and the agency will be full of enthusiasm that this will be a 'new look' and that they want us to give it a style that 'isn't like anything we've seen before' – all of that stuff. And you know that what usually happens is that after all the talk and discussion it ends up: 'Oh, well actually, we'd like it a bit like *Creature Comforts*!' It's part of the trap that we've got into. In some ways it's nice – it's very flattering for me – but there are other styles.

KM: *How did* Creature Comforts *come about? Was it the first thing that you did on your own here?*

NP: Yes, it was. At that time there were six or seven of us in the company and it had been a while since we'd done any small independent films and we were all ambitious to do something. So, since there were four different directors here, we decided to get together and apply to Channel Four with a number of projects which we could each direct individually. We spent months trying to think what this unifying series could be and all we could come up with was an idea of 'Lip Sync' – using animated lip sync – and that's what we called it, which wasn't a great title. The idea was that it was a development of the 'Conversation Pieces' idea, though some of the films didn't end up with any connection to that at all, like *Ident* and *Next*, the Shakespeare film. But Channel Four were happy to live with that, so we just went ahead and did our own films.

KM: *So you'd finished* A Grand Day Out *by this time?*

NP: Not quite. *Creature Comforts* was made in the rather long gap between finishing the actual film of *A Grand Day Out* and mixing the sound and music. I had spent six years trying to anticipate what it was going to be like when I finally graduated with this thing, and whether it was going to have any impact or not, and when it was finally finished all the limelight was stolen by *Creature Comforts*! It was my film, of course, so I didn't feel too bad about it!

KM: Creature Comforts *must have been made quite quickly.*

NP: From concept to finished print took about six months, which is very quick. We took three months to shoot and a couple of months to record the conversations and edit the soundtrack first.

KM: *How did you come across the idea for* Creature Comforts?

NP: It evolved over time. I was thinking about animals and how I could use them in a film and simultaneously wondering how I could use fly-on-the-wall recorded conversations in the tradition of Aardman. Eventually I got the idea of a film about a zoo. It was a subject which I hadn't seen dealt with very much at all. My mind went back to an art exhibition I once saw of paintings of animals in steel and concrete rooms.

I got a sound recordist to put a hidden microphone on me and I went to the zoo and tried to record the conversations of people looking at the animals. I just stood there among these people, recording what they were saying. The idea was to put the words of the people into the mouths of the animals as they looked at the people outside. I wanted the animals to be commenting on the people on the other side of the bars. It was a good idea, I thought, but it was extremely difficult. I didn't get any really good, concrete conversations. Everything was a little disjointed and the recording conditions were not much good because there was usually a fan going in the background or a waterfall, or something. I remember that after two days of recording all I had were two usable sentences! So I then thought: this is so difficult, why don't I simply interview people? It suddenly became more interesting. I tried to do the interviews myself, but I also hired a reporter who I thought might be better than me and she went out and recorded what people think about zoos. But it was pretty boring, really. Everyone said the same two things: 'It's nice to see the animals close up, especially for the children,' and, 'But it's a bit cruel.' And, in effect, that's all I got from hours of recording. As we weren't getting very far, we decided that what we needed to do was to find people in a situation somehow similar to that of animals in a zoo and interview them. We did try to ask people to pretend to be animals, but it didn't work. They just couldn't do it; it was like amateur acting. We needed it to come from the heart. They were saying what it was like for the animals in the zoo, but what we needed was people saying what it's like for 'me' here, in the first person.

KM: *So in the end you simply interviewed them about their own conditions?*

NP: Yes. I also asked them what they thought about zoos and then finally got on to asking them certain questions about where they lived. I happened to come across some people who, in a sense, seemed to be in a parallel situation to animals in a zoo: people visiting this country, or who were forced to be here for whatever reason, like the Brazilian guy who eventually became the Brazilian Jaguar. He was a student who I'd met before and I knew that for lots of reasons, particularly the climate, he hated living in Britain. So he was a good candidate. I also asked him about what his life was like in a student residence, about the food and that sort of thing. He went back to Brazil before the film was finished and I sent a tape over to him, but I've never heard back so I don't know what he thought of it. He works for an oil company now as a geologist and I did hear a story that when he goes to conferences he's asked to stand up and 'do the Brazilian Jaguar'!

KM: *What a peculiar type of stardom!*

NP: He was a real find . . . but one thing I've discovered is that you can use just about anybody. He was good because he helped to spice it up, but I found that almost anybody's conversation is funny if you put it in an animal's mouth, because you can have the animals doing things that the humans were not. You can have fun changing the context.

KM: *When you heard the voices did you think, 'Oh, that sounds like a gorilla, I'll make that voice a gorilla,' and so on? Did the voices suggest which animals they should be?*

NP: It was very much a matter of making the recording, listening to the tape and then deciding what animal they could be. But I did change my mind on a couple of occasions. At the very beginning I was thinking of making the Brazilian a penguin. Some were chosen for other reasons, like the gorilla. She was one of the last ones I recorded, I still hadn't got any apes and that's the only reason she ended up as an ape. In some ways I enjoy not making them what they suggest in terms of their voice because that's a conventional cartoon thing to do. People often do say that they fit well with the voices, but I really think you can make anything fit with anything. Sometimes it's funny because of the misfit – a big animal with a little voice, or whatever. Otherwise it's the typical kind of Disney thing: if you're a snake you have a hissing voice or whatever.

KM: *How much did you expect the enormous success of* Creature Comforts *and when did it first become apparent?*

NP: I guess it was at the same time when *A Grand Day Out* was first seen. All the 'Lip Sync' films and *A Grand Day Out* were screened at what was then the Bristol Animation Festival – now the Cardiff Animation Festival. That was the first public showing. Apart from the amateur film I'd had on the BBC as a child, that was my first taste of fame. Terry Gilliam was asked to review his favourite films from the festival on some movie programme and he chose *Creature Comforts*. He talked about it in such a dazzling, enthusiastic way that I thought: 'Is that me he's talking about?' I was one of his biggest followers, especially as a kid, and I've always loved his live-action direction as well.

KM: *Have you met him since?*

NP: No, I've never met him. But he was like ... I find it a bit embarrassing to repeat what he said – it was a very Pythonesque thing to say. He said, 'Nick Park should be made God tomorrow!' And this came completely out of the blue. I'd had no publicity at all before, and then to hear me talked about like that on TV was amazing! Then in the festival itself, it also went down very well and Ray Harryhausen, who was guest of honour at the festival that year, came up to me after the show and said in his heavy American accent, 'I've never seen Claymation so smooth!' And I thought, boy, it's like an angel coming down to me. It was beyond my wildest dreams. So in a way everything started to take off very, very quickly and suddenly, after that, there was the BAFTA award for *A Grand Day Out* and so on ...

KM: *And the following year both films were nominated for an Oscar and, of course,* Creature Comforts *won.*

NP: Yes, in fact they were both nominated for both awards. *A Grand Day Out* won the BAFTA and *Creature Comforts* won the Oscar. I think that's what caused an impact at the time, because suddenly I'd come from nowhere with two films finished and it made me look prolific.

KM: *Did you go to Hollywood for the ceremony?*

NP: Yes, I went over to both ceremonies, for *Creature Comforts* and the following year for *The Wrong Trousers*, which also won.

KM: *That first time in particular must have been very exciting.*

NP: It was, although you don't know how much of it to take with a pinch of salt. It's all to do with glamour and tinsel-town on the one hand; but on the other hand, it is the hub of the film industry and they do put their money where their mouth is – unlike the British. I think that's what I love about Americans: the top people in all the companies want to meet you and talk about your work and future projects. A lot of it doesn't come to anything, but at least they're doing it. For instance, I was amazed when I went on a tour of Disney and they took me to see the top man there, Jeffrey Katzenberg, and he was well aware of my work and of Aardman's work in general. He knew my name and the names of all the other good animators in Britain, even though we're in a different league. It was very impressive.

KM: *Were they trying to persuade you to make a feature film for them?*

NP: Of course. We haven't done anything yet, but I think people see the potential of what we're doing for feature-film work. We're in the middle of negotiating things at the moment; we've been seriously approached by nearly all the studios and we're talking to them. I can't go into any details now because nothing is finalized, but we hope to start developing something in the near future.*

[At this point the interview is interrupted by one of the assistant animators on *A Close Shave*, who wants Nick Park's advice on a particularly tricky bit of animation he has just completed. Nick reappears about three minutes later.]

* Since this interview was completed Aardman have entered into a development deal with Jake Eberts's Allied Film-Makers. Eberts was the founder of Goldcrest in the early 1980s and his recent credits as executive producer include Henry Selick's animated feature *James and the Giant Peach*.

KM: *Did you have a look at it?*

NP: Yes, I replayed it on the computer; every time we take a frame of film we also take a frame that is transferred on to a computer disk so we can look back at what we've done without waiting for the rushes.

KM: *And how was it?*

NP: It wasn't quite right and we both knew it straight away. It's a reshoot tomorrow.

KM: *A wasted day?*

NP: Not quite, only about four hours or so.

KM: *To get back to what we were talking about: if you do a feature, will it be with Wallace and Gromit?*

NP: Well, that's a big one. I think that after *A Close Shave* I'll have to review the situation and see how I feel about Wallace and Gromit. I do enjoy working with them, they're really nice. You'll have noticed that I tend to think that they exist and treat them very personally. I'm very affectionate towards them and I feel like they're my babies. But the problem is that the more ambitious the film gets – and this is a problem I'm having already on *A Close Shave* – the harder it is to control it all, and because of the way I feel about Wallace and Gromit, I do feel the need to control everything very tightly. So it might be best if we're doing a feature, especially the first one, to do something completely new and original, so that it isn't anyone's baby or anyone's personal style.

KM: *Would you direct it? I imagine that the studio would want you to.*

NP: Perhaps, but it could equally be Pete Lord, or it could be a joint effort with Pete.

KM: *Recently the profile of stop-frame model animation has been raised by Tim Burton's* Nightmare Before Christmas, *the first mainstream feature that's been made in that way for a long time. What did you think of it?*

NP: I was quoted on the poster from an interview I gave about it! The quote went: 'It more than lived up to my expectations. I was stunned!' I don't think I actually said that, though!

KM: *But were you stunned?*

NP: Yes, I was. I thought that, visually, it was very rich. Style-wise, I was interested to see that it was so Eastern European looking.

KM: *Yes, with the stitched-together character and the stylized landscape, that little twirl which always seemed to have the moon going down just behind it.*

NP: In that way it was very anti-Hollywood because they weren't trying to cover up the technique. It was a film *about puppets*: they were puppets and you were very aware of the material; it seemed to be influenced by traditional Eastern European puppet art. It also had something of that darker, nightmarish quality we were talking about earlier. It was meant to be for kids, but I'm not sure if it was, really – I think they'd find it too dark.

KM: *Technically, is it a lot to live up to?*

NP: Yes, they had the best animators in the world working on it. Lloyd, who's working on my film now, was one of them. He's doing my evil character.

KM: *It was impressive how much the camera moved and that they even blended in a bit of drawn animation along with the 3D stuff.*

NP: And as a musical I thought it was very ambitious. But what really startled me was the quality of it. With so many animators churning it out over such a short period of time – I think it took only about eighteen months – it really was of a consistently high standard. Henry Selick, who directed, handled it very impressively. What particularly struck me was the general 'choreography' of it; it really worked as a whole. It was like a piece of elaborate choreography and that's maybe what it was trying for.

KM: *What would you judge are its faults?*

NP: When I first saw it I couldn't fault it. It may have had faults, but I think I was so taken aback by the visuals that I could forgive it anything. I've now seen it about three times and I've actually appreciated it more every time, but the design is so dominant, the actual animation itself is so elaborate and the frame so busy that you miss what you're meant to be looking at. At times I was fighting to take it in. Also, I've never really been impressed with the story.

KM: *Yes, that's where I feel it's lacking. The story is thin and the jokes aren't funny enough.*

NP: That's what I thought too. It's not often funny, is it?

KM: *Did it teach you anything that you should be aware of when you make a feature?*

NP: I think that the film has problems, but I completely sympathize with them; that's why I'm not too ready to condemn it, because I'm very much in the same situation. I mean, how on earth do you pull this kind of thing off? It's daunting.

KM: *Are you surprised that Hollywood allowed* Nightmare Before Christmas *to be made?*

NP: Yes, I'm particularly surprised that Disney did it. I think it would have been very difficult to make if it didn't have Tim Burton's name on it.

KM: *This is maybe a good place to talk a little bit about money. Animation has the reputation of being expensive. How difficult is it to get finance for your projects?*

NP: Most animators have to do commercials just to exist, just to get by, and as a consequence we have probably the best commercials in the world in this country. The problem is that you can get stuck in that and, although some people are happy making commercials and have no desire to do anything else, most of us want to do our own films. There is really very little money for that – most of it comes from Channel Four and a little from the Welsh station S4C. Recently, the BBC have stepped in; they funded *The Wrong Trousers* and *A Close Shave*.

KM: *So how much does a short 3D animated film cost?*

NP: I'm not very good with figures. I'm a bit out of touch with the money side, but I do know that commercials don't really compare with short films. You're talking about £2,000 a second for commercials. Or is it more? I don't know. A thirty-second commercial is at least £60,000 – at least. And in comparison, *Creature Comforts*, which was five minutes, cost about £20,000 or £30,000.

KM: *How do* A Close Shave *and* The Wrong Trousers *compare?*

NP: *The Wrong Trousers* cost about £600,000 and *A Close Shave* almost twice that.

KM: *So, theoretically, you could do a feature for about £3–4 million?*

NP: Theoretically, but the main cost would be in terms of stress! Low living conditions! That's the problem, I think, and that's why we're always battling for more money because we nearly killed ourselves on *The Wrong Trousers*, we became so ill and over-worked.

KM: *How long did it take to make?*

NP: The filming alone took about thirteen months with a full-time crew of about ten. In comparison, there are thirty people on this one.

KM: *Had you decided that you wanted to do another Wallace and Gromit film when you finished* The Wrong Trousers?

NP: Yes. While we were over in Hollywood, with all these people phoning up, the thing that brought me back to reality was that I had commitments here. When I was over there with *Creature Comforts*, I had a commitment to come back and do *The Wrong Trousers* and when I was over with that, I had *A Close Shave* to come back to.

KM: *Did you know after* A Grand Day Out *that you wanted to use the same characters again?*

NP: Yes. It had taken me so long and, as I said, they were my babies really and even though I'd made *Creature Comforts*, which was in some ways a more personal film, I wanted to get back to those characters. I've always had this thing about wanting to create characters which people grow familiar with through a series or something – like the characters in the *Bash Street Kids*, for instance – characters everyone would come to know and see regularly. Wallace and Gromit were where I focused because I felt they had developed so far and I couldn't just drop them and do something else. I knew there was a lot more I could do with them. I've always liked the combination of comedy, thriller, adventure and science fiction.

KM: *Do you imagine ever franchising out the characters for someone else to make a series – say, a twenty-part series of five-minute films?*

NP: No, I couldn't see that at all. After *Creature Comforts* and *A Grand Day Out* we got quite a few people wanting to do that. They'd call up and straight away ask, 'How much would it cost for fifty-two episodes of that?' They were quite serious! Some of them even put their money on the table. But we knew that it would be impossible to do fifty-two, or anything like that. And, of course, as soon as they realized how long it took to do five minutes they went cold on us! Not that we wanted to do it, anyway. I always felt that if a series of *Creature Comforts* were made, people would say, 'It's not as good as the original,' and it wouldn't be, if you had to start mass producing them. The whole problem with this sort of animation is that it's very personal. Because it's clay, your animator has to be a good model-maker as well as having a good sense of cartooning in 3D. Also, on a big project the style has to be unified in some way which is very difficult, because it's hard to find good model animators and harder still to find good clay animators.

KM: *What is the material that you use for the models?*

NP: It's Plasticine – Harbutts Plasticine.

KM: *With* The Wrong Trousers, *did you do most of the animation yourself?*

NP: It was a split mainly between two of us. A guy called Steve Box did all of the Penguin, and the occasional bit of Gromit and Wallace asleep in the trousers. Overall we tried to split it 50–50, but in fact he ended up doing a bit more than me. Other animators were brought in to do bits and pieces, and Pete Lord and another animator helped out on the train chase at the

Nick Park working on *The Wrong Trousers*.

Steve Box working on *The Wrong Trousers*.

end which was very complicated. Overall, though, it was handleable. But the film we're doing now [*A Close Shave*] is a step up from that. The way that this one is being made, we're treating it as a kind of guinea pig before making a feature film in that we have had to step up operations.

KM: *How many animators have you got working on it?*

NP: Ian – who just came in – is an assistant animator, but we've got all three assistants actually shooting now, plus three main animators; that's seven including myself – when I get the chance.

KM: *So the assistants are actually shooting stuff.*

NP: Yes. They're doing bits where character isn't so important, although we're trying to shift one of the assistants into full-time animation, mostly handling Wallace. But at this stage I'm still having to come in and coach him quite a lot because it's quite hard trying to copy someone else's style. That's the thing about clay animation – it's like copying someone else's signature, or copying somebody's writing. It's a very personal thing.

KM: *Do you have problems with consistency?*

NP: Yes. One way that we deal with it is to give each animator a different character, like having Steve Box do the Penguin, and me doing Wallace and Gromit. That way you won't read the differences in style so much because it will in effect complement the characters. But I have such a firm idea of what I want in my head that I'm constantly coaching everybody – directing, I suppose.

KM: *Do you feel you're directing properly now for the first time?*

NP: Yes. I was directing before with *The Wrong Trousers* – which is why I ended up doing less that 50 per cent – but on this one I'm animating even less and directing a lot more, which I find exhausting because I'm simply going round sets looking at other people's work. I also find it slightly frustrating because I'd rather be doing it myself.

KM: *About a quarter of an hour ago one of the assistant animators asked you to have a look at what he'd done and you thought that it was wrong. Does that happen quite often?*

NP: Yes, but on this occasion it was quite easy because Ian could see how it wasn't working himself, which isn't always the case.

KM: *He'd spent four hours doing it. How much screen time was that?*

NP: It looked like about a second.

KM: *One second?! How can you look at a second and see that it's wrong?*

NP: Well, a lot can happen in a second. People are always amazed when we say that we do two seconds or three seconds a day. But in the world of animation time is condensed and that's what I like about it. You see, in animation you can punctuate much quicker in terms of storytelling, you can make points very directly and succinctly – you have to because it takes so long to do – and you have to get your timing just right. I think that's what it is: a kind of punctuation with the timing.

KM: *So when you storyboard, how much detail do you give?*

NP: Normally, I just do one storyboard picture per shot, but sometimes, if there is more than one event or action going on in that shot, I'll do two or three drawings.

KM: *But facial expressions and that sort of thing are left to the individual animator?*

NP: It's not as simple as that. What I try to do in the storyboard is sum up the basic thing that's going on – the key event. So if several significant things happen, and it might otherwise be misleading, I'll do a number of drawings. For instance, if it's a close up on somebody's face and they're smiling and then looking horrified, I might do just the horrified look, but I'd write underneath something like: 'Smiling Wallace – then looks horrified.'

KM: *What about the complex train chase sequence at the end of* The Wrong Trousers? *To what extent was that storyboarded?*

NP: I storyboarded all of the train chase before the script was even written, and it stayed pretty much as it was. For a long time I played about with the idea of the Penguin visiting

Wallace and Gromit on my own, and came up with some ideas, and I thought that because of the size of the Penguin it would be great if we could use toys that were scattered around the house – because as I've said, I love mechanical things in films and robot-like things – and eventually this idea developed into the train chase. Before the script was written I had story-boarded the whole thing. Then I went to see Bob Baker, a writer here in Bristol who Dave Sproxton introduced me to, and I put a lot of the key ideas that I had to him and he added the structure. I thought that he would be like any script editor and throw lots out, but he kept nearly everything in.

KM: *So you already had the idea of the Penguin as a crook, the electronic trousers and all that?*

NP: Yes, but we couldn't make a good story out of it; somehow it just wasn't adequate. We kept getting into problems and because we had spent so long on it and had written so many different versions, we eventually thought that either the Penguin or the trousers had to go. We couldn't get those two elements to

Sc 60. Shot 9. INT. DINING ROOM. NIGHT.
WALLACE REACTS HORRIFIED AT HIS APPROACHING FETE.

Sc 60. Shot 10. INT. DINING ROOM. NIGHT.
WALLACE HITS THE OFFICER'S AND FLIES INTO THE FOOD SERVING HATCH.
TRACK AND STOP.

Sc 61. Shot 1. INT. KITCHEN. NIGHT.
WALLACE IS PLUCKED FROM THE 'TECHNO-TROUSERS'.
YAAAAAARGH!

Sc 61. shot 2. INT. KITCHEN. NIGHT.
AND LANDS ON A VEGETABLE TROLLEY.
PAN WITH WALLACE

Sc 61. Shot 2 Continued.
WALLACE ZOOMS THROUGH KITCHEN TURNING AS HE EXITS A DOOR JAM.

Sc 62. Shot 5. INT. DOORWAY/STUDY. WITH
TRAIN ZOOMS TOWARD CAMERA.
ZIP PAN AS TRAIN APPROACHES

The Wrong Trousers.

Sc 62. Shot 3 continued.
PAN WITH TRAIN AS THEY SPEED INTO
THE STUDY AND ROUND A CORNER.

Sc 62. Shot 4. INT. STUDY. NIGHT
GROMIT SHEDS HELMET AND ATTEMPTS
TO CRAWL ALONG THE TRAIN.

TRACKING SHOT.

67

Sc 62. Shot 5. INT. STUDY. NIGHT
PENGUIN LOOKS BACK SURPRISED.

TRACKING SHOT.

Sc 62. Shot 6. INT. STUDY. NIGHT.
WALLACE OVER TAKES GROMIT WIELDING
A FISHING NET.

Sc 62. Shot 6. CONTINUED.
LEAVE HIM TO ME....
I'LL GET THE BOUNDER!
WALLACE RAISES HIS NET.

Sc 62. Shot 7. INT. STUDY. NIGHT
BUT... THE NET CATCHES THE MOOSE'S
HEAD.

Sc 62. Shot 8. INT. STUDY. NIGHT.
WALLACE IS YANKED INTO THE AIR.
"YAAAAAGH!

TRACKING SHOT.

Sc 62. Shot 9. INT. STUDY. NIGHT.
GROMIT RESUMES CREEPING UP
ON PENGUIN.

TRACKING SHOT.

68

Sc 62. Shot 9 continued.
HE'S DISTRACTED BY THE SOUND OF
WALLACE WAILING.
YAAAAGH!

Sc 62. Shot 10. INT. STUDY. NIGHT.
WALLACE HAS LANDED ON THE BACK
OF THE TRAIN. "YAAAAGH!

TRACKING SHOT

Sc 62. Shot 11. INT. STUDY. NIGHT.
THIS GIVES PENGUIN THE CHANCE TO
UNHITCH THE CARRIAGES.
WE ALSO PASS FROM STUDY TO LIVING ROOM.

Sc 62 Shot 11. continued.
THE GAP WIDENS AS GROMIT MAKES
A GRAB. BUT MISSES.

238 / THE DIRECTOR'S CUT

Sc 63. Shot 1. INT. LIVING ROOM. NIGHT.

PENGUIN CHANGES POINTS AS HE PASSES.

TRACKING SHOT.

Sc 63 Shot 2. INT LIVING ROOM NIGHT.

SEND WALLACE AND GROMIT OFF ON ANOTHER
TRACK.

TRACKING SHOT.

Sc 63. Shot 3. INT. LIVING ROOM. NIGHT.

GROMIT LOOKS AHEAD HORRIFIED.

TRACKING SHOT.

Sc 63. Shot 4. INT. LIVING ROOM. NIGHT.

THE END OF TRACK APPROACHES AND
THE FRENCH WINDOWS.

TRACKING SHOT

Sc 63. Shot 5. INT. LIVING ROOM. NIGHT.

GROMIT REACHES OUT...

TRACKING SHOT.

Sc 63. Shot 6. INT. LIVING ROOM. NIGH

...TO GRAB A BOX.

Sc 63. Shot 7. INT. LIVING ROOM. NIGHT.

EXTREMELY FAST GROMIT LAYS THE
SPARE TRACKS.

TRACKING SHOT,

Sc 63. Shot 8. INT. LIVING ROOM. NIGHT.

GROMIT STEERS THE TRAIN JUST
AVOIDING A CRASH.

TRACKING SHOT.

Sc 63. Shot 9. INT. LIVING ROOM. NIGHT.

HE STEERS THE TRAIN AWAY FROM
THE FRENCH WINDOWS.

PAN WITH TRAIN.

Sc 63. Shot 9 continued.

I MIND THE TABLE GROMIT.
PAN WITH TRAIN.

Sc 63. Shot 10. INT. LIVING ROOM. NIGHT.

TRACK IN TO TABLE AND CHAIR LEGS

Sc 63. Shot 11. INT. LIVING ROOM. NIGHT.

GROMIT HORRIFIED STILL LAYING
TRACKS MANICALLY...

NICK PARK / 239

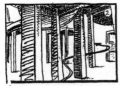

Sc 63. Shot 12. INT. LIVING ROOM. NIGHT.

GROMITS P.O.V. MEANDERING THROUGH
THE TABLE LEGS.

TRACKING SHOT.

Sc 63 shot 12Ⓐ LIVING ROOM. NIGHT

GROMIT LOOKS BACK OVER HIS
SHOULDER.

TRACKING SHOT

Sc 63. Shot 13. INT. LIVING ROOM. NIGHT.

WALLACE SNAKES THROUGH TABLE LEGS.

YAAAH! OOOOH! EEEEEEH! ERH: AAAAGH

* TRACKING SHOT.

Sc 64 Shot 1. LIVING ROOM/HALLWAY. NIGHT

WALLACE P.O.V OF GROMIT ENTERING HALL
TRAIN DISAPEARS AROUND WALL AND WALLACE
PASSES CAMERA

Sc 65. Shot 1. INT. DINING ROOM. NIGHT.

GROMIT SPEED OUT FROM HALLWAY INTO THE
DINING ROOM. LOOKS TO FRAME RIGHT.

Sc 65. Shot 2. INT. DINING ROOM. NIGHT.

PENGUIN COMES HURTLING ROUND THE BEND
TRIES TO BRAKE.
ALMOST GROMITS P.O.V.

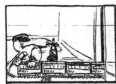

Sc 65. Shot 3. INT. DINING ROOM. NIGHT.

GROMIT CROSSES PENGUINS TRACK.
PENGUIN ABOUT TO COLLIDE WITH TRAIN.

Sc 65. Shot 3 continued.

WALLACE TRIES TO GRAB PENGUIN...

Sc 65. Shot 3 continued.

...BUT PENGUIN TRUNDLES ON ENGINELESS.

Sc 65. Shot 4. INT. DINING ROOM. NIGHT.

WALLACE HAS GRABBED THE ENGINE

TRACKING SHOT.

Sc 65. Shot 5. INT. DINING ROOM. NIGHT.

GROMITS TRAIN CURVES AROUND TO COME
UP PARALLEL TO PENGUINS TRACK.
GROMIT RUNS OUT OF TRACK AND DISCARDS

Sc 65. Shot 6. INT. DINING ROOM. NIGHT.

PENGUINS P.O.V. TROUSERS STEP ON HIS
TRACK. (WERE HEADING FOR KITCHEN)

TRACKING SHOT

Sc 65. Shot 7. INT. DINING ROOM. NIGHT.

PANICKED PENGUIN TRIES TO BRAKE AND
WALLACE AND GROMIT OVERTAKE.

TRACKING SHOT.

Sc 65. Shot 7. CONTINUED.

TROUSER FOOT COMES DOWN ON THE TRACK.
PENGUIN GOES FLYING.

Sc 66. Shot 1. INT. KITCHEN. NIGHT.

WALLACE REACHES UP TO GRAB PENGUIN.

TRACKING SHOT

Sc 66. Shot 2. INT. KITCHEN. NIGHT.

GROMIT ANTICIPATES A CATCH.

TRACKING SHOT.

Sc 66. Shot 3. INT. KITCHEN. NIGHT.

PENGUIN SAILS THROUGH THE AIR.

TRACKING SHOT.

Sc 66. Shot 4. INT. KITCHEN. NIGHT.

GROMIT SMASHES INTO KITCHEN UNIT CUPBOARD

TRACK THEN STOP.

Sc 66. Shot 5. INT. KITCHEN. NIGHT.

THE CRASH CAUSES A BOTTLE TO TOPPLE
OFF THE COUNTER.

Sc 66. Shot 6. INT. KITCHEN. NIGHT.

PENGUIN DESCENDS TRY TO FLAP ONE
WING.

Sc 66. Shot 7. INT. KITCHEN. NIGHT.

BOTTLE LANDS IN GROMIT LAP....

Sc 66. Shot 7 CONTINUED.

..PERFECTLY POSITIONED TO CATCH THE
PENGUIN AND THE DIAMOND.
ATTA BOY GROMIT LAD.

Sc 66. Shot 8. INT. KITCHEN. NIGHT.

WALLACE SLIDES INTO FRAME:
" WELL DONE! WE DID IT! "

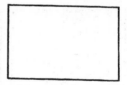

tie together. Then we found Bob, who managed to find a plot that brought the whole thing together.

KM: *In terms of both plot and characterization,* The Wrong Trousers *seems much more sophisticated that* A Grand Day Out. *Particularly noticeable are the pastiche elements, the film-noir references and, of course, the train chase, which is wonderful and complicated.*

NP: Yes, definitely, I think it was much more sophisticated. You see, *A Grand Day Out* was done virtually with string and nails, including the story. It was all a bit makeshift. I hadn't even finished writing it when I was completing it. It was up in the air and lacked all kinds of discipline. So I was determined that the next one should be a lot better. And, of course, I was lucky to get in the right expertise on *The Wrong Trousers*. I think it is by far a better film. But there are things that I like about *A Grand Day Out* – things that I was able to do because I had the time and I wasn't trying to fit a forty-minute film into a thirty-minute one – which is what I was trying to do on *The Wrong Trousers*. And *A Close Shave* is even worse! It's a feature film in thirty minutes!

KM: *One delightful aspect of your films is the tiny details, such as the titles of the books that Wallace reads:* Sticks *and* The Republic *by Pluto. This is what makes it fun to watch the films over and over – you spot more every time. Do those little details arise spontaneously as you're making the film?*

NP: They tend to come while we're getting things together, perhaps while the props are being made. But sometimes they happen at the last minute. I'll be about to start and I'll think, 'Oh, that's a great idea for a title of a book or for a headline on Gromit's newspaper!' I'm constantly talking to the model-makers and they come up with their own ideas. I'm glad you notice those little things; that's what I hope for. I want the films to have a personal touch about them, a hand-made quality.

KM: *In* The Wrong Trousers *the lighting is quite sophisticated and the camera moves a fair bit, which gives the film a cinematic feel.*

The Wrong Trousers: Gromit and the Penguin.

NP: That's something we strove for. I don't know whether I made a decision to do it, or if it just happened. I think it was a natural thing, really. I think that it was a sensibility that crept in. I didn't decide: this film is going to be like that, feature-film-like in quality, or whatever. It all became like that. The script seemed to demand it. The whole concept of a 'diamond-heist' film lent itself to that sort of treatment and I enjoyed referring to different genres. I find it very exciting to make an animation film of this type, full of all these quotes, because I've never seen anything like that before. There's bits of *The Third Man* and Hitchcock in there.

KM: *Specific references?*

NP: No, they're never very specific. I feel it's just playing around with ideas, skimming across the top of these things and using them where we want to. You don't very often see model animation which is well lit, do you? For me that's part of the comedy of it; I love the idea that you're making a thriller and it all looks authentic, but the lead character is in fact a Plasticine penguin!

KM: *I heard somewhere that* A Close Shave *was influenced by David Lean's* Brief Encounter.

NP: Yes, I have said that, but it could be misleading. The reference is there, but the script has evolved so much that it's almost untraceable. If it's there at all, it's on the romance side. I've always loved that film and had it in the back of my mind while we were writing it. We watched it a lot when we were developing the idea. Bob Baker and I came up with the story for *A Close Shave* together from scratch, rather than me having lots of ideas first. This film also contains many references to the previous two. I didn't notice them when we were writing it, but I see them now it's been shot. It's funny how it works like that. In *A Close Shave* it feels like I've been exploring new places which already existed in Wallace and Gromit's world. But *Brief Encounter* . . . there are no railway stations. I tried to get one in, but it didn't make it into the final script. The main influence is the idea of repressed, very English love. We borrowed the style: they say very little to each other, but say a lot at the same time. It's a spoof of sorts.

KM: *And, of course, the music adds to that – its quite 'big' and cinematic.*

NP: Yes, very much so. That's Julian Nott. I love his music.

KM: *It must be very hard to move the camera in animation. It must redouble your problems.*

NP: Yes, it is difficult. If I move the camera it needs to move one frame at a time, like the characters. What that means, though, is that you think much more about the consequences of a camera move than you would in live action, and in some ways maybe that's good discipline. One of the major differences between my films and contemporary animated feature films, like Disney's, is that because of all the developments in computer animation it is very easy for them to move the camera – or at least the 'point of view'. It's the easiest thing in the world once you've got the program to have the camera floating around, spinning around. To begin with, everybody loved it, but the problem might be that it all becomes a bit meaningless and you don't think about why

A Close Shave.

you're doing it. I'm not trying to oppose computer animation or anything, but I have been to shows of the latest in computer animation where I felt that there was a lack of awareness of what the camera – or 'point of view' – was doing.

KM: *Do you think that Wallace and Gromit have developed as characters through the films they've been in?*

NP: Yes, I think that even in *A Close Shave* they have developed. They're becoming more and more subtle, and as they have new experiences you have to think, 'What would they do in this situation?' The more experiences they have, the broader they become. In *A Close Shave* Wallace is falling in love and has to cope with a new villain, and I think that we see a little bit of Gromit that we didn't know about as well.

KM: *Virtually the last shot in* The Wrong Trousers *shows the Penguin behind bars and as the camera pulls back we see that he is not in jail but in a zoo. Is that a comment by you as an animal lover – or a reference to* Creature Comforts?

NP: I am an animal lover, and I suppose it is a comment on how I feel about zoos, although I'm not an activist or anything. I can see the dilemma and realize that zoos are now a situation we're stuck with. I don't tend only to make statements condemning things; I'm being more ironic than that. I remember that the original script opened with the Penguin escaping from the zoo and I was going to do it like *Mission Impossible* or *The Great Escape*, where you start off with the control towers, the search-lights and the prisoner going along the barbed wire – and then you see that it's a penguin escaping from a zoo! When we lost that opening I put that shot in at the end because I thought it was funny and it was a comment on zoos being prisons. I found the idea funny that zoos are where bad animals go.

KM: *Do you think that the great animal-loving British public responds to that – which perhaps explains part of the popularity of your films?*

NP: I think with Gromit, yes. We are a nation of dog lovers and so many people have said, 'My dog looks at me just like

Gromit does!' But from what I've picked up, I think the broad base of the appeal is the characters. People see something real in them which they latch on to and identify with, or see in others. Maybe it is that the characters tend to ask for sympathy from the viewer – maybe.

KM: *Would you say that the humour in these films is very British?*

NP: I think so. What I tend to do is mix something that's fairly subtle with something that's very brash, almost slapstick, clowning-type humour – like when Gromit gets hit by the jam, which is on the same level as Tom and Jerry. But *Creature Comforts* is much more subtle; it's all to do with character and you need time to watch it.

KM: *Could you say a little more about the animators who you feel have influenced you?*

NP: I don't mean to sound pompous, but I don't think I have an influence really. I don't think I look to anyone in animation. Perhaps, if I have to cite someone, I should say Peter Lord – I've always been challenged and influenced by him. I hope that doesn't sound too sycophantic.

KM: *What do you think of the vision of Disney in drawn animation like* Aladdin *or* The Lion King?

NP: I haven't seen *The Lion King*, but I saw *Aladdin* and *Beauty and the Beast*. I find them quite challenging and I like to look at them from the point of view of learning a lesson. They are very well directed. It seems to me that that's where the skill of Disney really lies, in telling a story. They're very good at that. I get turned off by some of the things in them, though – the sanitized stories and the sickly-sweet characters. Sometimes they still seem to be doing the things they were bad at years ago!

KM: *They haven't left the 1940s?*

NP: Yeah, with characters with waists *this* thin and eyes *this* big, who pout and flutter their eyelids to look pretty. I used to think, 'Who likes this stuff?' And they're still doing it!

KM: *I read recently something Tim Burton said about animation: one thing that makes it difficult is that everything has to be so thoroughly pre-planned so that when you come to shooting you're simply executing, and that if you have any new ideas you can't really use them because it will interrupt the delicate equilibrium of what you've already planned. Do you agree with that?*

NP: No, I don't feel it works in that way. I am thinking up new ideas a lot of the time and when I start shooting it's not just a matter of executing what's been put down on paper or on a storyboard; if that was the case it really would be boring. There is so much room to improvise, to change something spontaneously. Even though the storyboard is set in stone, and we try as hard as we can to sort out the structure and everything in advance so that everyone has something to look at and knows where they're going, the animation is in no way sorted out, because a lot of that comes down to improvising – the animator improvising on the set. Even though I talk things through with the animators, they are like directors directing actors. In fact, you could say that they have to be like actors themselves. You talk through each scene with them and talk about the motivations, because they've got to get inside the scene and the character to pull it off.

KM: *So the animator has a lot of room to improvise within the storyboard when they're on set?*

NP: Yes, even though as a director I've got a very strong idea of what I want. My difficulty is being open to new ideas that might be just as good or better. I'm learning all the time how to tell the difference between something that's new and something that's just bad. Because we can't keep reshooting and there's great pressure to go with the first take, that's the problem with this kind of animation, because you can't test it much. You've got to go for it; there's not time to reshoot, so we've got to make sure that we thoroughly understand what's needed. But things don't always work out and that leads to frustration.

KM: *You're having to learn to trust others with your creations.*

NP: Yes. But I find it very, very difficult to trust anybody with Wallace and Gromit, especially. Nevertheless, it's working out well. They're all good animators, though some I would trust with some things more than with others, and some are better at other things. That's what I'm learning. As in acting; you don't just hire an actor to tell them what to do. You also hire them for what they can bring, and that's quite exciting. I think that, in that sense, what I'm doing is very akin to live action. I should also say that we don't just shoot to the frame what we want; we're shooting a little bit more all the time which leaves room for improvisation in the editing room.

KM: *Yes, tell me how much goes on in the editing room. I'd always assumed that, in animation, the editor simply pieced things together. If, for instance, you've got a conversation between two people, do you shoot both ends completely and intercut in the cutting room?*

NP: No, there isn't that flexibility, but you'd be amazed by how much there is, even though at most we have only two takes and usually only one. With conversation it's a lot more difficult because you have to decide in advance exactly what you want in order to get the lip sync right – and, of course, the lip sync takes so long that we don't do more than we possibly have to.

KM: *How long were you in the editing room with* The Wrong Trousers?

NP: About a month.

KM: *And do you have close involvement in the sound?*

NP: Yes, I'm involved in all aspects, really. When you're doing the animation you're often thinking of the sound effect that will make it work – it's the other half of what will make it work. I've always used Adrian Rhodes for my sound and Julian Nott for music – we were all at NFTS together. Adrian's got a 'good eye' for sound. We think on the same wavelength and because he's had the history of doing *A Grand Day Out*, he knows the nature of the world of Wallace and Gromit. We try to make the sound somewhere between realism and 'cartoonishness'.

KM: *You're now at work on the third Wallace and Gromit film,* A Close Shave. *Why did you decide to do another one?*

NP: Three seems to be a more complete number for anything, and I did feel that we'd just started with Wallace and Gromit. After the success of *The Wrong Trousers* I thought, 'Boy, I can't leave it like that!' So although I was actually eager to do something else, I didn't feel I could put them to bed yet.

KM: *Will this be the final one?*

NP: I think we'll probably leave it at three for now and maybe look at using the same characters in a different way, perhaps in a feature film. We don't know really yet. I want to see how I feel after this.

KM: *Apart from the possible feature film, are there any other new directions you'd like to explore?*

NP: Well, I've been working now for a while on longer format films – half-hour – with a large crew and, of course, a feature film would be even bigger, so I'd love to do something much simpler, like *Creature Comforts*, again – not necessarily like it, but a short one-off idea like that.

KM: *You'd like to get back in there and do it all yourself again?*

NP: Yes, and it would give me a chance to change tack a bit, as well. I'd like the opportunity to try something else other than animals talking and Wallace and Gromit, because that's all I've done in the last five years.

KM: *Would it still be humorous?*

NP: Probably. I don't think I could stop doing funny things. I find it easier and more rewarding to do comedy.

KM: *Do you see your films as being for children?*

NP: No not all – nor adults, really. I don't think of either audience. I *do* think of an audience, but I think of myself as it! So I suppose in that sense I am making the films for myself. I think of an audience full of me!

WRITING

11 On Writing

Robert Towne talks to Mark Cousins about *Chinatown*

ROBERT TOWNE: As we go through *Chinatown* I'm hoping that I myself can find out something because I think that ideally every effort either to write a movie or deal with a movie is in some sense an act of discovery. Even when you think you know where you are going when you start a script, if you are lucky or if you have done your job well, then you will be surprised, if not by where you end up then by many things along the way. Did you ever read those comic books where they have about fifty numbers and you connect the numbers and it creates a face? That's all you really have to do. One of the problems with trying to analyse something is that you want to be sure that people don't feel that this was all foretold. Movies and scripts are a little bit like wars in that you can prepare for them, and then all you can do is just hold on to survive; it's only after the fact that somebody can describe what happened. Being a participant in the battle, you really don't often know exactly what happened. I think it was Wellington who said a war was like a ball, that you didn't dance every dance and you couldn't possibly be in all parts of the ballroom at once, so your view was necessarily limited. That's the way it was with *Chinatown*, both in the writing and in the production.

This afternoon, something oddly appropriate happened. I was having my photograph taken outside the Sheraton Hotel, and there was a lone piper playing by the fountain. This is not because I'm in Edinburgh, but I have always been dramatically affected by the sound of the bagpipes. I think it's one of the most compelling sounds in the world. I think it's because it is hard to analyse something like that, but you sure know why people would go into battle behind it. It is both very rousing and very sad. I mention this because when I was working on *Chinatown*, at a point of unusual difficulty for me, I was, for a variety of reasons, exiled from the mainland of California. I went to Catalina Island, which is a little island off the coast of Los Angeles, existing very much even today as the mainland did fifty or sixty years ago at the time of *Chinatown*, with its climate and landscape. Catalina is shaped sort of like an eight and I was working at the isthmus, which is a little eighth of a mile of land that separates the windward side of the island from the leeward side. I had a cottage that was overlooking this place and it was there that I was writing. One afternoon I was struggling with a scene and I heard the sound of a bagpipe, a lone bagpiper right in the centre of the isthmus. I walked outside and looked down and about a hundred feet below there was a lone bagpiper playing. I don't know how or why he ended up on Catalina Island, but he would play about three times a week and you could hear that pipe for probably five miles out to sea. So, a lot of this film was written hearing that piper and when I heard that piper today, it brought me back to the time that I was working on it.

The genesis of the film came about partly because I was unable to get a movie going called *The Last Detail*. The screenplay was written for Columbia Pictures at a time when we had just been given a kind of freedom in Hollywood to use language we hadn't been able to use: explicit treatment of sex and violence that hadn't been permitted before.

I don't know how many people have seen the film, but it makes very explicit use of language and at that point David Beagleman, who was the then head of Columbia, called me and said, 'Robert, we'd like to make this movie but let me ask you something candidly. Wouldn't it be better if you used twenty "mother-fuckers" in this film rather than forty? Wouldn't it be more dramatic?' and I said, 'Yes David, it would be more dramatic, but it's kind of the point that the use of this language is because these fellows can't do anything else but swear. They are essentially impotent, under the thumb of an authority that will make them whine and wail and swear, but do nothing other than their job and so it would be immoral in that sense: to cut the language because it would suggest that they were actually going to do something' – and that killed the film for a while.

At that time there had been a variety of things going on in Los Angeles. The kind of destruction and despoilation of the city that had continued unabated since *Chinatown*, and that, combined with a photo-essay in a local magazine, made me realize that there was still enough left of the city actually, judiciously to photograph and suggest the past which I had missed. At that time, fortuitously, I happened upon a book called *Southern California Country: An Island on the Land* by a man who is now dead called Kerry McWilliams. He wrote what I think still is the single finest book on Southern California ever written and maybe ever will be written. It's just extraordinary and in it there is a chapter called 'Water Water Water' about the destruction of the Owens Valley and how water from the Owens Valley was siphoned off from the valley 225 miles down from Central California – bypassing Los Angeles – to the San Fernando Valley. The San Fernando Valley was arid sheep-farming country which the land speculators bought up quietly, secretly, and then caused panic in the city of Los Angeles by fomenting a drought. They then made millions and millions of dollars as a result and the Owens Valley was destroyed. There are many books on the subject, but it was actually rather new to me. The fallout of this episode was, oddly enough, that water could have been used in both places, but in order to speculate they had to do it quietly which meant that the water had to come down, and not be used in the city on the way down. What's more they had to have the dams at the terminus, not the origin. Terminus dams were then dirt-banked and inadequate to hold the flow of water, and as a result the San Frasceto – or possibly the San Norman – dam broke.

Living in that area were five hundred Mexicans who did not speak English and when the County Sheriffs went out there to warn them to leave, they thought they were just being hassled by a bunch of Gringos and so they stayed and were drowned. There is an echo of this in the expanded version of the script when Mulwray expresses a refusal to build another dam, and Escobar, a Mexican character who is police chief and who had relatives drowned in that dam, has no sympathy or regret for the death of Mulwray. In any case, that fascinated me and I hoped to dramatize the formation of a city on a basis which was deeply destructive both for the city that was destroyed and the city that would gradually grow like a cancer. That was really the beginning of it for me, and I thought I would couch it as a detective movie because I didn't feel that a polemic on water and power would really sell very well. I thought that a mystery just following water – you turn on a water faucet and water comes out – wasn't very mysterious but you could make it into a mystery, and it would be a real crime, although not a crime as in most detective stories where it involves something more ostensibly exotic like a jewel-encrusted bird. Whatever it was, I wanted a real crime, and then I wanted a real detective. While still wanting to use the traditional genre of the detective story, I wanted to inform it with the reality I remembered – if not from the 1930s then the 1940s which was close enough – what detectives were *really* like then. As much as I admire Philip Marlowe and loved Chandler's evocation of the city, successful private detectives were not tarnished knights who refused to take divorce work and dressed shabbily. They were peepers, hired to catch people *in flagrante delicto*, and have photographs taken and do all the correspondence stuff that is made fun of in divorce cases. There were several models for Gittes in the past of whom I knew, so I made my detective a dapper guy who would basically take only divorce work and that – plus having worked with Jack Nicholson for years in acting class watching him work and using what I knew of him – was the beginning of *Chinatown*.

It may seem strange, but one of the basic structural problems that I had to deal with first – although it is embarrassingly obvious after the fact – was what scandal do you deal with first, the water-and-power scandal or the incest? The more serious, the more important one is the water-and-power, but the more dramatic one is the incest. I got it right finally because one led rather nicely into the other and the underlying notion and horror that most people can identify with of a man violating his own child, awful as that is, is not nearly as significant as the larger crime of a man who is willing to violate everyone's child, namely the future, and ruin a place that was probably arguably one of the nicest places to live on earth. So that really was the beginning. At a certain point I had to leave my home, partly because I was broke and it was cheaper to work on Catalina, and there was the piper. So with that, I more or less completed the film, except for the last little bit. A friend of mine who had an apartment loaned it to me – I was moving around and had no real home at that point. This was Curtis Hanson, who has just directed *River Wild* and has done some wonderful other things, and he told me it had been inhabited years ago by John O'Hara when he was doing *Pal Joey* in LA. So I completed it. I have been asked several times today if I thought the film was going to end up being whatever it was. I can only say that after both the writing of it and the production of it, up until the very day that I saw the answer print, I was just hoping that I had a career left. I really thought it was a fucking mess and I was just hoping that I wasn't going to get killed. It started off very ambitiously, but once you get embroiled in the thicket of a melodrama you just think, 'Oh Jesus Christ, I hope this is more fun for people to see than it is to write'. That's pretty much the beginning.

My wife said to me the other day that she thought that the movie was really about Noah Cross, and I think she's right, and we can use that as an organizing principle to see the kind of shadow that Cross casts even in scenes where he isn't seen.

Maybe we can go through it and also discuss incidental things that related to Roman with whom I worked on the shooting script after having done two drafts and who was, and is for that matter, my collaborator. As much as we infuriated one another, he was inextricably a part of the process, and probably the best collaborator I ever worked with, as infuriating as the little fart is! But he would say the same about me too ... it was a funny time.

CLIP: OPENING SCENE OF *CHINATOWN*

A couple of things here. One of the things that Roman Polanski would say, and it's always important, is that you really cannot or should not introduce a character or even a location without repeating it, almost like a refrain in music, because it loses its significance if you just have the character show up and never recur. Sometimes one does it by instinct which I did in this case, and I tried to take it out but Roman said, 'No, no, it's important.' I think movies are most effective in the use of the refrain and I think it's what sets them apart from novels and even the stage. You can take a movie, for example, like *Angels with Dirty Faces*, where James Cagney is a child and says to his pal Pat O'Brien, 'What do you hear, what do you say?' – cocky kid – and then as a young tough on the way up when things are going great for him he says, 'What do you hear, what do you say?' Then when he is about to be executed in the electric chair and Pat O'Brien is there to hear his confession he says, 'What do you hear, what do you say?' and the simple repetition of that line of dialogue in three different places with the same characters brings home the dramatically changed circumstances much more than any extensive diatribe would. You understand automatically the irony inherent in this same kind of buoyant statement under the changed circumstances, and that is also true even in the repetition of a scene.

If you go forward a little bit in the film – this is just an odd piece of history – he talks about Los Angeles being a desert and

Chinatown: Gittes and Seabiscuit.

thematically that is terribly important. The other thing that is important is something that never really got there. Gittes is a sort of dapper pimp and he is holding a racing form there with the horse Seabiscuit on it, and if you listen in the morgue scene you will hear Joe Hernandez calling a race with Seabiscuit in it, but it never again made the film. The intent was to suggest that Gittes's affection for this little horse – who was so much smaller than other racehorses and who broke down and came back – was a kind of early warning suggestion that he was not immune to class. It was an attempt to suggest that when he became convinced that Mrs Mulwray was classy, he would begin to feel the same way about her. It didn't work out, but that's one of those things.

If you go forward through the surveillance scene to the point where we see the stills of Mulwray with John Huston – Huston's first entrance. He is a villain and everything that is going on in the movie that Gittes does not know about is related to this man here and the bond issue; everything you've seen – the way the city council is behaving, passing the ordinance – all of this is being controlled by this man here who is the villain. Detective movies have certain things in common with dreams and with Oedipus Rex. As far as dreams are concerned, there is nothing extraneous in a dream. It is all your own story, your creation; you observe yourself going through a dream, even though while you are dreaming you may not know where the story is going. To be really effective in a detective movie, which is most like a dream with puns and visual repetitions, there can be nothing extraneous because unlike life, its reality is that everything fits, everything has a meaning, everything has a pattern – just as in your dreams. As far as Oedipus goes, Oedipus determines to find the killer of the king and he has the killer in front of his eyes – basically himself – from the very beginning, though he doesn't see it. Similarly, most detective movies that are satisfying, generally speaking, have the villain appearing almost from the beginning, and only the detective doesn't see it. He is blind to what is right in front of his face. Mary Astor as Brigid in *The Maltese Falcon* is, after all, the villain and she's the one who shows up in the beginning in Sam Spade's office. Lauren Bacall's sister is almost the first person you see in *The Big Sleep* and she is the murderer of Shaun Regan and the origin of everything that set him on his adventure. This is also the case here. It is so striking it is unavoidable. Poe's *Purloined Letter* is almost a paradigm of a detective movie. There is a letter in plain sight on the wall for

Chinatown: The villain's first appearance.

Dupin, but he only finds it at the end. It's almost as if there are rules for a detective movie that can be extrapolated, and that's one of them – whether you come by it through instinct or you come to realize it.

MC: *You say that you shouldn't find anything extraneous in a detective movie but is there not a case where a detective, in the process of investigation, might be led up a blind alley and is actually on the wrong lead?*

RT: That's true, but you are talking more about an investigation as in *French Connection* where you might go up a blind alley. In a classic detective movie, generally speaking, the hero, like Oedipus, shares to some extent the responsibility for the crime, by either a failure to see it or hubris of some kind that he can solve a problem. In attempting to solve it, he becomes part of the problem, and this is the case in *Chinatown*. I got the notion for the title from a Hungarian vice cop who actually sold me a dog who ended up getting a credit on *Greystoke* and who was for many years the love of my life; I've always felt a little guilty for stiffing him with that credit for *Greystoke*. But I asked the vice cop where he was working and he said Chinatown, and I said, 'How do you like it?' and he said, 'It's terrible. You go down there and you have no real idea of what is going on, so the best thing to do is nothing because you don't know what the hell is happening.' That's sort of emblematic for the whole city, with the manipulation going underneath with Cross and in a larger sense, it stands for the futility of good intentions. With the best will in the world, Gittes tries to make things right and screws it up. As I said, in a classic detective movie I think that – and I don't mean every movie that involves detection is like that – where the detective is the kind of central figure involved in an investigation, he is really investigating his own limits to act in a way that is meaningful and positive.

CLIP: GITTES TELLS CHINAMAN JOKE IN HIS OFFICE

I would probably have been roasted today for the Chinaman joke, but aside from its intrinsic entertainment value and because I like racist jokes, it was emblematic of the time: a kind of naked racism that was rampant in the thirties that was not disguised. It's like the attitude to women, which was 'Sophie, go to the ladies' room, you can't hear this.' Those are attitudes that did exist and I think it's important in doing any period piece really to try not to revisit that time and kind of clean it up and make it as it is now with our allegedly enlightened attitudes. The other side of it was that people were not nearly so much victims; they could call someone a name and they wouldn't sue you for it. They would either punch you out or do something else. So, it sets up the time, and it also sets the crudeness of the man. It's an attempt really to suggest what this pimp in his suit is like when he is involved with a woman of some substance and elegance. A nice piece of casting on Roman's part with that lawyer who is nervous and sweating about being in the room with a guy like Gittes. It was nicely done.

Let's go to the scene with John Hillerman. Gittes goes to Hillerman's office, the Department Head, and investigates the room. You see here who works his way into Mulwray's office – who is not there – and Gittes sees that it says '7 Channels Used'. In other words, when we saw him following Mulwray from the water bed to the ocean to various places – confused a bit by

Chinatown: Gittes and Evelyn Mulwray.

the scene in Echo Park with them rowing around with water everywhere – this is a clue, saying that seven channels were used when emptying water out of the reservoir. He doesn't know what that means now; again this is the first scene in the Water Department and it's nicely reprised later. It's important to say that in a complex story, a secondary character like the one that Hillerman plays increases your understanding so much by the fact that you are dealing with the same character in the same location. It makes it that much easier for you to absorb the information that comes your way.

CLIP: SCENE IN WATER DEPT. YELBURTON ENTERS

He [Nicholson] very carefully takes some of Mulwray's cards when he goes, running into that guy there, Mulvihill, who he knows is a hood working for the Water Department. This scene is interesting for the use of the chammy there. You hear this squeaking on the car and this is the third time he turns to hear this. Roman is wonderful at taking his time. It was written that way, but he actually did it that way, which is unusual. It was a time when you could hear the sound of a chammy. You could hear sounds that you cannot hear now: leaf-blowers and everything else are all going.

Now we get to the pond. The solution to the crime is right here – Mulwray's glasses in the salt-water fountain which he sees a glint of. The potential solution is constantly before his eyes.

Now you are going to see Evelyn Mulwray. It is an interest-ing scene. She says she will drop the lawsuit and Gittes is confused and says he can't afford to do that because, in effect, it will ruin his reputation. He says he has been made to look like a jackass and somebody was out to make her look bad. It actually occurs to her that he is right, but there is not much to do about it. We go on from here to the reservoir where he very nicely uses the card that he had taken from Yelburton and there he meets his old nemesis.

CLIP: GITTES GOES TO RESERVOIR AFTER THE DISCOVERY OF THE CORPSE. CONFRONTATION BETWEEN PERRY LOPEZ AND JACK NICHOLSON

Anthea Sylbert did a superb job with the costumes. You can almost see on the big screen the difference in fabric between Perry's clothes and Jack's – the hang of the shirt, that kind of starchy look on Perry's shirt and that soft, fuller thing on the soft collar and the colour of Jack's suggests somebody who has done well for himself without it being glaring.

There's a gag about the Chinese spinning in the laundry here, just to remind you that this is a constant and ongoing leitmotif.

CLIP: MULWRAY'S BODY IS DISCOVERED

There is another major change in the plot, where Evelyn Mulwray, confronted with the choice between going further with something she wants to say nothing about, lies and hopes that Gittes will back her up, which he does. That thereby begins the complicity on which their relationship is built. I think it is plausible because she certainly doesn't want to get into the fact that she is dealing with her daughter.

Chinatown: Clothes make the man: Perry Lopez and Jack Nicholson.

MC: *Coming back to two things you mentioned in these two scenes: the use of the business cards and also the growing complicity between the two central characters. How much of that was mapped out in detail right at the beginning of the script and how much of it fell as you were doing it?*

RT: I remember the complicity happened as I was writing it. Confronted by that inquest or preliminary, I realized that that's probably what would have happened. It just came out of the character's mouth as I was writing it. The card ... I don't know. When I was doing the scene it didn't develop in the same way as this did which was quite a surprise. I may have thought of it just prior to writing the scene. The guy is routinely looking for any target of opportunity to get something that he can subsequently exploit.

MC: *When Jack Nicholson goes to the office that Hollis Mulwray used to work at and he opens the book and finds the '7 Channels Used', he walks away and leaves the book open. Is that supposed to imply that he has in some way had an effect in the killing of Mulwray, because he has actually left this evidence that Mulwray is on to them?*

RT: Mulwray is already dead by this point, although Gittes doesn't know it. This is ten in the morning. He goes to the house at eleven and at noon the body is discovered. He goes and she says he is attending lunch, so the man is already dead. We obviously don't know this.

CLIP: NOSE-SLITTING SCENE

I've been asked a number of times about that little piece of violence. It just came out of nowhere, really. I remember thinking about something really horrible, something that would appeal to your imagination, and I thought of all kinds of things like slitting cheeks, or ears, but there is something about the nose that for a detective is irresistible. Just slitting a nostril seemed to be horrible and I guess I was right because other people reacted in the same way. For a movie with such little

Chinatown: The nose-slitting scene.

actual violence in it, it had a huge impact. At the time people said it was so violent they couldn't look at it. When you think about movies over the last twenty years it is really nothing by comparison and yet it still has its effectiveness because most of the time when you are seeing the kind of violence displayed now it is so grand that it loses its reality completely. You are lost in wondering about all the special effects associated with it, and the buckets of blood and the body parts that go flying around the screen. That sort of takes you out of it, whereas here it doesn't take you out of it because it is so brief and because you actually think it could happen: just a little nose slit, and you start thinking, 'God, I wouldn't like that happening to me.' It really informs the potential for violence throughout the rest of the movie and it scares you and continues to scare you because it appeals to your imagination and you think, 'God that must really hurt.' Then the other thing one should say is that from this point most directors would try to get rid of this Band Aid that Nicholson wears as soon as possible. Roman, to his everlasting credit said, 'No, it would be a mess, and we are going to keep it on him.' Jack agreed and so he is one of the few leading men who goes through a movie with a Band Aid patch across his face. It actually gives ballast to the reality of the thing and it makes you fear a little bit more for the potential violence that you are afraid is coming. It has, in the parlance of our time, a resonance.

MC: *Was Polanski already on the film when you were doing this little act, because Polanski is obsessed with knives, right from his first shorts through all Polanski's life. He must have loved that part.*

RT: I guess he did, but frankly, no, he was not. It was before. The nostril ante-dated Roman. It doesn't seem as if it did, but it was certainly made for him. The length of the knife, however, was Roman's choice.

MC: *How about the 'midget' line?*

RT: We put it in during a rewrite, and Roman didn't seem to object. I remember years ago a friend, Jay Siebring, who was a hairdresser and not a very tall man – one of the people murdered at Sharon Tate's house – was talking to Roman one day and Jay said, 'Hey man, do you think you're too short?' and Roman said, 'No, but if I was any shorter . . .'

CLIP: ENVELOPE SCENE

This scene here is critical because Noah Cross begins to cast his shadow again here; you see that Evelyn Mulwray starts coming unglued over the envelope with the name 'Cross' on it.

CLIP: GITTES DISCOVERS CROSS AND MULWRAY WERE PARTNERS

We go into this second scene with Hillerman which again repeats the location and setting, and that's the scene where Jack accuses Hillerman of complicity. Hillerman, in covering up a conspiracy to dump water in an LA river, owns up to the fact that they've been supposedly irrigating property. There is an extraordinary amount of information conveyed in here: that Mulwray and Cross were partners, and that the entire history of the Water Department is done contrapuntal to the marvellous secretary who is absolutely infuriated with Gittes's fussiness. She enables us to get through what is a mouthful of information, and Roman's willingness to play that out over the photographs allows you to take enjoyment from the scene and at the same time be given what is absolutely vital information. In terms of a writing problem and a directing problem, this scene is pivotal. While it may not seem as dramatic or flash as other scenes, it is one of the more important scenes in the movie in terms of solving a problem.

We go to Gittes's office where Evelyn Mulwray again speaks about her father. She lights two cigarettes and in doing so offers to hire him. By this time Gittes knows who Cross is because he has seen the photograph in the office, and he has seen the photographs that Walsh has taken. He knows that it is Noah Cross and in going to meet him he now knows that he has seen him. This is a critical scene.

CLIP: GITTES MEETS CROSS (HE IS EATING A FISH WITH ITS HEAD ON WHICH GITTES COMMENTS ON)

Cross's entrapment by Gittes with the photographs by Gittes was not something I planned in the beginning of writing the scene, it just evolved and you realized he would know. He had the pictures and so he sort of let Cross go down the garden path. 'When was the last time you saw him?' – a natural question – then, 'You lied to me because it was five days ago!' I didn't know that's how it was going to come out, I was just writing it and that seemed the natural way to do it. One of the problems in writing a melodrama – for me at least – and trying to have the scenes organic is that you know you have to accomplish certain things, but you don't know how you are going to do it. You have to let the scenes run, and you stumble across that place where the story point is made most natural and work it into the fabric of the structure.

Gittes then goes up to the hall of records, not a scene that most detectives end up doing terribly dramatically.

Chinatown: Gittes meets Noah Cross (John Huston and Jack Nicholson).

CLIP: GITTES LOOKING INTO THE HALL OF RECORDS (WITH ALAN WARNICK) USING A RULER TO SCAN DOWN PAGES ACCURATELY

We got to the old folks' home where Roman has that wonderful old man goosing the nurse. Most people miss it. Then Gittes asks the man that he has come to see about the fact that his father needs to be admitted to a home. He says, 'Do you accept people of Jewish persuasion?' Evelyn Mulwray is of course shocked – and he says, 'Well, don't feel bad about it, neither does Dad.' Again, it is one of those times in the history of LA where there were things like 'No Dogs or Jews Allowed' written on country club signs. It was pretty blatant and being about virtually the only Jew growing up in San Pedro I became aware of this at a fairly early age. It is an attempt to let people know what the times were like. That was part of it, part of the prejudices that were accepted without thinking and were useful to use.

There is an echo of that gunshot here and she touches her eye then we get to the bathroom scene. He evades her question about what happened in Chinatown and she says if this kind of thing happens to you in the course of a day, in the afternoon or evening, it's amazing that you are able to get through a day.

CLIP: EVELYN MULWRAY SAYS TO GITTES, 'THAT'S A NASTY CUT' LEADING TO LOVE SCENE

In this scene we have a deliberate use of something that I had seen in someone's eye to suggest, in a sense, her vulnerability and a tainted family. Of course she is eventually shot through the eye, although that was a complete accident because I didn't write it with her being shot initially.

I always thought the boldness of Roman starting a love scene in light from a bathroom was very good. It was written that way, but he lit it like a bathroom, not like a love scene.

CLIP: FILM SPINS FORWARD (GITTES KNOCKS OUT EVELYN'S TAIL LIGHT TO MAKE HER CAR MORE IDENTIFIABLE AND EASIER TO FOLLOW)

He knocks out the tail light to follow her in the car and that is again a technique that was used at that time by detectives.

CLIP: FILM SPINS FORWARD

This is the confrontation scene where Evelyn says, 'It's my sister, my daughter . . .' and there are a couple of things to point

Chinatown: 'That's a nasty cut' (Faye Dunaway and Jack Nicholson).

out here. There is again an identical repetition of a setting and a scene – you saw through water darkly the glasses at the very beginning, and here he picks them up; he could actually have picked them up all along. Now Gittes is convinced that as he was murdered at the house, then she did it.

CLIP: 'SHE'S MY SISTER, MY DAUGHTER . . .' SCENE

I always felt on reflection that in the playing of this scene there was a couple of moments more over-the-top than I would have liked. It's really saved by her reading of 'Or is it too tough for you?' For me, it takes the edge off it. It is a critical line-reading at a critical point, probably the most critical line-reading in the movie. If we go on to where she gets to the glass, this is an absolutely diabolical moment in terms of plotting, because nobody had a fucking idea how to deal with this.

CLIP: AUDIENCE DISCOVERS THAT MULWRAY 'DIDN'T WEAR BIFOCALS . . .'

To establish a smoking gun it's not enough to get the glasses in there, it had very clearly to be John Huston's glasses, so one guy wearing bifocals and one not was something we arrived at in trying to get that scene to work.

CLIP: GITTES DISCOVERS THE TRUTH ABOUT THE DIFFERENT SPECTACLES

And now you know that Gittes knows . . .

CLIP: ACCUSATION SCENE: 'YOU KILLED HOLLIS MULWRAY IN THAT POND.'

That's basically the heart of the story right there. Renoir once said, 'Everyone has their reasons,' which is probably the single smartest thing anybody ever said about anything. You see it every day, that kind of infinite capacity for people to rationalize their behaviour. In the course of my life I have found it particularly true of people who long for power and who want to rationalize; they have a need from time to time to rationalize how they've gone about getting it. It's the same thing here, and to me this is a story that was set before the Second World War with a detective who is used to all kinds of cynical chicken-shit things, but incest, this kind of infinite desire for power, these are things beyond his ken. It would have been beyond the ken of most of us prior to the Second World War and prior to all the monstrosities we were exposed to after it. In that context he is rather naive even though he thinks he is a wise guy. That capacity for evil is something he doesn't have in him and he doesn't have the ability to imagine that kind of grand design in someone else. Generally, people who scheme at that level can't be punished, so society ends up rewarding them, putting their names on streets and buildings as great founders of the city. Basically, Gittes is being had and from that point on he can't control what happens, as indeed he couldn't from the very beginning, and the story unwinds. We go now to Chinatown and her death.

MC: *You key in at some point in the film what the horn of the car she is driving sounds like, and right at the end the thing that tells me she has died is the horn. Had you worked all that out beforehand?*

RT: Yes. At the time when I did the rewrite for the ending I did do that. She puts her head on the horn in the earlier scene so that you know.

MC: *It's a very memorable effect.*

RT: I think we are inundated by the use of sound like that all through the film, from the chammy to the horn to the fly buzzing and all of those things. What's that George Lucas effect where they absolutely deafen you before the start of the movie by advertising the sound system? It deafens you and desensitizes you to little things that are significant. Sound in a movie is hugely undervalued in the sense that it is the great common denominator. You watch a movie and you are in all parts of the theatre and nobody will see the picture in quite the same way: you'll get distracted, you'll drop your popcorn, you'll be looking at your girlfriend. Whatever it is, you might not see something but everybody will hear the same thing at the same time. That was the power of radio and it's the power of sound in film. It gives you that extra little distance if properly used, and it's underappreciated really.

CLIP: SHOOTING SCENE AT END OF FILM

That's the end of the picture.

FILM-MAKING

Wong Kar-Wai.

Christopher Doyle (self-portrait).

12 Don't Try for Me, Argentina

A Journal of the Shooting of Wong Kar-Wai's *Happy Together* by Christopher Doyle

Edited and introduced by Tony Raynes
Photographs by Christopher Doyle

Wong Kar-Wai entered the Hong Kong film industry as a scriptwriter, but stopped pre-scripting his own films when he embarked on the second, *Days of Being Wild*. Since then he has begun each film with only a few key elements in place: the basic story idea, the choice of settings, the leading actors, and some specific images, words and pieces of music. The shooting and editing of the film is then an aleatory process, in which all concerned discover only gradually where the film is taking them and what it's 'really' about. It's unlikely that Wong would be able to make films this way if he weren't also his own producer . . . and if he didn't have two more or less permanent collaborators at his side throughout. One of the latter is the designer/editor William Chang, who has worked on every Wong Kar-Wai film since the first, *As Tears Go By*. The other is the cinematographer Christopher Doyle, who has shot everything since *Days of Being Wild*.

Chris was born in the suburbs of Sydney and began travelling the world as a merchant seaman in his late teens. He did various exotic jobs in far-flung countries and somewhere along the way took a degree in art history at the University of Maryland. He got into still and movie photography by accident, as a side-effect of his involvement with avant-garde theatre and dance troupes in Taipei in the late 1970s; the first feature he shot was Edward Yang's début, *That Day, On the Beach*. A brief stay in France led to work on Claire Devers's film *Noir et Blanc*, but most of the films he has shot have been Chinese. He normally operates his camera himself. Aside from Wong Kar-Wai, he has worked with Stanley Kwan, Chen Kaige, Patrick Tam, Shu Kei and Stan Lai, among others. He has recently worked with Park Ki-Yong in Korea, and has a directorial project of his own in development with a Japanese producer.

Alongside his cinematography, he is a prolific still photographer and collagist and an increasingly prolific writer. Several books of his photos and essays have already appeared in Chinese and Japanese, and more are on the way. This journal, written during and after the making of Wong Kar-Wai's *Happy Together*, is his first comprehensive account of the making of a film. It not only records the production from the cinematographer's point of view, but also offers a great deal of insight into the unique process which brings a Wong Kar-Wai film into existence.

Happy Together turned out to centre on one man's struggle to regain mental and emotional equilibrium after the bad ending of an affair. Lai Yiu-Fai (Tony Leung) and Ho Po-Wing (Leslie Cheung) arrive in Argentina from Hong Kong as lovers, but Ho suddenly goes off on his own. He becomes a good-time boy in Buenos Aires, turning the odd trick for fun and profit. Broke and more upset than he first realizes, Lai takes jobs in the city – first as a tango bar doorman, then as a cook – to earn money for his ticket home. But Ho turns up on his doorstep, bruised and bleeding from a beating, and they try living together without sleeping together. Eventually the break becomes final. Lai's attempts to put himself back together are aided (unwittingly) by Chang (Chang Chen), a young backpacker from Taiwan who wants to visit the southernmost tip of the continent – 'the end of the world' – before going home. For his part, Lai decides he must see the huge Iguaçu Falls before leaving. When Lai finally gets out of Argentina he passes through Taiwan and goes to look for Chang . . . The film had its première at the 1997 Cannes Film Festival, where it earned Wong the Best Director prize.

Chris's writing started out Jarmanesque and has become more and more Bukowskian. It needs only a little more editing than a computer spell-check can give it.

Tony Raynes, 1997

14–15 August: Hong Kong – Amsterdam – Buenos Aires

Another thirty-six-hour flight into everything I've spent more than half my life flying away from: mediocrity rather than identity, borrowed values rather than ideas of one's own. All the reasons I hated and left Australia so long ago come closer with each time zone and more terrifyingly magnified through the bottom of each in-flight glass. *Don't try for me, Argentina* . . . I don't know how I'm going to try for you! Going there we gain a day. Leaving, we lose nothing.

30 August 1996: The Breakdown

Did a story breakdown for WKW today, and turned it into as good a synopsis as I could. It looks a little feeble in this form: few 'motivations', little apparent action, no subplot. Thank God we're all self-assured and intuitive enough to believe that something interesting will eventually evolve from this. It reads like this:

The blue-green magnificence of the Iguaçu Falls. Pull back to reveal that the image is in fact a souvenir lampshade by a messy bed in a love hotel. Two silhouettes overshadow the Falls and the desolate room. A red convertible crosses the brilliant white expanse of the Salta salt flats, just this side of the Bolivian border. Tony and Leslie are loving and partying their way south. At noon on 23 September (the vernal equinox) they cross the Tropic of Capricorn. Now there is no turning back!

Their sex that night is abrupt and violent. They part in the morning. Leslie is in tears. Cut to Buenos Aires. Leslie is distraught, but hesitates to throw himself from the La Boca Bridge.

Tony gets off a bus in La Boca, holes up in the Hotel Rivera. Plays at love and odd jobs. A good fight is as welcome as a good fuck. His self-respect diminishes with every glass he knocks back.

Leslie works in a gay tango bar. Dancing and tricking his night away without reflection or remorse. He plays hard to get when Tony crosses his path again, but softens to his loneliness. He steals first a Rolex, then a passport from one of his tricks; the pawn money will pay for Tony's ticket home.

His hands crushed by the angry trick, Leslie retreats to the Hotel Rivera, where Tony nurses him. Then Leslie betrays what begins to look too much like love by running off with a cheap Milonga pimp. Back north . . . a Bolivian border town. Wild, colourful lights pattern the ceiling and walls. Leslie, stoned, stares through the waterfall lamp at the predicament he has fallen into. His Milonga trick has passed out or OD'd. Leslie flees once more, not forgetting his one-ounce stash of coke. No Rolex to get him out any more, Tony agrees to rendezvous with Leslie at the Iguaçu Falls . . .

It's going to be a very visual 'landscape and spaces' kind of film, which should make me happy enough. William Chang and I will have more than enough to occupy our days.

Still Again

I carry a 35 mm still camera on the set most days now, partly in my own interest, but often also because there's no other photographer on set. The photos on these pages could not have been taken by anyone else, not because I'm better than other photographers but simply because I'm in the middle of whatever is going on and sometimes have the chance to capture what I see.

'No One Speaks English . . . and Everything's Broken'

The whole of Buenos Aires is a Tom Waits song. What used to be 'The Paris of the South', with the tenth-highest living standard in the world, has been reduced to a hallucinatory exchange rate, an infrastructure as bad as the food and an impossibly low minimum wage which makes exploitation, corruption and a 'parallel service sector' inevitable. The streets all run north-south–east-west: grids of boredom and artificial restraint imposed upon every town in the country. This plan is not just a topographical legacy from Spanish colonial times but a blueprint of the Argentine mind, which is proud to be third-class European.

Robert Rauschenberg said you're not an artist if you can't walk a block and come up with five new images and even more ideas. Edward Steichen said you can photograph a world in your room . . . and later Robert Frank and others showed us how. Here, I'm starting to wonder if I'm losing my mind and eye. I haven't taken a single 'personal' image since I got here. Somehow I just don't 'see' this place. It just doesn't 'talk' to me. Shit.

Balut Bus
We're going north-west, via Rosario Cordoba and Santiago del Estero, on Green Bus Balut. It's a thirty-hour ride to Jujuy, with only two stops en route. My visions of either running into Brad Pitt and Bertolucci on location or being crammed in with coca-chewing peasants laden with livestock and provisions turn out to be wrong: this is a modern touring coach. Its number is 100, which, my Chinese assistant assures me, is very auspicious. I drag myself up the front to check how 'auspiciously' we're doing. We're travelling Argentine style: no streetlights, no headlights, lots of traffic that shouldn't really be on any road, lots of horn.

Tropic of Capricorn
The northern province of Jujuy borders Chile to the east and Bolivia to the north. We're scouting it in a dilapidated taxi, looking for a route and a reason for Tony and Leslie to have come to such a place. The first road sign we've seen in hundreds of kilometres reads 'Tropic of Capricorn'. I was once a sailor, but too green to remember how we navigated by Capricorn or any of the other stars. Wong, though, is impatient for new

ideas: 'I need to know the metaphysical meaning of the Tropic of Capricorn . . .' And he isn't joking: 'You've got until this time tomorrow . . .'

Surfing the Tropics

What we call 'the tropics' lie between the imaginary lines of the Tropics of Cancer and Capricorn, respectively 23 degrees 27 minutes north and south of the equator. These points represent the northernmost and southernmost points at which the sun can be found overhead on the longest day of the year. As they call it here, 'the day when walls have no shadow'. The zodiac sign of Capricorn is represented by the knees in the human body. It's an earth sign which holds things and gives formation to water. Henry Miller sees Capricorn as a manifestation of the poet alienated from society, creating his own destiny and ultimately finding renaissance in death – which sounds more like what we're looking for and expecting of Tony and Leslie in the story. That's all I have for Wong by noon the next day.

First Day Shoot

The first day of filming is not really a shoot, more an affirmation that we're here. We pick up 'ambience' shots in and around the stinking, oil-slicked port called La Boca and the façade and roof of the Hotel Rivera (= Riviera), where Tony and Leslie will make love. Don't really know what I'm doing. Just playing it by ear, trying filters and film speeds, not looking for inspiration so much as a few visual ideas. Finally we get lucky with a bus disgorging passengers and turning under the derelict bridge into a vast expanse of sunset light. It's loneliness, departure, loss incarnate. At last I have a visual theme to build on, a direction in which to explore the 'character' of this place.

Storm Warning

Haven't seen Wong for days now. He's locked up in some hotel room, sorting through the jumble of images and ideas we've

Exploring the character of the place.

accumulated since we arrived. He's getting keyed-up for the flash flood that the actual filming will have to be.

Kafka's Watch
We've always talked more about music and literature than about the content, intent or the 'meaning' of our films. Wong pretends to have a structure, although we all know it will change day by day. We never know what the story will eventually become or where the search for it – what I call the journey – will take us. The worst thing is not knowing how long it will take. I often feel like Kafka's watch or some other useless thing. When we work this way, my role's sham: I pretend to know how the morning sun will fall or how many lamps it will take to light a room, but all I really know is how I see the space and what I hope I can do with it.

Empty Shots
What do we call our trademark shots in English? In Chinese, they're *kongjing*. They're not conventional establishing shots

because they're about atmosphere and metaphor, not space. The only thing they 'establish' is a mood or a totally subjective POV. They're clues to an 'ambient' world we want to suggest but not to explain.

Monday Morning

WKW's most famous quip about his reason for working in Hong Kong rather than Hollywood or anywhere else is: 'I'd rather work with first-class gangsters than bad accountants. Gangsters have more pride, they're more ethical. Even if they fuck you, they'll kiss you first.' So . . . we drop the local production crew. The money questions were always awkward, and their explanations got just a little too weak. A commission or mark-up is understandable, but they have quoted us $1,500 a day for use of a bar location whereas the owner turns out to be happy with $500 or less . . . Should we blame the Central Bank of Argentina or Alan Parker?

Dances with Wolves

Flak from the fired production house is stalling us; they've alerted the unions and other authorities, made some notably non-specific threats and blocked our access to a number of locations. And we're making very slow progress with the work permits. More than half the crew have to go to Uruguay today to get new fifteen-day tourist visas when they re-enter Argentina. We've been warned this may be the first of many such trips. Expecting the worst, we've started to bribe our way forward for the best.

It's All About Angles

Wong's toothache has affected his ear. His normal 'tall-man-avoiding-low-ceilings' walk is pronouncedly lop-sided these days. Maybe that's the only way to see this place: from unexpected, unusual angles, not just 'through a beer or wine glass darkly', as all of us have tended to since we got here.

Leslie Needs Love

Leslie in high heels walks like a trick-tired whore. He looks great as a redhead, but his make-up looks pasty: a bit like a weekend cross-dresser hiding five o'clock shadow. But Leslie is worried: 'Am I convincing enough? Not just camp?' He really wants to know. Actually, he needs more to be convinced than 'convincing'. And so we preen and powder and switch to a modified bouffant and mother-of-pearl glam look. 'Am I a woman? A real woman?' he asks his mirror more than us.

Our nagging suspicion that we're finally making the *Days of Being Wild* sequel which so many have expected from us for so long clicked when Leslie started humming the theme from *Days* as he prepared for a shot today. Checking his costume and make-up in a wall mirror, he turned exactly like Carina Lau in *Days* and mimicked her glorious 'How do I look?'

10 September: Who's on Top?

We do a Polaroid session to give the lovers a 'past'. We look almost as if we know what we're doing, and they look as if they've been at it on and off for years. The evening passes in semi-drunken speculation about who exactly gets to 'do' who.

Hotel Room

We discuss the film's structure, fairly sure that sex should start the film, but also that in the chronology of their days together Tony and Leslie should be seen fucking only on their last night as a couple. Should we go for a 'down' effect or should we film it as if their love will never die? Should it be the antithesis of the 'down' that is to come or should the relationship be a roller-coaster of conflict from the start? We go with the 'up' tone. They do too. Their first kiss is very mellow and natural. It starts to feel like this film is about intimacy, not sex.

Tony and Leslie try to touch and feel their way around the bed, each other and the scene. William has suggestions. Wong and I are not much help. We clear the room. It's just 'the boys' and the two of us. Don't know how or why (we've never resolved it), but Tony is 'on top'. Don't know how or why either but the position I take for myself and the camera is as discreet and evocative as a camera position can be. It's a beautiful and sensual scene.

But Tony is devastated when the scene is done. 'Wong said that all I'd have to do was kiss Leslie,' he confides to me. 'Now look how far he's pushed me.'

My Gaffer Loves My Focus-Puller

Wong has appropriated the names of my crew members for Tony and Leslie's characters. We end another love-hotel sequence with a close-up of their names cut into a heart shape in the wooden wall: 'Po-Wing loves Yiu-Fai forever'. My focus-puller loves my gaffer, and we never even guessed!

Space

We came to Argentina to 'defamiliarize' ourselves by moving away from the spaces – and hopefully the preoccupations – of the world we know so well. But we're out of our space and depth here. We don't even know the city well. So why do we still tend towards bars, barber shops, fast-food joints and trains? What happened to the inspirations from Manuel Puig's structures and Julio Cortazar's conceits? We're stuck with our own concerns and perceptions. If it's true that every artist basically has only one thing to say, then . . . we'd better do our best to say it more eloquently this time!

Friday Night, La Boca

Everyone else's Friday night bash is our logistical nightmare. The birthday dance at 3 Amigos versus the 'lowlife' party at Il Piccolo across the street. Street kids cruise our equipment; we try to tie it down. The street is raucous and violent, and there's nowhere to put our lights. The 'rush' of getting in and out as quick as we can energizes my mini-crew. We're so guerrilla and unobtrusive that one bouncer tries to cosh us for running out without paying our tab!

Wong Kar-Wai working out 'who's on top'.

Five Stars Minus Four

Spent most of the evening waiting for William to turn Leslie's five-star room in the Kempinski into something tacky and non-descript. He re-wallpapers two more rooms and I add a lot of orange to the fluorescent light in the bathroom. I've done a rush-job English text for these two scenes, which show Leslie with an American John. Everything that Leslie hasn't already claimed for himself, our American bit player is doing his best to forget. In the script I call him White, with apologies to Tarantino. The actor has so much 'attitude' and needs so much to 'communicate' that we're all calling him 'Mr Hollywood' before the night is done.

Style

We've gone for 'high-key' colours and lighting this time, and lots of grain to boot. I'm pushing the filmstock so much that we're losing the blacks. Is it the exposure? The locations? Or the lack of budget for the lights we need to maintain the tone we're after? I won't know until we get back to Hong Kong. Here all we see is a video transfer of *some* of our negatives.

When one of the Argentine lighting crew says, 'Your style is like not lighting at all!' our line producer Jacky suggests we just steal some table lamps from our serviced apartments and leave the generator at home.

Jazz

If only film was jazz, if only we could 'jam' . . . We get closer to this with each film; my camera becomes more and more of a musical instrument. On and off, different film speeds, frame changes in shot . . . these are my key and register shifts. I riff, you solo, we jam towards a free form that we believe a film can be.

Director for a Day

Wong is holed up somewhere reworking the script and schedule. Leslie has to leave very soon, and there's to be a general strike on Thursday and Friday. As if boring us to death, delaying us to death and cheating us to death weren't enough, these bastards now want to mobilize us to death. We've been here for forty days now, but we've worked for only ten. Today, William Chang and I take over. It's like a music video shoot. We suggest a situation and some dialogue, choose a space and let the actors do the rest. We don't know what it means or where in the story it might go . . .

Fat Man's Feet

We're shooting lots of anecdotal shots, trying to outline the development of Tony and Leslie's relationship. Scene 27A Take 3 is OK, and so we move on to 27F. No one except Wong has any idea of how these numbers come about or what they mean. But our tastes and telepathy are close enough to agree that 'B' should be brightish and that 'D' should be a twilight shot. I'm working off instinct and the possibilities of the space. I have no idea what Wong is working off . . . The structure and implications of his films are like a fat man's feet: he doesn't really know what they look like until the end of the day.

Hotel Rivera

First day in Hotel Rivera – our main location, at last! We come to grips with the fickle power supply and offers of blow jobs from the live-in whores. We're just about done with cajoling and bribing the rest of the residents when someone who looks like an escapee from *Pro Wrestling Live!* emerges from the end of the hallway and threatens to shoot out all our lamps – not to mention us too – if we don't piss off. We make frantic calls for our bodyguards and the police, then ask ourselves why we don't have our own armed protection.

Depressed

I always get depressed when I miss the timing on a complex shot. I know that it's excusable, since we don't have rehearsals and generally 'shoot from the hip', but it's a bitch to come so close to great and then have the film run out or the actor's timing lose sync with mine. Our kind of camera-work is

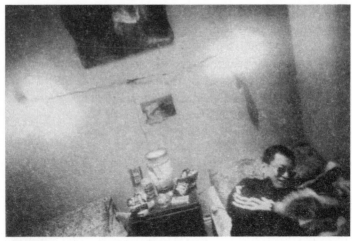
Wong Kar-Wai in the Hotel Rivera.

'anticipation and response'. I need to follow the actor/dancer as much as I need him/her to 'lead'. And I can't ask for another take most of the time; I'm afraid that would slow us down.

28 September: Film Roll 218, Sound Roll 90, Scene 29F

We're on our sixteenth take of a shot in which Tony's hands clasp his head. In, then out of focus for most of the shot . . . on a 14mm lens. 'Smoother,' demands Wong from the monitor room next door. Smoother is everything I want to be, I'm thinking. But I'm tired and the shot is complex. All I can say is, 'I'm only human.' The thirty-plus kilos of my camera, magazine and filmstock address me like an anxious lover from the bed. Don't know why I'm this way. I just have to get it right this time.

3 Amigos

There's something ominous about the number three in this film. It comes before 'four', which is a homophone for 'death' in Chinese. Is 'death' where Tony and Leslie's love is taking them? Outside the 3 Amigos cabaret bar, bus number 33 is about to stop. This is the third time I've put the same lens on the same camera in the same part of the same street. They dance to a song called 'Milonga for 3'. Now Wong is talking about adding a third character to the story: 'We need a third character to catalyse the film and their love . . .' I've heard this kind of stuff before; it looks like we're in for the long haul. It's all getting a little too 'mystical' for me with all these 3s . . .

Old Bridge at La Boca

We have more bridges in this film than a hundred calendars could use. Our two lovers quarrel and go their separate ways at dawn on a bridge. The location is not just a metaphor, it's the shadow on their loves . . . On the bridge in heavy morning traffic I can't hear a word the actors or director say. I guess at when and where they'll move, and when emotions seem close to bursting I pan discreetly away – but what should be a smooth transition turns into a quick pan. It's not a stylistic choice: I'm barely balanced on two apple boxes, and they're shifting from under my feet.

Trainshopping

We check out tomorrow's location, the vast Retiro railway station and its even vaster men's toilet, where Leslie will be cruising and dealing dope to make ends meet. We're not quite sure how we're going to handle the space or the situation, but I doubt we'll be as explicit as the fat black cock the guy in the urinal next to mine is shaking at me.

Boulevard of Dreams

There's indolence in the clouds . . . and cynicism in the air. My crew's hearts are drained sallow by all these empty days. Implications about all we could or couldn't do. Incriminations. Threats. I walk Corrientes Avenue. The so-called 'street that never sleeps' is as tired as I am. More listless, lonely . . . dazed. Its souls are as lost as the glory of its past. Its neon colours are

Wong Kar-Wai working out how to handle the scene.

faded, and tango bars are gone. This film is one long dark street tonight . . . not my kind of *Boulevard of Dreams*.

Dunkin' Donuts
Can't work out why people queue outside Dunkin' Donuts on Florida Street downtown. There's no crowd inside, but at least thirty in the cold outside. Are donuts aphrodisiacs here? Are there uses for donuts only Argentines know?

Homophobe Again
My camera assistants from Hong Kong are young and dedicated. They married early. They are very 'straight'. Weeks of complaining about how bored they are here earned them a night out on the town last night. When I ask them how well they 'scored' they mime puking gestures and tell me they had to drink their beer through straws and couldn't even use the toilet. It turns out they went to a gay bar by mistake. We've been filming two men simulating blow jobs and anal sex for weeks now, and 'my boys' still think you can get AIDS from a beer glass or a sweaty handshake.

Cinema X

A little too much of the wrong-coloured light distracts me when I view the rushes of our gay-cinema scene. No one else will see these images the way I do, but *I* see them this way. Why did I accept 'realism' instead of making 'poetry'? It's the little details that hurt the most. Consoling myself with a 'you learn by your mistakes' isn't going to change the scene or the light.

Walk on the Wild Side

'I hope you're treating her well . . .' Wong takes me aside for a confidential word. 'She' is my local so-called girlfriend, an Argentine Chinese who takes her virginity as seriously as her first-year medical college exams. 'The whole town is on to you two,' warns Wong. 'Watch your step.' I'm sanguine until I learn that her father is the branch chief of Taiwan's infamous Bamboo triad gang.

1 and 2 October

We discuss 'pick-up shots' to fill in the details of Tony's life in Buenos Aires. Wong's list includes: 'pizza', 'phone-card', 'cigarettes' and 'abattoir'. I'm confused. 'Why abattoir?' Wong laughs. 'That's what I wanted to ask you! Where else could someone go if they'd failed at suicide?' I ask if he's ever been to one, and he replies that he hasn't. I tell him, 'It's all blood and pieces, stench and sound. It's cathartic, to say the least.' He says he doesn't want catharsis, finding it too 'obvious'. I tell him to wait until he sees the blood and guts before he talks about anything being 'obvious'.

Abattoir

An old vegetarian like me just has to laugh: our meat-eating crew is wilting, throwing up at the sounds and smells of the slaughter of cows. I always believed that, 'If you can't kill it, you don't deserve to eat it.' If killing cows is disturbing, what do war and abortion do to your daily life? Tony (who has to play a slaughterhouse worker) gets drunk. The crew members are coating their stomachs with yoghurt and scrubbing their hands very hard.

Hospital

Leslie's hands have been crushed by one of his jealous tricks. We're not shooting sequentially, and so Leslie's in and out of the plaster casts on his hands six or seven times a day. It's time-consuming and frustrating. 'I can't pee when I'm wearing them,' Leslie complains. One of the gayer members of the crew volunteers to help him with his fly. Leslie suggests that it's really a job for line producer Jacky . . .

Overcompensating

We've been joking lately about how many shots we're doing per scene. 'Our basic two?' I ask about the passport scene. 'No,' replies Wong, 'I want to make it more choppy – at least one cut per phrase.' We end up with fourteen different angles for five lines of dialogue. 'I think we've overcompensated this time,' I say after the fourteenth shot.

Signature Style

At first we hesitated to repeat our 'signature style', but eventually it was just too frustrating not to. We do more and more in-shot speed changes as the film goes on. From 'normal' speed to 12 frames per second or 8 frames per second . . . or the other way around. And our notionally taboo wide-angle lenses are being brought in more and more often to make a 'flat' image more 'interesting'. I've always associated our 'blurred action' sequences with the adrenalin rush triggered by fear or violence. This time around it's more 'druggy'. We change speed at 'decisive', 'epiphanal' or 'revelatory' moments. The actor moves extremely slowly while all else goes on in 'real time'. The idea is to suspend time, to emphasize and prolong the 'relevance' of whatever is going on. This is, I'm told, what a hit of

Leslie Cheung's bloody hands.

heroin is like. The bitch for the actors is knowing how fast or slow to speak.

Money Makes the World Go Round

None of us is sleeping well these days. Everyone feels down. Forget 'devotion', forget 'idealism'. We only work well when we work . . . and we've worked only 10 per cent of the time we've been here. Our energy dissipates with these constant questions and doubts. My camera and lighting crew have no money to eat, and since we're not shooting that's all they want to do. I'm not sure if I'm more loyal or just less energized than they are. It's always been this way on the films I've done with WKW. The money I could have made by *not* doing the WKW films could keep me for years. But we've come so far together, and if I really cared about the money I would've gone into real estate long ago.

Wong's difficulties may be partly self-inflicted and his methods irresponsible to everyone but himself. But every film is a journey, a choice. And we chose to help that journey happen and so, as far as we can, we should accept what the choice entails. But I should also take care of my crew, who always follow my lead. I have to speak out for them. In my experience, it will make no difference. But tonight I must make a stand.

Star System

Leslie is back, but not for long enough to make the trip to the northernmost border where we planned to shoot the opening scenes. These days Wong is regretting his preference for working with stars. They consume most of our budget and our energies, and their comings and goings force us to change story lines and even dictate how much sleep we can get. We have to accommodate their schedules . . . and pamper their moods. The one consolation is that we get the last word. At the end of the day, we're the ones who get to throw them on the (cutting-room) floor.

Dead Again

We're still stuck in the same ten by twenty-foot room in the Hotel Rivera we've been in for the past month. We have no scaffolds, so no top shots, no way to get a little distance and no way to shoot from across the road. The only part of the room we haven't already shot twenty times is the washbasin/shaving-mirror corner by the door. Wong is frustrated: 'Where the hell is Tony going to die?' All I can suggest is that the blue – tiles and shower curtain – will go well with the blood. 'We can't afford two days' blood,' is his cryptic answer. A production assistant explains that the 'cut-throat make-up' is $300 a pop. Wong tells me that we'll save the cut throat and blood for a later day; I'll have to match it with what we shoot today.

This is what any cameraman most hates to hear. It's so difficult to match parts of scenes shot days, weeks or even months apart. It's too easy to mess up little details or the light, and almost impossible to maintain continuity. I hear myself thinking out loud: 'Why can't we do the whole scene when we have the blood?' The answer is that we have only so many more days with Leslie before he has to return to Hong Kong. I should've known.

Mosquito Capital of the World

4 a.m. on what the script describes as 'a pampas road far into the countryside'. Our 'road movie' is taking shape in bits and pieces by a slip road two hours south of Buenos Aires. Leslie sleeps/Tony eats. Tony drinks/Leslie sulks. Tony tries to thump some sound out of the car radio/Leslie can't read the map. They argue. Leslie leaves. Tony cries. We start shooting just after dawn has broken. Leslie leaves Tony in a fog both real and metaphorical across a vast, grassy space dissected by the approach roads to the Patagonia Highway. This distances are huge. Leslie walks and Tony chases. Everyone's out of breath. We're almost out of film, each take is so long. I sit in the long grass trying to keep my hand-held camera a little steadier than my nerves. Five seconds into the next five-minute take, my hand

stings. Then my left cheek . . . and my right ear. I hear the sounds of many hands slapping much flesh. My assistant slaps my thigh. There's a sudden piercing pain in my balls. Wong himself finally can't take it any more. He shouts out, 'Cut!' I jump up screaming, 'Welcome to the mosquito capital of the world!'

Tony Leung and Leslie Cheung at the Tropic of Capricorn.

The Metaphysical Meaning of the Tropic of Capricorn II

It's been six weeks since we first set ourselves this intractable problem. We're now twenty days too late for the solstice, and a thousand kilometres too far south. It's 5 p.m., and the sun is going. We need an immediate solution. How to light the Tropic of Capricorn is like asking how to screen darkness, how to frame a memory or how to colour loss – all those unanswerable questions that camera-people have to address somehow. We decide on a 'line of light' to suggest passing through this imaginary Tropic. You'd need arcs or strobes for that kind of effect even in this feeble, fading light. We have two 1,000-watt 'sunguns' (hand-held battery lamps) . . . and a make-up mirror which barely fills my hand! There are no natural motivations for the sun to make such a shadow or line, and we have no physical references like a signboard or a sundial. All we have are a flat plateau and the sun setting behind a couple of groves of trees. 'Just flare the lens,' says Wong, to no one in particular. 'We have no other choice.'

So, trees and flare it is. A stretch of open road. Sunlight flickers through the trees and flares the lens (with a little help from the make-up mirror). I change film speed and aperture. Tony and Leslie look enigmatically into the light; they're over-exposed for a few seconds – increase frames per second – the image darkens a moment and they look at each other in romantic slow motion. It looks great on the video monitor. Wong smiles: 'OK!'

Haven't You Ever Seen a Wong Kar-Wai Film Before?

We shoot Tony driving through the morning mist, then lock down the camera and wait for the light to change so that we can repeat the shot later with Leslie driving in a slightly different light. 'Why wait?' the continuity girl is asking. 'There are half a dozen shots we could do in this free time!' She's Chinese, but grew up here. That's no excuse as far as we're concerned.

A chorus starts up: 'Haven't you ever seen a Wong Kar-Wai film before?'

Repetition may be the basis of Wong's style . . . but judging by the blush in her cheeks we won't need to ask that particular question of her again.

Days of Being Tired

Our third twenty-hour shoot in as many days. Leslie must leave tomorrow. We hustle to get his half-dozen scenes done in a single night. Leslie's in a buoyant mood. Happy to be leaving, relishing all the chaos his departure will cause. My gaffer and I are so tired we spend two hours trying to convince each other that we actually agree on where all three of our lamps should go. 'Compromise, Chris!' exhorts Wong. 'It won't matter how good or bad the light is if we don't have an actor to stand in it!'

Rushes
I don't know why I bother going to see rushes. I usually sleep through them, and the good labs are always somehow two hours out of town. We all laugh at the 'silly' bits and make a few in-jokes. They give me the lab technical data . . . which I always manage to lose. Technicians smoke and shuffle their feet, waiting for instructions I can't or don't know how to give. I never know how to talk about what we see – at least, not intelligently or technically enough to be of much use to anything but this diary.

The Back of Leslie's Head
Leslie's gone (again), but we still need him for this and that. Obviously we can't do dialogue or close-ups, and so we cast for the back of his head. All sorts and sizes of contenders come to the office, some so brave their determination could bend a fork. One of them is asking, 'You don't want me to sing or dance?' An assistant replies, 'No, it's posture that counts,' dismissing him with a Polaroid snap, a telephone number and the classic, gruff, 'We'll let you know.'

Short Ends
We're reduced to counting our filmstock by the foot. My assistants are running up a sweat just keeping the fifty-foot 'short ends' in the magazines. We average only one take per magazine – sometimes two. Take a smoke or beer break and wait for my clapper-loader to prepare the next. We're running out of old stock, and it's just too expensive to buy more here. We test a replacement which will need finer tuning and extra lighting for it to match the tone of the rest of the film.

Wo Jintian Bu Shouhua

My clapper-loader has a sign taped to him: *Wo Jintian Bu Shouhua* ('I'm Not Speaking Today'). Everyone is asking why, but no one can or will explain. I suggest that the director gets one too, and he immediately slaps the clapper-loader's sign on me.

11E, Scene 3, Roll 417

Tony scores hash in the men's toilet of Retiro station. He commits himself to the task a little more diligently than the scene strictly requires. 'Just to ease the pain in my ribs,' he claims. The next scene will show him leaving Buenos Aires by boat. The sea is calm, but the harbour stinks. We get an unexpected 'alternative ending' when Tony throws up and slumps miserably over the side of a trawler heading out to sea.

Top-heavy and Round-footed

I'm faint. My feet seem to roll under my weight. I totter and stagger, top-heavy with a stifling cold. Illness, tiredness and going to the toilet are rarely accounted for in scripts, and so there's no one and no time to feel sorry for me. But I do feel apologetic and remorseful that my work tonight will be less smooth and interpretive than I expect it to be.

Another Star System

Many Westerners are surprised to discover that our stars don't have private trailers or secured resting places and take their meals on the sidewalk or in the local greasy spoon along with the crew. Today Tony wants to move out of his five-star hotel suite and into the serviced apartments with the rest of us. This happens because Leslie has gone, and the question of 'face' has gone with him. I wonder if it's the camaraderie or just the mahjong games and the home-cooked Chinese food he really wants.

'Wong wants me to give Tony more *presence*.'

Tony's Presence

Wong wants me to give Tony more *presence*: 'He's so unfocused and so de-energized these days.' No one dares tell WKW that four months here has done that to him – and to the rest of us as well.

October Ends . . . November Never Will

Christmas in Argentina no longer sounds like a crew in-joke. Shirley Kwan and Chang Chen have arrived to join the cast – or what we're starting to call the 'casualty list'. They idle in their rooms waiting for their roles to materialize while WKW hides in nearby coffee shops hoping for the same. We stop shooting for the umpteenth time to 'save money', to 'acclimatize our new stars'. Now that they're here, we fret over what to do with them and over the thematic justifications for them to even be here at all.

15 November: Tony and Chang Chen

Hotel Rivera – we all hope for the last time. I have to leave for my so-called 'Masterclass' at the London Film Festival. The plane leaves at 11 p.m. I should finish by 9 at the latest.

It's 9.03 p.m. Wong insists that I shoot one more scene: 'This shot's important!' I can't recall one that isn't. Chang Chen is playing Tony's co-worker in some yet-to-be-decided job. (We later settle on a restaurant kitchen.) They've been drinking too much. Chang gets Tony back to his place; it's as much of a mess as Tony's ramblings are. Chang finds Leslie's yellow jacket there and innocently tries it on. Through a drunken haze, Tony imagines that Leslie has come back to him.

We cover every scene in two or three shots, but Chang Chen is not used to our shooting style. Ten takes into the first shot, I'm sweating more out of frustration than the physical exertion of the shot. At 9.17, we're on to the second shot. Wong is still not happy with Chang's approach: 'You're acting like you know what you're doing!' By now I'm so pissed off that I feel

Wong Kar-Wai with Chang Chen.

like quipping, 'So do you!' back to Wong. I hold off, starting to find Chang's awkward and unpredictable rhythm. But my assistant is putting focus in places I don't think it should be. By the time we start the third shot, I'm barking at Jacky, 'Get production to hold the plane for me – I'm already an hour late!' I try to see my light and not my flight, forget the exhaustion, get the shot.

Out of Love

I once claimed my best work was done when I was saddest and just 'out of love'. I was very much in love with Denise when we started this film and so I half-expected that it wouldn't be so good. But she seems to have taken my metaphors too seriously, and I've been away from Hong Kong for too long. An old boyfriend wants her back . . . she has to move on. She breaks the news to me during my flying visit to London. When she says, 'It hurts, but I have to leave you', it *does* hurt more than she or I imagined it could. But when she adds, 'At least now I know you'll make a better film!' I know it's time to get philosophy out of the bedroom and to keep my bullshit to myself.

The Eyes of WKW

Every other day WKW says, 'You're my eyes' – especially if we're 'stealing' a shot or having to move too fast to set up the TV monitor. Sometimes it sounds encouraging, sometimes more like a threat. Most often it's a huge responsibility. But sometimes I wish I could be his mind too. Then maybe I could help more with the 'creative blocks' and move the film along!

Chance and Accidents

All camera-people have a love–hate relationship with the TV monitor which allows the director – and just about anyone else who's interested – to 'monitor' what the camera's eye sees. Wong says, 'Don't change a thing' as often as he says, 'That angle's not interesting enough.' Today what he liked most was what he saw on the monitor when my assistant laid the camera on Tony's bed when I took a break to go for a pee. We messed up the bed a bit more, half-covered the lens with a dirty shirt and some underwear – and the style for a whole sequence was born. Sure, this 'style' is a mirror for the 'discarded' feeling Tony has now that he's broken up with Leslie for the umpteenth time. But it wasn't intellectualized into being, or even planned. It just seemed visually more interesting and unexpected, and solved the problem of how to picture this minuscule space which we've been in and out of for thirty days by now.

'Style' is more about choice than concept. It should be organic, not imposed.

Early Start

We're not sure if we got up at 5.30 or 6.30. We're in Argentina. The Iguaçu National Park is in Brazil. The gates open at 7.30. Because we can't agree whether they're an hour ahead of or behind us, we'll be either an hour early or at least an hour late. We're confused and worried. We want an empty, lonely Falls; no tourists distracting us (or, ultimately, the audience) from Tony's troubled, emotional state.

The Devil's Gorge

No video, no photo, no place I've ever been has prepared me for the Falls. The roar, the rush, the energy – just where we're standing. There's water everywhere. Tony falls twice, gets soaked to the skin. Bright dawn sunlight makes rainbows around our feet, but Tony is shivering in the shadows.

I ask William if this is a real or imaginary part of the film. We're on our own again today; Wong's still working out whether this is a flash-forward dream sequence or the last stop on Tony's physical and spiritual journey and another possible ending for the film. We decide to shoot it both ways.

Helicopter

Waited in the heat of the afternoon for our Bell Jet III helicopter to be done with its tourist customers and free for us. It takes an hour to get its door off and set our camera rig in place. I hang halfway out of the door with only a jerry-rig frame to support my camera and a seat belt to keep me from falling to a spectacular death. The take-off turbulence is like a roller-coaster rush. I go straight into 'cameraman' mode, looking through the viewfinder rather than straight down. The rig shakes violently. My assistant double-checks the seat belt clasp. The down-draught from the Devil's Gorge exerts a powerful centrifugal force, and the rig won't let me tilt down enough to fill the frame with as much cascading water as we want. And so on the second run we tilt the whole helicopter 35 degrees on its side

Tony Leung at the Devil's Gorge.

towards the gap. I feel like I'm bungee-jumping as we drop at 160 kph 100 feet towards the rocks.

The Sun Never Sets on a Wong Kar-Wai Day

Down to Tierra del Fuego, 'the end of the world'. It's 10 p.m. summer time. The sky is still daylight blue, and I'm getting disorientated by the lack of sleep and the rising moon. What does 'the end of the world' look like? It's only when you get there that you realize it's as abstract as the Tropic of Capricorn. 'Infinite horizons' looks like a great idea on paper, but 'World's End' stickers and T-shirts don't work here. How to say visually that this is 'the end of the world'?

Wong Kar-Wai at the end of the world.

Good Luck in Bad Weather

The sea is calm enough for Wong to complain that my tele-photo shots are 'too steady' to match the style of the rest of the film. I 'rough them up' a bit by rocking the boat in one direction and the camera in the other. We go down to our favourite 8 or 12 frames per second and pan randomly from the sky or sea to Chang Chen on the rocks by the 'lighthouse at the end of the world'. Seabirds shit on my lens and equipment and on Wong. We're circling erratically in a little yellow boat around a pensive and stoic Chang.

We need to change the magazine . . . but the spare stock is on the naval boat that's accompanying our tiny fishing vessel. And they won't budge as we make our slow way against one of the most infamous currents in the world. I complain that we'll never get the shot in time if they don't come to meet us half-way. Through the walkie-talkie, though, comes word that the naval captain can't reverse, only go straight ahead. No wonder they lost the Falklands War! Are Argentine sailors afraid to go south in case they fall off the edge of the world?

Back on ship and into port just as a wild storm starts to hit the coast. The captain retrieves his 'Canal Beagle' cap from Wong, who is reluctant to part with it. It's brought good luck to such a difficult shoot.

7 December: Some of Us are Done

Wong leaves for Hong Kong tonight. William has already gone to do Leslie's concert costumes. Christmas is looming and flights are overbooked. Wong has left me here to shoot a week of 'empty shots'. By 10 December, I guess I'm done.

Real Time

It's early 1997. Chang Chen is twenty years old, the age at which Taiwanese males are obliged to begin military service. Since it's also the age at which the teenage girl population of Taiwan has fallen for him, half of the entertainment industry is pulling strings to keep him out of the army for the moment, so that he can pursue his career as an actor and singer.

We're in Taiwan for a couple of days to shoot another possible ending for our story. Tony has come to Taipei to look for Chang Chen; he finds the family's noodle stall, but the only trace of Chang himself is a photo of him by the lighthouse at the end of the world, stuck to a mirror by the phone. Tony steals it.

Taipei hasn't changed much. Film remains an amusement for the gangster fraternity and amateur auteurs. Everything is ad hoc and totally haphazard. We fumble through regardless, ending with shots of Tony riding the notorious new elevated railway through the rain.

The Edit

Sleep, love and consciousness get lost in the rush to meet impossible deadlines for Cannes. Wong is editing on an Avid computer, William is at the Steenbeck. I'm doing a video transfer. Music and voice-overs are going in, scenes and whole characters are coming out. The first cut – a week ago – was three hours long.

Now it's down to ninety-seven minutes and there's no more Shirley Kwan. We play and replay the Iguaçu Falls sequence to let the image and music re-energize exhausted bodies and minds.

'The fat man's feet' are showing now. We start to see what the film is about. Wong says it falls into two parts: the first is 'action' and the second is the characters' reflection on what they've said and done. He feels that what Chang Chen gives Tony (and what Tony gives Leslie) is not 'love' but 'courage' – a 'will to live'. It's our brightest film in all senses of the word and looks like having the happiest ending of any WKW film. It's also much more 'coherent' than our other films, and very lyrical. Of course, the traditional WKW themes of 'time' and 'loss' put in appearances. And there are plenty of great lines, my favourite being: 'Starting over means heading for one more break-up.'

Upside-down
Today (6 April) we're shooting in Hong Kong. The film needs some reference to where Tony has come from, his reflection on his own space. He's looking back from Argentina, on the other side of the world, and so we turn the camera on its head and shoot the streets of Hong Kong upside-down.

The Future
Our interiors are consciously 'timeless', they're not 'logically' lit. Time of day is not a concern in this film. Tony and Leslie's world is outside space and time . . .

Wong says it's only as he edits the film that he finds the true meaning of much of what we've shot. We didn't really know what certain details or colours or actions meant at the time we filmed them. They anticipated where the film would take us. They were in a sense images from the future . . . from the time we've only just reached.

The tango: 'outside space and time'.

13 Paul Thomas Anderson talks to Mike Figgis

MIKE FIGGIS: *I thought your film was fantastic.*

PAUL THOMAS ANDERSON: Thank you.

MF: *One of the best films I've seen in a long time, just the whole way you made it. So, is it something you'd been with for a long time?*

PTA: Long, long time. When I was seventeen I wrote a short film called 'The Dirk Diggler Story', and shot it on videotape. I was a big fan of *Zelig* and *Spinal Tap* and it was that format, fictional documentary. Also I was seventeen, so I was completely immersed in watching porno, in a horny-young-boy way but also in a film-maker's way. I wanted to make movies and here were these terrible movies, but I also got off on them, they were so goofy and bad. Plus I lived in the San Fernando Valley, which is the capital of porn production. So it was always peripherally around me. There were warehouses near where I went to high school, some of them had signage, then there'd be one that didn't, but it had a ton of expensive cars parked out front. So you're thinking, 'What the fuck is going on inside of that one with no sign?' It's because they were making porno movies. So the story obviously stuck with me for nine or ten years. I was twenty-five or twenty-six when I made *Boogie Nights*.

MF: *That's your first feature?*

PTA: Actually, my second. *Hard Eight* was my first one, I wrote and directed it.

MF: *Is that a good film?*

PTA: It's a great film.

MF: *How would I see that now?*

PTA: You can see it on tape or laser disc, or I just did a retransfer for a DVD, which I'm excited about. It was financed by people whose roots were in bad television, *Baywatch*-type stuff, and they decided to try and get into movies. Clearly they hadn't read the script. I delivered the movie and they were really confused. All I could do was point to the script and say, 'This is what I shot, this is what you paid for, this is what you agreed to.' And this argument would always come up – 'Well, the script is not the movie, and the movie's not the script.' I had the most horrendous, terrible time in the editing process. I fought, and I was fired off of it, then eventually got it back. So now the movie is my movie, it's out there – with the exception that the title was 'Sidney', and it was changed to *Hard Eight*.

MF: *I just had a similar situation. I spent two and a half years on one movie, Mr Jones. Now they've actually asked me to re-cut it, do a director's cut.*

PTA: Oh, great.

MF: *And I've discovered the footage all still exists, they don't throw anything away. So I think I'm going to do it. At first I thought, 'Fuck it, I don't know if I want to revisit all of that.' Then I was lying in bed thinking about certain scenes. I remembered shooting them, thinking, 'This is good.' So I thought, 'No, life is about closure, and I would like to finish this.'*

PTA: You'll feel great. I had to spend all my own money to finish *Hard Eight* after I got it back. But I did it, and now I'm happy. It came out last February and died an instant death, because it was always a bastard child for this company. They'd had so much trouble trying to get me to make their cuts. They were saying, 'We don't like the movie, we don't like you, we don't even care that Sam Jackson and Gwyneth Paltrow are in it. We're not going to do anything for it.' It got amazing reviews, almost as good as *Boogie Nights*, but it played for about a weekend and then it was gone. Now, a lot of people have found it on video because of the success of *Boogie Nights* – frustrating that it's on video, but that's fine. And the company that paid for it, Rysher Entertainment, went out of business – which is wonderful. The greatest part about the day they went out of business was that *Daily Variety* published a chart of Rysher's film history, what the movies cost and what they made. And at the very bottom, the lowest-grossing movie in Rysher history was my movie. So I was so happy that I aided their downfall in some way. 'My movie made ten thousand dollars and it cost you guys two million.'

MF: *So why are you especially excited by the DVD release?*

PTA: My cut came out in the theatres, and that's what was put on video. But they brightened it up, because that's the tradition, 'It's got to be brighter.' And they did it behind my back. Then when I got my laser disc at my local video store it was like, 'This is my cut but it sure doesn't look like the movie I made.' So Columbia Tri-Star Home Video had the rights, and I convinced them, they were kind enough, to sink a couple of extra bucks into it and release it properly on DVD, with some commentary and extra scenes – to really preserve it properly. It wasn't good enough for me that my cut was preserved when the colour was all wrong.

MF: *When* Leaving Las Vegas *came out on laser disc – director's cut, wide screen, blah blah – some real film buff from Birmingham, England, called me and said, 'You know the frame line is right across the eyes?' I'd never seen it, didn't know it was out. But they'd got it out in time for Christmas. So I went out and bought one. It was Super 16, and they'd done a wide-screen version where they'd just literally and arbitrarily sliced through it. They hadn't racked it, it was just a complete mess. I couldn't believe what I saw. So I got the negative out and forced them to do it again. But people had already bought it. You have no control, unless you're Kubrick and you watch every frame . . .*

PTA: I watched every frame in the process of *Boogie Nights* towards the end. But I think I drove a lot of people nuts, like 'Why do you have to sit here all day?' 'Because it will be wrong otherwise.' It's not distrusting people, it's just that things get handed down in an assembly-line nature, it goes from one lab to another, one transfer house to another, and honestly, it's just that mistakes get made on order forms because people don't pay attention. There's no conspiracy – although generally if it comes across someone's desk, they want it brighter. It's just about keeping on top of basic POs – okay, this has got to be blue and it's green. I've only made two movies but I can't imagine being able to make as many as I'd like to make, because it takes so much time.

MF: *And there's a certain point when maybe you have to let go. Because if obsessively controlling the detail of a film stops you making the film . . . well, there's nothing quite as close to watching paint dry as film-making.*

PTA: Or watching paint not dry.

MF: *Exactly. What was the time-span on* Boogie Nights?

PTA: We started shooting in July of 1996. We shot until October and then edited until October 1997. We finished everything a week before it came out – we waited till the last minute.

MF: *And your first movie?*

PTA: I shot that in twenty-eight days, then I had three weeks to cut it. But then came the mêlée with Rysher, which lasted a year, essentially. I thought the movie had been taken away from me, and the only way I could deal with that was to go make another movie. So I started prepping *Boogie Nights*, but in the middle of that I essentially stole back my work print elements on *Sidney* [*Hard Eight*].

MF: *How did you do that?*

PTA: I had a dupe work print made. I submitted it to Cannes, and they invited it to come into Un Certain Regard – a big deal. So I called Rysher and I said, 'Listen, I know you guys own it. But I took my dupe work print, I submitted to Cannes, and it's in. It's a big mistake if you guys don't give me some money and let me finish the movie.' And they said, 'No, we don't care.' What was great is that we ended up going to Cannes, and Rysher had made their flyers promoting the products they were unveiling at the Festival. And my movie was nowhere to be found on their product list. It's like, 'You guys have a movie in the Official Selection . . .' Of course, I didn't want to go into the Grand Palais with my dupe work print, so I had said to Rysher, 'Let me have the original negative elements.' But they'd already cut negative on their version, so I couldn't just match up my dupe work print to the negative.

MF: *That would cut into your shots . . .*

PTA: Exactly. I had to go to alternate takes, which weren't always as good. There were three or four very long Steadicam shots and, of course, they cut right into the middle of those.

MF: *Can you splice back in now?*

PTA: You can, but pretty much always you'll lose a frame. I had to do it. I had to go through the whole movie and lose a frame at the head and tail on either side of each shot, pretty much. It made for a great study in what one frame is. Because a lot of times you cruise along, taking your frames off, and you think, 'I don't miss them.' Then you get to one, and you find that one frame makes all the difference. It's insane. You don't want to believe it. But in one or two scenes, there's a slight rhythm change that will always stick with me. It was the best I could do.

MF: *You know how films are speeded up for cable? Scorsese pointed this out. Say the cable schedule slot is two hours and twenty-two minutes. And maybe the movie is running two hours and thirty-two. They get a calculator out and say, 'What speed would this have to run at in order to fit in the slot?' Then they use a harmonizer to take the voice back down to the original key, so we don't notice. But everything is speeded up.*

PTA: Oh, shit. Maybe there is a conspiracy.

MF: *The conspiracy is capitalism because there's no cohesive system.*

PTA: There you go.

MF: *One thing about* Leaving Las Vegas *that pissed off the technical community was the 16 mm. Because everyone's invested in lightweight 35 mm. The last thing they want to hear is Super 16. 'Fuck off, Super 16, we don't want to know, we don't have the cameras, we don't have labs set up for that.'*

PTA: But single-handedly you made that a viable format. You convinced everyone else. Super 16 has taken off now, in terms of the potential for independent movies to possibly break out.

MF: *If there's a problem with budget and schedule, that's the way to go, without a doubt. Stocks are good enough now to blow up from Super 16.*

PTA: No director has final cut, projectionists have final cut. Theatres are so fucked. This THX is the biggest scam going. THX doesn't mean anything, it means that George Lucas gets a cheque to say that some theatre is now THX-approved. It sounds good, but it's bullshit. Not to mention the projectors. You spend all this time, you want the film to look right. A few months after *Boogie Nights* came out, my girlfriend and I were walking by a theatre on the 3rd Street Promenade in Santa Monica. I said, 'Let's look in.' It was a Fuji print and it just looked terrible. The scope, the ratio were fucked up.

MF: *That's because New Line have a Fuji deal.*

PTA: Yes. But now I got rid of that.

MF: *Did you?*

PTA: Oh, yes, I said there's no way I'm making a movie with you guys again unless you get all Kodak prints. So they signed off, which is good. At the same time, I was thinking, when I was watching my movie on 3rd Street, 'If I can't enjoy anything about this bad Fuji print, and this bad mono soundtrack, have I done my job?' This movie should still come off, the story should still work. So do I want to be the guy who's got a Kodak print that's precise and perfect, and that's the only way it can work? Or do I want to be the guy who says, 'Yeah, I know it looks like shit and it sounds like shit, but you liked it, didn't you?'?

MF: *My first American movie was* Internal Affairs. *Years later I'm in Cuba doing a commercial, and I'm at the airport waiting to meet a plane, because my crew's coming in. It's delayed, so I'm hanging outside and a guy tells me, 'The drivers will be in that little hut there if you need them.' So I'm standing by the hut and I hear Andy Garcia's voice and I think, 'That's* Internal Affairs.' *I go in and they're all watching a little black-and-white telly, a broadcast of a bootleg print of* Internal Affairs. *It looks terrible. I'm stunned and I start to say to the guys, 'You know, that's –', and they go, 'Shut up, we're watching this movie.'*

PTA: But in that case it's probably a better feeling even than going to the Hollywood première at Grauman's Chinese.

MF: *Were you happy with* Boogie Nights?

PTA: Yes. There's probably a couple of things I'd like to have done differently, but it's not like I didn't stick to my plan that I had. The first assembly of the movie was three hours and fifteen minutes. And I took about a half-hour out of it, it's now two hours thirty-seven. But the *Boogie Nights* that's out there is the director's cut.

MF: *The scene with the firecrackers – was that always written in?*

PTA: Yes.

MF: *That's impressive. I enjoyed the scene more than most things I've seen in cinema, just because it's such a funny idea.*

PTA: Well, the idea comes from two places. It's a distant piece of background action in a movie called *Putney Swope*, directed by my idol Robert Downey Senior. I called Bob up and said, 'This is the greatest fucking thing, I want to take it and run it through a whole scene, make it foreground action. And I want to say that it's my idea.' He said, 'Great.' Also, my dad was in early television in Cleveland in the mid-sixties, he was the horror talk-show host. He would introduce bad horror films like *Beast from 50,000 Fathoms*. And he was one of the first guys to chromakey himself inside the movie and comment on how bad the dialogue was and so on. He would constantly blow stuff up with firecrackers, take little skulls and throw firecrackers at them. So it's a combination of those two father figures with firecrackers. There it is in the movie.

MF: *What experience did you have with actors prior to making movies? Have you acted?*

PTA: No, but it's always been my favourite thing in movies. I love the pizazz and the cool camera stuff and that's why I'm a director, but I'm just an actor-freak fan. My first experience with actors really was on the short film that I made. Philip Baker Hall who's in *Boogie Nights* and *Hard Eight*, he was in it. He was the first real actor that I met, and he introduced me to how to look at acting and how to write for acting. For my first movie I had Gwyneth Paltrow and Sam Jackson and John Reilly and Philip Baker Hall. You can't get into it any better than that.

MF: *No, you can't. I've had such a crush on John C. Reilly. I met him on* Internal Affairs. *And for some reason he couldn't do the part I wanted him to do. His voice is just brilliant. I was so pleased he was in your movie.*

PTA: He's the main man of *Hard Eight*. John is my best friend. A listing of the people whom I see the most and who are my friends would be all actors. So I get sick of agents and directors saying, 'Oh, actors are crazy, all the great ones, we love them, but they're crazy.'

MF: *There's such a clear division now between film-makers who like toys for boys, and that rarer breed who are actors' directors and who are story-driven. One of the things I loved about your film was there's a real gentleness about it, which I found really moving. Because I'm so fed up with the way films are going. I really don't like movies any more.*

PTA: I don't know, I want to be with you there, but I'm scared to say that, because I feel like I'm bad-mouthing the cause. Even though I know in my back pocket that there's shit out there – yes, it sucks – I almost want to keep it to myself, because I don't want anyone to see our collective cards. But, yes, we're fucking up like crazy, and I wish it wasn't going on. The action genre, that little club, is fucking up lately. I love those movies, and I want them to succeed, I want to see good action-adventure films. I wanted *Godzilla* to be wonderful, I love monster movies.

MF: *That department is a committee film-making process. That's like the sacrifice that cinema has made. OK, you guys, you can have that genre because that's money and everything.*

PTA: I think it's unfortunate because there is an intelligent Godzilla movie to be made, an intelligent action-adventure film. But that genre's getting killed by committee. I've wanted for a long time to make a real romantic comedy in the most traditional way. I mean, I'd fuck it up in an untraditional way, but I'd dive into it thinking it was traditional.

MF: *I want to do a smart thriller. I love the genre. You can do what you like, you can make a surreal film – because once you're in the genre, people don't care what you bring in with it, as long as the dynamics work. All those genres, the horror film, the monster movie, they're great. Are you going to do one?*

PTA: Absolutely. I've got a million ideas and scripts I've tossed around and played with. I write my own stuff.

MF: *I've found (and you may find) that the limitation of being a 'slash', as we're called – a writer-director – is that you're tied to the project you're tied to. But if you've got a quick brain, you might have six of those ideas, and it maybe takes eight years to realize them. That's a little bit depressing. I'm desperately trying to find writers now, so I don't have to commit myself to every script. I can oversee. I'm trying to come up with a script factory, where we have script meetings, talk about it, come back a week later with a couple of scenes, and divide them up, so there's maybe three of us writing together. It's an experiment, but I can't carry on being the assigned writer.*

PTA: What about television? Have you ever –

MF: *I think television and video and disposable non-sacred formats are wonderful for storytelling.*

PTA: I've been thinking about this for a while, and then *The New York Times Magazine* asked me and a bunch of other people to write about what our dream TV shows would be, if we could create them. I gravitated instantly to the variety show. Look at *Boogie Nights*, there are so many actors in it. I'm saying the variety show could be the perfect place where actors and directors could go – so that, say, John Reilly doesn't have to do *Armageddon* to support his family. He can just come to the show for three or four months. And Bill Macy can do the same, or Heather Graham – like a pit-stop for great actors who want to keep their wheels turning, get paid a little bit of money, and not have to go sell their souls in crap. I think you'd have enough interest from some really talented actors.

MF: *I love ensemble. I think that's healthy. The problem with film is it's on the altar and it takes a long time and it slows us down. And creative people are fast and tend to fire things out quickly.*

PTA: What's the fastest you ever made a movie?

MF: *The last one was a four-week shoot. Three, four months editing.*

PTA: See, that's pretty good.

MF: *So satisfying. I want to ask you about the porn industry. You said earlier that you got fascinated as a willing participant, as a teenager. What do you think about the way they're made? Could they be better?*

PTA: Oh yes, God, there's so much to talk about here. Porno movies could and should be a genre. There's a whole series of John Holmes movies about 'Johnny Wad' – it was a character he created, a suave, sophisticated detective, a bit James Bond, a bit Sam Spade. The Brock Landers stuff that Dirk Diggler creates was modelled after that. These were essentially murder mysteries, but they were also fuck films. So you wanted to watch him solve the case or defuse the ticking bomb just as much as you wanted to see him fuck the beautiful girl.

MF: *Were they well made?*

PTA: Well, they pull it off because they're actually sexy. They were on film and certainly it helps that the girls are at least natural. My hormones go towards, 'Oh, she's pretty. And, no, she doesn't have enormous fake tits. There's a little zit on her butt, she's got a little tummy. It's natural.' The same thing with the guys – the guys are not appealing in porno today. They're like fucking robots, chiselled to perfection. There's nothing you can relate to, it's like watching space aliens. The Johnny Wad stuff pulled it off because it didn't take itself too seriously. And John Holmes was quite an actor, really natural. The main thing about them is that a lot of the sex doesn't happen for the camera. Most porn actors now complain that every position in porno is completely uncomfortable. Seventies porno was much more 'Let the camera figure it out'. It was a bit more hand-held, and trying to get into the spot where you got the good juicy close-ups. Somehow it comes out more sexy and natural. Nowadays they're in contortions that are clearly guided towards the camera. It doesn't come off in any way. And the goal of a porno movie should be to give you a boner.

MF: *What else? I mean, my experience of porn movies is being in Hamburg, in some generic concrete block of a hotel, away from people you love, alone in a bedroom. And there's a porn channel and you find yourself watching it. You end up with such a feeling of loneliness and desolation, and at that point, it's almost as if we have a duty here as film-makers. Somebody should be making better stuff that doesn't leave you quite so devastated.*

PTA: Well, I think some of that devastation comes from just watching the sadness in a lot of the performers' faces nowadays. You instantly think, 'Who are they? How did they get there? How can I help?' And it's almost like they're looking into the lens going, 'Save me.' It's funny because, late sixties, early seventies, this sort of porn was fashionable and OK to see in the theatre, it was a date movie. *Deep Throat* was the highest-grossing independent film of all time. *Behind the Green Door* was happening. But *Midnight Cowboy* was also happening. Had it not been for video, I think more porn movies would have come closer to legitimate, traditional narrative stuff.

MF: *It kind of did in other world cinemas – like* Ai No Corrida *in Japan, in France, and in Spain, such as in what Pedro Almodóvar does.*

PTA: Totally. Or even in *Betty Blue.* One example I've used before – not to be salacious or anything – but how interesting it would have been to see Forrest Gump and the Robin Wright character making that baby that we see in the end. How does Forrest Gump have sex? And it's not trying to give you a boner, to show you Tom Hanks and Robin Wright, in bed. What could be more –

MF: *Human.*

PTA: Right. What could be more of a revelation of a character than watching them have sex? That says a lot about someone, how they touch another person in bed.

MF: *I have a theory. Because the way that porn treats the sexual act influences TV and mainstream cinema, it's almost as if actors imitate porn movies when they do sex scenes – which is then what young women and men watch, and they think, 'Oh, that's how sex is.'* So real people end up impersonating porn. You think, 'Hang on, this is all wrong.'

PTA: Totally. I wrote a scene in *Boogie Nights* for Don Cheadle's character Buck and his wife Jessie. They're lying in bed, they decide to have sex, they suggest to each other, 'Maybe we can try to do this, like, real.' But Don fucks up a little bit because he starts to say, 'Baby, oh baby, yeah' – and then he catches himself, and then she starts doing it. It's a funny, small, tender scene where you watch these two people who are so caught up –

MF: *You didn't shoot it?*

PTA: No. We rehearsed it and it was great, but I knew it would never be in the movie.

MF: *Why? I think that's very strong.*

PTA: I thought it was taken care of in other places – porno people trying to be real people. But it is funny, I've been in a situation with a girl and suddenly you think, 'Where did this Elizabeth Berkeley *Showgirls*-sex thing come from? Do you think this flopping around that you're doing is making me excited?' I think porno movies have trained a lot of young people how to have sex, unfortunately – especially the new ones. I think it would help if they were shot on film, I really do. It's more expensive, it requires more of a plan. And I think they fail to plan. Video is a blessing and a curse. It's created an assembly-line mentality. If the concept is that you're making a movie for a consumer – well, the consumer is at home with a fast-forward button. This guy wants to fucking see some dick and some pussy and he wants to see it now. And he's going to fast-forward past all this other shit.

MF: *I don't know about the economics, but there's a huge market comprised of captive audiences in hotel rooms, where you can't fast-forward.*

PTA: Now they have these different systems of Pay-Per-View. There's one where you can click the button and get two or three minutes free, so you can preview it. Within those two or three minutes, you'd better see some fucking or else they're going to go to Pay-Per-View channel two, and if they see fucking, they're going to stay right there. That's why a lot of the Pay-Per-View stuff now is basically highlights. They usually stay away from stories and just do best-of stuff, so you know you've got a constant-fuck thing going.

MF: *I think if I had the balls I'd make one. Just to try it.*

PTA: But I think you have had the balls to put sex scenes in your movies that are explicit. You've injected a bit of porno – in the best possible way – into some of your films.

Walter Murch.

14 Sound Design

The Dancing Shadow by Walter Murch

It disappeared long ago, but in 1972 The Window was still there, peering blindly through a veil of dust, thirty-five feet above the floor of Samuel Goldwyn's old Stage 7. I never would have noticed had not Richard pointed it out to me as we were taking a short cut on our way back from lunch.

'That was when Sound was King!' he said, gesturing dramatically into the darkness.

It took me a while, but I finally saw what he was pointing at: it looked like the observation window of a dirigible from the 1930s, nosing its way into the stage.

What is now Warner/Hollywood Studios had been built originally for Mary Pickford when she founded United Artists with Chaplin and Fairbanks. And it was there, on Stage 7, that Samuel Goldwyn produced one of the earliest of his many musicals: *Whoopee* (1930), starring Eddie Cantor and choreographed by Busby Berkeley. In 1972, Stage 7 was temporarily functioning as an attic, stuffed with the mysterious lumbering shapes of disused equipment, but forty-two years earlier Goldwyn's director of sound Gordon Sawyer had sat at the controls behind The Window, hands gliding across three Bakelite knobs, piloting his Dirigible of Sound into a new world . . . a world in which Sound was King!

Down on the brilliantly lit floor, Eddie Cantor and the All-Singing, All-Dancing Goldwyn Girls had lived in terror of the distinguished Man Behind The Window. And not just the actors; musicians, cameramen, director, producer, even Goldwyn himself – no one could contradict it when Mr Sawyer, dissatisfied with the quality of sound he was getting, would

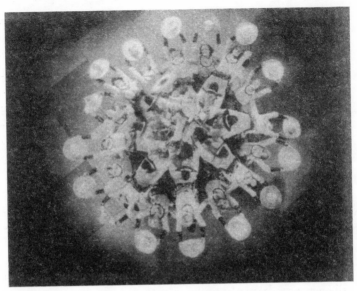

Whoopee.

lean into his microphone and pronounce dispassionately, but irrevocably, the word 'Cut!'

As far as Richard was concerned it had all been downhill from there.

His father, Clem Portman, had been head of the sound department at rival RKO studios, just down the street from Goldwyn, and had helped to create the sound for such films as *King Kong*, *Gunga Din* and *Citizen Kane*. Richard had followed his father's pioneering footsteps and become a mixer himself, one of the best in the industry. On that day in 1972 we were on our way to finish the soundtrack for *The Godfather*.

The situation was not quite as bleak as he liked to imagine, but the late 1960s and early 1970s in Hollywood *were* a relatively quiet period in the evolution of film sound. The stereo magnetic soundtracks of the roadshow films of ten years earlier were no longer being produced (the last one was made in 1971), along with the diminishing fortunes of the film industry in general. Dolby and digitalization were yet to come. The release format for the sound of *The Godfather* would be virtually identical to the format used on *Gone With the Wind*, made thirty-three years earlier.

So forty-five years after his exhilarating coronation, King Sound seemed to be living in considerably reduced circumstances. No longer did The Man Behind The Window survey the scene from on high. Instead he was usually stuck in some dark corner of the stage with his little cart. The very idea of him demanding a 'Cut!' was inconceivable. Not only did no one fear his opinion; they hardly consulted him and were frequently impatient when he *did* voice an opinion. Forty-five years had turned him from King to footman . . .

At least that was how it seemed to Richard.

There is something feminine about sound's liquidity and all-encompassing embrace that might make it more accurate to speak of Sound as a Queen rather than a King. But still, was Richard's nostalgia misplaced? What had befallen The Window? And were Sound's misfortunes really what they appeared to be, or was she a Queen for whom the crown was a burden, and who preferred to slip on a handmaiden's bonnet and scurry around incognito through the back passageways of the palace?

A brief venture into our own biological histories might provide a clue.

Four and a half months after we are conceived, we begin to hear. It is the first of our senses to be connected up and functioning. And for the next four and a half months we luxuriate in a continuous bath of sounds: the song of our mother's voice, the swash of her breathing, the piping of her intestines, the timpani of her heart. All during the second half of pregnancy Sound reigns as a solitary Queen of the Senses: the close and liquid world of the womb makes Sight and Smell impossible,

Taste monochromatic, and Touch a dim and generalized hint of what is to come. Whatever we think of our universe at that point – and there is no doubt that we *are* thinking – comes to us primarily through the graces of Sound.

Birth, however, brings with it the sudden and simultaneous ignition of the other four senses, and an intense jostling for the throne which Sound had claimed as hers alone. The most notable pretender is the darting and insistent Sight, who blithely dubs himself King and ascends the throne as if it had been standing vacant, waiting for him.

Surprisingly, Sound pulls a veil of oblivion across her reign and withdraws into the shadows.

So we all begin as hearing beings – our four-and-a-half month baptism in a sea of sound must have a profound and everlasting effect upon us – but from the moment of birth onwards, hearing seems to recede into the background of our consciousness and function more as an accompaniment to what we see. Why this should be, rather than the reverse, is a mystery. Why does not the first of our senses to be activated retain a lifelong dominance of all the others? The reasons, no doubt, go far back into our evolutionary past, but I suspect it has something to do with the child's discovery of causality. Sound, which had been absolute and *causeless* in the womb, becomes something understood to happen *as the result of*. The enjoyment a child takes in banging things together is the enjoyment of this discovery: first there is no sound, *and then* – *bang!* – there is.

Anything in our experience that first seems to be absolute and self-sufficient, and then is suddenly revealed to be only part of a new, larger context, must suffer an apparent reduction in importance, and this is what may have happened with hearing relative to the other senses.

Something of this same situation marks the relationship between what we see and what we hear in the cinema. Film sound is rarely appreciated for itself alone, but functions largely as an enhancement of the visual. By means of some mysterious perceptual alchemy, whatever virtues the sound brings to the film are largely perceived and appreciated by the audience in *visual* terms – the better the sound, the better the image.

At any rate, in our deepest secret biological histories there lingers an equivalent of The Window, relic of an age when sound's rule was absolute. The analogy is not precise, but may be close enough to help determine whether Richard's nostalgia was justified, or whether sound gains more by giving up her crown than by keeping it. It is enough for the moment to note that this is an open question, and that the issue of causality has something to do with it.

Just as Sound had been the Queen of the senses through lack of competition, what had given film sound its brief rule over the image was the fact that no one had yet figured out how to cut it, or mix it. As a result, everything had to be recorded simultaneously – music, dialogue, sound effects – and once recorded, it couldn't be changed. The old Mel Brooks joke about panning the camera to the right and revealing the orchestra in the middle of the desert was not far from the truth. There was a cumbersome six-disc system, operated by wooden pegs, that gave some ability to superimpose and dissolve, but for the most part Clem Portman, Gordon Sawyer and Murray Spivack had the responsibility for recording Eddie Cantor's voice *and* the orchestra accompanying him *and* his tap dancing, all at the same time, in as good a balance as they could manage. There was no possibility of fixing it later in the mix, because this *was* the mix. And there was no possibility of cutting out the bad bits, because there *was* no way to cut what was being chiselled into the whirling acetate of the Vitaphone discs. It had to be right the first time, or you called 'Cut!' and began again.

Power on a film tends to gravitate towards those who control a bottle-neck of some kind, around which manoeuvring is

difficult. Stars wield this kind of power, extras do not; the director of photography usually has more of it than the production
designer. For the technical reasons just mentioned, film sound
in its earliest versions was one of these bottle-necks, and so The
Man Behind The Window held sway with a kingly power he
has never had since. And he could have remained enthroned
for ever if there had been no further developments beyond the
original Vitaphone technique.

But there is a symbiotic relationship between the techniques
that we use to represent the world and the vision that we
attempt to represent by means of those techniques: a change in
one inevitably results in a change in the other. The sudden availability of cheap pigments in metal tubes around 1870, for
instance, allowed the Impressionists to paint quickly, out of
doors and in fleeting light; and face to face with nature they
realized that shadows come in many other colours than black,
which is what the paintings of the previous 'indoor' generation
had taught us to see.

Similarly, humble sounds had always been considered the
inevitable (and therefore mostly ignored) accompaniment of
the visuals, stuck like an insubstantial, submissive shadow to the
object that 'caused' them. And like a shadow, they appeared to
be completely explained by reference to the objects that gave
them birth: a metallic clang was always 'cast' by the hammer,
just as the village steeple cast its shape upon the ground.

The idea that sounds could be captured, preserved and
played back later was not only considered impossible; it was
hardly considered at all. In fact, sound was the prime example
of the impermanent: a rose that wilted and died as soon as it
bloomed.

Magically, sound recording loosened the bonds of causality
and lifted the shadow away from the object, standing it on its
own and giving it a miraculous and sometimes frightening
autonomy. King Ndombe of the Congo consented to have his
voice recorded in 1904, but immediately regretted it when

the cylinder was played back and the 'shadow' danced on its own, and he heard his people cry in dismay: 'The King sits still, his lips are sealed, while the white man forces his soul to sing!'

The true fluidity of sound was not fully realized until the perfection of the sprocketed 35mm optical soundtrack (1928), which could be edited and put in precise sync with the image, opening up the bottle-neck of the inflexible Vitaphone process. This opening was further enlarged by the innovation of re-recording (1929–30) whereby several tracks of sound could be separately controlled and then superimposed and recombined. Vitaphone itself had faded from the scene by 1931, but as with any rapidly developing technology, the reality was more chaotic than it seems at a distance of almost seventy years – in 1929 there were more than thirty-five competing systems (from Bell-o-tone to Vocafilm) of which only one, RCA Photophone, has survived more or less intact. In addition, these developments took some time to work their way into the creative bloodstream. As late as 1936, films were being produced that required only seventeen additional sound effects *for the whole film* (instead of the thousands that we might have today). But the possibilities were richly indicated by the imaginative sound work in Disney's animated film *Steamboat Willie* (1928) and De Millie's live-action prison film *Dynamite* (1929). Certainly they were fully established by the time of Murray Spivack and Clem Portman's ground-breaking work on *King Kong* (1933). The optical soundtrack was the equivalent of pigment in a tube; and sound's fluidity, the Impressionists' coloured shadow.

In fact, animation – both of the *Steamboat Willie* and the *King Kong* variety – probably played a more dominant role in the evolution of creative sound than it has been credited for. With live action, the documentary illusion of 'what you hear is what you get' could be maintained – for a while, anyway. In the beginning, it was so astonishing to hear people

Steamboat Willie.

King Kong.

speak and move and sing and shoot each other in sync that almost any sound was more than acceptable. But with animated characters this did not work, since they are shadowy creatures who make no sound at all unless their creators create the illusion of it through *sound out of context*: sound from one reality transposed on to another. The most famous of these is the thin falsetto that Walt Disney himself gave to Mickey Mouse, but a close second is the roar that Murray Spivack provided King Kong.

At any rate, the construction of a film's soundtrack began to be a much more elaborate, time-consuming process, one that involved more and more people in various departments, and began to extend over the length of the entire film-making process. The good old days of *do it right the first time* and The Man Behind The Window were gone. To Richard's regret, the days of *fix it in the mix* had begun.

But there was another innovation that was to accelerate and deepen the process even further; one that has a personal dimension for me – magnetic sound.

In the early 1950s, when inexpensive tape-recorders were first becoming available to the public, I heard a rumour that the father of a neighbourhood friend had actually acquired one. Over the next few months I made a pest of myself at that household, showing up with a variety of excuses just to be allowed to play with that miraculous machine: hanging the microphone out the window and capturing the back-alley reverberations of Manhattan, scotch-taping it to the shaft of a swing-arm lamp and rapping the bell-shaped shade with pencils, inserting it into one end of a vacuum cleaner tube and shouting into the other, and so forth.

Later on, I managed to convince my parents of all the money our family would save on records if we bought our own tape-recorder and used it to 'pirate' music off the radio. I now doubt that they believed this made any economic sense, but they could hear the passion in my voice, and a Revere recorder became that year's family Christmas present.

I swiftly appropriated the machine into my room and started banging on lamps again and resplicing my recordings in different, more exotic combinations. I was in heaven, but since no one else I knew shared this vision of paradise, a secret doubt about myself began to worm its way into my pre-adolescent thoughts.

One evening, though, I returned home from school, turned on the radio in the middle of a programme, and couldn't believe my ears: sounds were being broadcast which I had only heard in the secrecy of my own little laboratory. As quickly as possible, I connected the recorder to the radio and sat there listening, rapt, as the reels turned and the sounds became increasingly strange and wonderful.

It turned out to be the *First Panorama of Musique Concrète*, a record by the French composers Pierre Schaeffer and Pierre Henry, and the incomplete tape of it became a sort of Bible of Sound for me. Or rather a Rosetta Stone, because the vibrations chiselled into its iron oxide were the mysteriously significant and powerful hieroglyphs of a language which I did not yet understand, but whose voice none the less spoke to me compellingly. And above all told me that I was not alone in my passion.

What had conquered me in 1953, what had conquered Schaeffer and Henry some years earlier, was not just the considerable power of magnetic tape to capture ordinary sounds and reorganize them – optical film had already had this ability for decades – but the fact that the tape-recorder combined these qualities with full audio fidelity, low surface noise, operational simplicity, the ability to record over the same piece of tape again and again, and above all, low price and availability. The earlier forms of sound recording had been expensive, available to only a few people outside of laboratory or studio situations, noisy and deficient in their frequency range, and cumbersome and awkward to operate. And once recorded, you could not erase and start again.

The tape-recorder extended the magic of sound recording by an order of magnitude, and reduced the size and cost to the extent that a ten-year-old boy like myself could think of it as a wonderful toy: the tape-recorder encourages play and experimentation, and that was – and remains – its pre-eminent virtue.

By the 1960s, magnetic sound had completely replaced the optical process (except in the final theatrical release-print) and the tiny transistor was busy replacing the bulky and unreliable vacuum tube. The dismantling of these two old bottle-necks and the resultant 'democratizing' of the craft of film sound opened up more creative possibilities, but proportionately reduced sound's kingly power.

Yet at the same time, the studios were suffering one of their periodic financial troughs, and research and development budgets had been cut back or eliminated.

It was just around this time of simultaneous expansion and stagnation that I was hired to create the sound effects for and mix *The Rain People*, a film written, directed and produced by Francis Coppola. He and I were recent film-school graduates and were anxious to continue making films professionally the way we had made them at school. Francis had shot *The Rain People* using all his own miniaturized equipment and saw no reason to stop now when it came to post-production. He felt that his previous film (*Finian's Rainbow*) had become bogged down in the bureaucratic/technical swamp at the studios, and he didn't want to repeat the experience.

He also felt that if he stayed in Los Angeles he wouldn't be able to produce the inexpensive, independent films he had in mind. As a result he, fellow film student George Lucas and I, and our families, moved up to San Francisco to start American Zoetrope. The first item on the agenda was the mix of *The Rain People* in the unfinished basement of an old warehouse on Folsom Street.

Ten years earlier this would have been unthinkable, but magnetic sound and the transistor had opened things up to such an extent that it seemed natural for Francis to go to Germany to buy – almost off the shelf – mixing and editing equipment from KEM in Hamburg and hire a twenty-five-year-old ex-film student to use them.

Technically, the equipment was state of the art, and it cost a fourth of what comparable equipment would have cost five years earlier, if you could have found it at all. It was high-speed multi-track equipment with 'rock and roll' erase/re-record and video playback. This halving of price and doubling of quality is familiar to everyone now, after twenty-five years of microchips, but at the time it was astonishing. The frontier between professional and consumer electronics began to fade away.

In fact, it faded to the extent that it now became economically and technically possible for one person to achieve what several had before, and the other frontier between sound-effects creation and mixing also began to disappear.

From the beginning, the Zoetrope idea was to try to avoid the 'departmentalism' that was sometimes the by-product of sound's technical complexity. That tended to pit mixers, who were brought up mainly through the engineering department – direct descendants of The Man Behind The Window – against the people who came up with the sounds, who were mostly from editorial backgrounds. It would be as if there were two directors of photography on a film – one who lit the scene and one who photographed it – and neither could do much about countermanding the other.

We felt that, given the equipment that was becoming available in 1968, there was now no reason for the person who came up with the sounds and prepared the tracks not to be able to mix them. The director would then be able to talk to one person about the sound of the film the way he was able to talk to the director of photography about the look of the film. Responsibility for success or failure would lie squarely with that one person, and because communication problems would be reduced or eliminated, the chances of success would be increased.

So the films *The Rain People*, *THX-1138*, *The Conversation*, *American Graffiti*, and *Godfather II* were all done in this manner, which has subsequently been followed on most of Francis Coppola's and George Lucas's films in the intervening years, as well as those of Saul Zaentz (*One Flew Over the Cuckoo's Nest*, *Amadeus*) and Phil Kaufman (*The Right Stuff*, *The Unbearable Lightness of Being*). In general, it has become the standard approach to film sound in the San Francisco area.

Originally, we had no name for this approach, although my credit on some of the early films was 'sound montage', which had mostly to do with the fact that I was working non-union at the time and didn't want to raise any unnecessary flags.

On *Apocalypse Now*, however, in addition to picture editing and re-recording, my other task was to develop a design for the use of the film's quadrophonic sound in the three dimensions of the theatre: when should the sound (for dramatic reasons) focus down to a single point; when should it expand across the front of the screen to stereo; and when and how should it use the full dimensionality of the entire theatre? No dramatic film had been released in this format before, so we were moving into uncharted waters. I thought I was doing a job similar to that of a production designer, except I was decorating the walls of the theatre with sound, so I called what I did sound design.

The name stuck, and has since been used by many others, not without controversy. One friend (a mixer) said, only half-jokingly, 'If someone on one of my films gets the credit sound designer, I call myself the sound redesigner.' Frequently, the name is used by people who simply *design sounds* (that is, create special sound effects that could not be found in libraries) rather than those who *design and execute the overall soundtrack*.

Short of restricting sound design to its original meaning on *Apocalypse Now*, it is this latter definition that I would encourage: someone who plans, creates the sound effects and mixes the final soundtrack, and thereby takes responsibility for the sound of a film the way a director of photography takes responsibility for the image. In other words, it is the original Zoetrope method that we started with in 1968, which was the direct descendant of the way we had done things in film school.

Actually, it sounds very close to reinventing, with modern techniques, The Man Behind The Window. But the name 'sound designer' does uniquely describe a role that has been made possible only by the more recent advances in sound-processing technology. And if present trends continue, this blurring between creating, editing and mixing will only increase – how far, it is hard to say. The sound editor using a digital workstation is now able, routinely, to combine sounds in ways that were formerly practical only in the mixing theatre. And vice versa: mixers can quite easily create and edit sounds with the tools that are increasingly at their disposal.

All of the techniques that early on liberated the shadow of sound to dance on its own also progressively increased the number of people involved and thus diminished the kingly power of The Man Behind The Window. But they repaid what was taken away ten times, a hundred times, in creative power – in the increased fluidity and malleability of sound. Now the digital and automated grandchildren of those same techniques have the potential to restore to one person the control that could only formerly be exercised by several, but not at the expense of the all-important fluidity and malleability of the sound.

Beyond the controversy, though, of who is called what, or who does what job, the important thing is the final soundtrack and its internal balance and clarity, its relationship to the picture, and the creative possibility of reassociating sounds with images that are different – sometimes astonishingly different – from the objects or situations that gave birth to the sounds in the first place.

It might have been otherwise – the human mind could have demanded absolute obedience to 'the truth', but for a range of practical and aesthetic reasons we are lucky that it didn't. The reassociation of image and sound is the fundamental pillar upon which the creative use of sound rests, and without which it would collapse.

This reassociation occurs for many reasons: sometimes simply for convenience – walking on cornstarch, for instance, happens to record as a better 'footstep in snow' than snow itself; or necessity – the window that Gary Cooper broke in *High Noon* was not made of real glass, the boulder that chased Indiana Jones was not made of real stone; or for moral reasons – crushing a watermelon is ethically preferable to crushing a human head. In each case, our multi-million-year reflex of thinking of sound as a submissive causal shadow now works in the film-maker's favour, and the audience is disposed to accept, within certain limits, these new juxtapositions as the truth.

But beyond all practical considerations, this reassociation should be done, I believe, to *stretch* the relationship of sound to image wherever possible; to create a purposeful and fruitful tension between what is on the screen and what is kindled in the mind of the audience. The danger of present-day cinema is that it can suffocate its subjects by its very ability to represent them: it doesn't possess the built-in escape valves of ambiguity that painting, music, literature, radio drama and black-and-white silent film automatically have, simply by virtue of their sensory incompleteness – an incompleteness that engages the imagination of the viewer as compensation for what is only evoked by the artist. By comparison, film seems to be 'all there' (it isn't, but it seems to be), and thus the responsibility of film-makers is to find ways within that completeness to refrain from achieving it. To that end, the metaphoric use of sound is one of the most fruitful, flexible and inexpensive means: by choosing carefully what to eliminate, and then adding sounds that at first hearing seem to be somewhat at odds with the accompanying image, the film-maker can open up a perceptual vacuum into which the mind of the audience must inevitably rush. As a result, the film becomes more 'dimensional'. The more dimensional it is, the more impact it has on the viewer, the more it seems to speak to each viewer individually, and the more the sound can become a representation of the states of mind of the central characters, approaching the pre-verbal 'song' that Stephen Spender called the base ground of poetry: 'a rhythm, a dance, a fury, a passion which is not yet filled with words.'

Every successful reassociation is a kind of metaphor – what Aristotle called 'naming a thing with that which is not its name' – and every metaphor is seen momentarily as a mistake, but then suddenly as a deeper truth about the thing named and our relationship to it. The greater the stretch between the 'thing' and the 'name', the deeper the potential truth.

The tension produced by the metaphoric distance between sound and image serves somewhat the same purpose, creatively, as the perceptual tension produced by the physical distance between our two eyes – a three-inch gap which yields two similar but slightly different images: one produced by the left eye, and the other by the right. The brain is not content with this close duality and searches for something that resolves and unifies those differences. And it finds it in the concept of *depth*. By adding its own purely mental version of three-dimensionality to the two flat images, the brain causes them to click together into one image *with depth added*. In other words, the brain resolves the difference between the two images by imagining a dimensionality which is not actually present in either image, but is added as the result of the mind trying to resolve the differences between them. The greater the differences, the greater the depth. (Within certain limits: cross your eyes – exaggerating the differences – and you will deliver images to the brain that are beyond its power to resolve, and so it passes on to you, by default, a confusing double image. Close one eye – eliminate the differences – and the brain will give you an image with no confusion, but also with no third dimension.)

There really is, of course, a third dimension out there in the world: the depth we perceive is not a hallucination. But the *way* we perceive it – its particular flavour – is uniquely our own; unique not only to us as a species but also in its finer details unique to each of us individually, because everyone's eyes are a different distance apart. And in that sense it *is* a kind of hallucination, because the brain does not alert us to what is actually going on. It does not announce: 'And now I am going to add a helpful dimensionality to synthesize these two flat images. Don't be alarmed.' Instead, the dimensionality is fused into the image and made to seem as if it is coming from 'out there' rather than 'in here'.

In much the same way, the mental effort of fusing image and sound in a film produces a 'dimensionality' that the mind projects back on to the image as if it had come from the image in the first place. The result is that we *actually see* something on the screen that exists only in our mind, and in its finer details is unique to each member of the audience. It reminds me of John Huston's observation that 'the real projectors are the eyes and ears of the audience'. We do not see *and* hear a film; we hear/see it. This metaphoric 'distance' between the images of a film and the accompanying sounds is – and should be – continuously changing and flexible, and it takes a fraction of a second (or sometimes even seconds) for the brain to make the right connections. The image of a light being turned on, for instance, accompanied by a simple *click* – this basic association is fused almost instantly and produces a relatively flat mental image.

Still fairly flat, but a level up in dimensionality: the image of a door closing accompanied by the right 'slam' can indicate not only the material of the door, but also the emotional state of the person closing it. The sound for the door at the end of *The Godfather*, for instance, needed to give the audience not only the correct physical cues about the door, but it was even more important to get a firm, irrevocable closure that resonated with and underscored Michael's final line: 'Never ask me about my business, Kay.'

That door close was still related to a specific image and, as a result, it was probably 'fused' by the audience fairly quickly, although it required a few more milliseconds than the simple click of the light switch. Sounds, however, that do not relate to the visuals in a direct way function at an even higher level of dimensionality and take proportionately longer to resolve. The rumbling and piercing metallic scream just before Michael Corleone kills Solozzo in *The Godfather* is not linked directly to anything seen on screen and so the audience is made to wonder at least momentarily, if perhaps only subconsciously, 'What is this?' The screech is from an elevated train rounding a sharp corner, so it is presumably coming from somewhere in the neighbourhood (the scene takes place in the Bronx). But precisely *because* it is so detached from the image, the metallic scream works as a clue to the state of Michael's mind at that moment – the critical moment before he commits his first murder and his life turns an irrevocable corner. It is all the more effective because Michael's face appears so calm and the sound is played so abnormally loud. This broadening tension between what we see and what we hear is brought to an abrupt end with the pistol shot that kills Solozzo: the distance between what we see and what we hear is suddenly collapsed at the moment that Michael's destiny is fixed.

(This moment is mirrored and inverted at the end of *Godfather III*. Instead of a calm face attended by a scream, we have a screaming face in silence. When Michael realizes that his daughter Mary has been shot, he tries several times to scream, but no sound comes out. His face is contorted by grief and anguish, but the scream that you would expect to hear with such a face is missing. In fact, Al Pacino was actually screaming when the film was shot, but the sound was removed in the editing. Even though we are dealing here with an *absence* of sound, a fertile tension is created between what we see and what we would expect to hear, given that image. Finally, the scream bursts through, the tension is released, and the film – and the trilogy – is over.)

The elevated train in *The Godfather* was at least somewhere in the vicinity of the restaurant, even though it could not be seen. In the opening reel of *Apocalypse Now*, however, the jungle sounds that fill Willard's hotel room come from nowhere on screen or in the 'neighbourhood', and the only way to resolve the great disparity between what we are seeing and hearing is to imagine that these sounds are in Willard's mind; that his body is in a hotel room in Saigon, but his mind is off in the jungle, to where he dreams of returning. If the audience can be brought to a point where they will bridge such an extreme distance between picture and sound with their own imagination, they will be rewarded with a correspondingly greater dimensionality of experience.

The risk, of course, is that the conceptual thread that connects image and sound can be stretched too far, and the dimensionality will collapse. The moment of greatest dimension is always the moment of greatest tension.

I might add that in my own experience the most successful sounds seem not only to alter what the audience sees, but to go further and trigger a kind of *conceptual resonance* between image and sound: the sound makes us see the image differently, and then this new image makes us hear the sound differently, which in turn makes us see something else in the image, which makes us hear different things in the sound, and so on. This happens rarely enough (I am thinking of certain electronic sounds at the beginning of *The Conversation*) to be specially prized when it does occur – often by lucky accident, dependent as it is on choosing exactly the right sound at exactly the right metaphoric distance from the image. It has something to do with the time it takes for the audience to 'get' the metaphors: not instantaneously, but not too long either – like a good joke.

In all of this the question remains: Why do we generally perceive the product of the fusion of image and sound in terms of the image? Why does sound usually enhance the image and not the other way around? In other words, why does King Sight still sit on his throne and Queen Sound haunt the corridors of the palace?

In his recent book *Audio Vision*, Michael Chion describes an effect – what he calls the 'Acousmêtre' – which depends on delaying the fusion of sound and image to the extreme by supplying only the sound (most frequently a voice) and withholding the image of the sound's true source until nearly the very end of the film. Only then, when the audience has used its imagination to the fullest, as in a radio play, is the real identity of the source revealed, almost always with an accompanying loss of imagined power of the source of the sound: the Wizard in *The Wizard of Oz* is one of a number of examples cited, along with the Mother in *Psycho* and Hal in *2001* (and although he didn't mention it, Colonel Kurtz in *Apocalypse Now*). The 'Acousmêtre' is, for various reasons to do with our perceptions – the disembodied voice seems to come from everywhere and therefore seems to have no clearly defined limits to its power – a uniquely cinematic device. And yet . . .

And yet there is an echo here of our earliest experience of the world: the revelation at birth that the song which sang to us from the very dawn of our consciousness in the womb – a song which seemed to come from everywhere and to be part of us before we had any conception of what 'us' meant – is the voice of another and that now she is separate from us and we from her. We regret the loss of former unity – some say that our lives are a ceaseless quest to retrieve it – and yet we delight in seeing the face of our mother: the one is the price to be paid for the other.

This earliest, most powerful fusion of sound and image sets the tone for all that is to come.

15 Clint Eastwood on Directed By . . .

You want me to talk about the directors I've worked with? Let's start with those I didn't get the chance to be directed by. Howard Hawks, for example, the first director I ever met! It was a brief meeting. I was helping him round up his horses when I was about sixteen, seventeen. John Ford? I never met him but, sure, he's one of the ones I'd like to have worked with. I saw a lot of his movies when I was young.

I saw all the big hits like everybody else: *Grapes of Wrath*, *Gone with the Wind*, etc. I also saw comedies like *Sitting Pretty* and westerns like *Winchester 73*. Very few foreign films were imported in those days, but I do remember seeing an Australian movie, *Forty Thousand Horsemen*. There was a lot of action. It was also the first movie where I heard actors use bad language. They'd say 'Damn!' or 'Hell!' That wasn't allowed here. The Hays Office saw to that. I can't remember who the director was.* At the time, I didn't care who directed what.

Going back further, I remember Preston Sturges's comedies. I liked *Sullivan's Travels*, Joel McCrea especially. Maybe he didn't have the stature of Gary Cooper, but he always gave the impression that more was going on inside him than he was revealing. There were also fantastic character actors in Sturges, Capra and Hawks movies. They all had interesting faces. It's very comforting for a director to know he can rely on the same actors movie after movie. I tried to do the same in *Every Which Way . . .* and *Bronco Billy* by getting together people like

* Charles Chauvel (1940).

Sullivan's Travels: Preston Sturges's stock company of character actors.

Geoffrey Lewis, Bill McKinney and so on. Someone like Ford liked the same faces around him. When you're an admiral, you play the part. You don't ask any questions. Ford wasn't the kind of director to analyse what he was doing with his actors. He knew their capabilities and what they could bring him. Could I have joined his gang? I don't think so. I'm not the gang type.

I met Capra when I was making *High Plains Drifter* in Mono Lake, North California. I was staying in Silver Lake, four houses down from Capra, and I got the chance to talk to him. Afterwards, every time I came by, I paid him a visit. He was always pleased to see me, but I never worked with him. Did Capra ever see *Bronco Billy*? I don't know. When I read the script, I thought 'Capra could have made this'.

Capra's movies have an underlying energy which, although it's difficult to define, he alone possesses. Anyone can shoot a scene, but like all the greats, Capra added something which was neither written nor visualized, but which permeates all his work. All the greats had this gift to some extent or other. It depended on the material, their enthusiasm, the problems they had to solve.

Hitchcock? He was with another studio when I was under contract at Universal. Years later, I met him once, shortly before he died. I got a call from his office: 'Mr Hitchcock would like to see you. His health isn't good, he may not make the movie, but he'd like to talk to you about the lead part.' We had lunch at the Universal commissary. It took us ten minutes to walk from the door to the table. He walked very slowly and carefully. He ordered his usual lunch: steak and tomatoes. He was still in full possession of his mental powers. He talked brilliantly and I fell under his spell. The movie was set in Finland or Norway, on a train. He'd seen a few of my movies, notably *Misty*. We had a good time. But how could I have been his man? I was a generation too young!

The same goes for Ford and Capra, who were retiring when I was starting out. Anthony Mann? Yes, I'd like to have worked with him at his peak. I liked his movies a lot, especially the westerns with Jimmy Stewart. Nick Ray also did some good things but I never met him. Same with Sam Fuller. He was preparing a film at RKO, *The Run of the Arrow*, and I tried unsuccessfully to get a meeting. I only met him much later, in France.

At the time, Mann, Ray and Fuller were looking for new sources of inspiration and went to make movies in Europe. The top man was Elia Kazan. Ever since *On the Waterfront*, he was the director everyone wanted to work with. The trouble was he did his casting in New York and other places. I never managed to make a movie with him. The same applied to Stanley Kubrick. I saw *The Killing* when it came out. I would have liked to have worked with him, but the opportunity never came up.

On the other hand, I did get to meet Billy Wilder when he was casting *The Spirit of St Louis*. As often happens in Hollywood, the press was full of stories about him looking for an unknown to play Lindbergh. All the young guys, especially the gangly ones, were chasing the part. I met him once . . . just for a handshake, not even an audition. His films had marked my youth: *Double Indemnity*, *Sunset Boulevard*, and so many others. I don't understand why he stopped working so soon. I don't know the circumstances, but I find it amazing that a man of his talent hasn't been more productive in the last twenty years.

I desperately wanted to be in Raoul Walsh's *The Naked and the Dead*. My agent couldn't get me an audition so I didn't get to meet him. Small agencies had no power. Walsh was a fantastic character. And he'd been an actor as well. It's always good to work with directors who've been actors. They're much more receptive. When I gave Don Siegel a part in my first film, *Misty*, I told him that way he'd learn to be more tolerant towards his actors while I'd learn what it's like to be a director. Often an actor only worries about his performance and his character. He doesn't realize a director can only spend 5 per cent of his energy on him, the other 95 per cent being devoted to the crew, the other actors and all the rest.

In my time, Universal mainly made B movies. They had a stable of actors under contract: Rock Hudson, Tony Curtis, Jeff Chandler, Rory Calhoun . . . But they couldn't afford stars like Cooper or Gable. I played a small part in *Away all Boats*, and Gable was offered the lead. I was in the studio commissary when he came in. It caused a sensation. No one at Universal had seen such a great star. But, in the end, the part was played by one of the house actors, Jeff Chandler I think.

It was a good period, but Douglas Sirk was the only important director. Universal gave him all their prestige movies, big melodramas like *Magnificent Obsession* and *Written on the Wind*. I tried to get a meeting but failed. When you were under contract, you thought you could get meetings anywhere, at least with the house directors. You even thought you had the edge over actors from outside, but that wasn't the case at all. Sometimes directors were suspicious precisely because you were under contract. Familiarity breeds contempt. They could see you any time, but actors from outside had the advantage of novelty.

In those circumstances, it wasn't easy to get work with the greats. But I did work with William Wellman at the end of his career, on *Lafayette Escadrille*. It wasn't a great movie, the script wasn't up to scratch, but it was a period when Wellman, the eternal rebel, was trying something new. Perhaps he wanted to do something he hadn't been allowed to do before. I remember we had a conversation on the set of *The Ox-Bow Incident*. It was one of my favourite films. He was surprised by my opinion, because it was a financial disaster. He said it was Mrs Zanuck's fault. Everyone at the studio was very proud of the movie, but when Darryl screened it at home, his wife said, 'But this is terrible! How can you let them lynch Dana Andrews and Anthony Quinn?' The rumour spread that the movie was jinxed. So it only got a limited release. It was only when the

Wellman's *The Ox-Bow Incident*.

movie was praised by the French critics that Fox tried to run it again in New York. But that didn't work either. The movie had been shot fast, in less than thirty days, like a commando raid. That's how Wellman worked best. To save time on *Lafayette Escadrille*, he used two cameras to cover the same scene, something he'd never done before. His idea was that there'd be no continuity problems. He was right, but I think it meant making too many compromises with angles and lighting. I've used two cameras very rarely, usually only for angles and lighting. I've used two cameras very rarely, usually only for action scenes. I prefer using several lenses rather than several cameras. Wellman retired after *Lafayette Escadrille*, but I carried on seeing him and his family. He gave me a lot of encouragement during *Breezy*. He liked the film a lot, and wrote me some very nice letters. I think that because he was married to a woman much younger than himself, he identified with the William Holden character. He had a big influence in encouraging me to become a director.

I couldn't work with the greats every day. Which is why I worked with unknowns or semi-unknowns, such as Sergio Leone, who only had a couple of toga movies under his belt. *Fistful of Dollars* was his first big break. *The Colossus of Rhodes*, I admit, didn't make much of an impression, but people said he had a great sense of humour. I'd already realized this reading the script. I told myself I should maybe try something new and, if it didn't work out, I could always say I'd had a good vacation in Spain.

Sergio cast me after seeing an episode of *Rawhide*. Anyway, he didn't have much choice: the film was being made on a shoestring. An American representing the producer even asked me whether I could bring my own costume. I was amazed, but I went off and bought some clothes in a shop on Santa Monica Boulevard. I bought a pair of trousers and washed them over and over again to age them, and grabbed the boots and gunbelts I used on *Rawhide*. I put them all in a rucksack and headed off to Europe! And I finally met Sergio. He was a character. I didn't speak Italian and he didn't speak English. Our interpreter was a Polish lady, Elena Dressler, who spoke six or seven languages. She'd been in a German concentration camp and was liberated by the Americans. One of the assistants spoke English and would give me all the necessary instructions. After a while, Sergio and I got to understand each other quite well. The only time we really used the interpreter was when I wanted to cut dialogue I believed irrelevant. We talked a lot, discussed what we were doing, and ended up coming to an agreement. I was playing the character as I saw him, very controlled, with the minimum of gestures. The opposite of playing to the gallery! I showed no emotion whatsoever. If I'd tried to be as baroque as the others, it would have been ridiculous. Sergio understood what I was doing, but when the producers saw the rushes, they thought I was doing nothing, that it was a disaster. When the film was cut together, they changed their minds.

It was fun working with Sergio after *Rawhide*, where the stories were so conventional. I remember that Lee Van Cleef thought Sergio was completely crazy when we started making *For a Few Dollars More*. Maybe Sergio's methods and ideas weren't very orthodox, but they helped me discover another point of view. He was a great admirer of the masters of the western, Hawks and Ford. But he had his own vision of what a western should be, and some of his ideas were truly crazy. Sometimes I'd have to intervene to keep the ship on course. But we made a good team. We were on the same wavelength. Sergio liked to say there were fights on the set; but that wasn't true in this case. Later he got a little jealous because I was more prolific than he was. It was neither his fault nor mine. After the premiere of *Bird* at Cannes, I went to see him in Italy and we spent a great day together. I think he held it against me for having turned down Charles Bronson's part in *Once Upon a Time in the West*, then the part of an Irish gangster in *Once Upon a*

Eastwood with Siegel on the set of *The Beguiled*.

Time in America. I would have liked doing *Once Upon a Time in the West* if I hadn't done the three westerns before. It was time for me to move on and try something new.

When *Coogan's Bluff* came up, Don Siegel heard I'd asked to see some of his movies. The only one I vaguely knew was

Invasion of the Body Snatchers. They screened for me his two previous movies for Universal, *Madigan* and *Stranger on the Run*. When he found out about this, Don asked to see the films I'd made with Sergio. He liked them, and that's how our association started.*

We only had one argument, right at the beginning. Don always insisted on writing the story where it was set. If the story was set in New York, then he'd go and live there. I'm the opposite. I prefer concentrating on the story and making the necessary adjustments afterwards. He liked going to the locations and planning everything around them. This is what happened on *Coogan's Bluff*. The problem was, Don got so involved in the geography that he completely forgot about the story. When he came back, the script had to be rewritten, which is what we did together.†

Don always needed an opponent, either the studio or a producer. This went back to his fights with Jack Warner, and usually the enemy was the producer. When we were getting ready to shoot *Dirty Harry*, I said to him, 'Now you're your own producer, you won't be able to find any scapegoats.' He laughed, but ended up blaming the production manager! Don never liked production people. He must have known them when they'd been assistants or secretaries, and he treated them like they still were.

Don hated the old studio system. And I showed him how to escape it. I'd come up the ladder while the new system came into being. My power wasn't linked to any particular studio. This was the age of Frank Wells and John Calley. They didn't tell you how to do your job; they just let you get on with it. But Don was used to endless interference from studio executives. When I was at Universal, I used to slip into the back of the

* Eastwood dedicated *Unforgiven* to 'Sergio and Don'.

† See Siegel's account of the same episode in his autobiography *A Siegel Film* (Faber and Faber).

screening rooms where executives were watching rushes and listen to what they said. There'd be at least twenty of them and right in the middle, forced to listen to their idiocies, would be the poor director. We had a bit of that on *Coogan's Bluff*, but managed to get away from it afterwards. At Warner's it was completely different. When I got Don to come over for *Dirty Harry*, all they said was 'Now it's up to you.' All of a sudden, Don had more time than he'd ever had before in his life. Seven or eight weeks seemed to him an eternity. Don could be anything but extravagant. He was always grumbling but, my, he was efficient! He knew what he wanted and he knew how to take decisions. He kept to his budget and to his schedule. His frugality rubbed off on me, I'm sure. On *Escape from Alcatraz*, I persuaded him to shoot in the air-shafts where the escape happened. Why spend a hundred thousand dollars building a set?

Don knew exactly which shots to shoot. But he wasn't rigid. He could add or change a shot at the last moment. I've worked with directors who are completely pole-axed if you suggest a change in a scene. I bumped my head while we were shooting *In the Line of Fire*. To hide the bruise, I asked Wolfgang Petersen whether I could enter a shot from the right rather than the left. Wolfgang had a lot of trouble reorganizing the scene, because he'd imagined it all from the one angle. A detail had changed and it threw him off balance. This was never the case with Don. Sergio would have taken time to think and then probably have said OK, but Don wouldn't have blinked an eyelid. He believed that there were no rules, or if there were rules, they were made to be broken.

16 Making *Tarnation*

Jonathan Caouette talks to Jason Wood

The feature debut of Jonathan Caouette, *Tarnation* is a raw, extremely personal and sensual display of self-destruction and rebirth that announces the arrival of an exceptional new cinematic visionary. Interweaving a psychedelic whirlwind of snapshots, Super-8 home movies, answering machine messages, video diaries, snippets of eighties pop culture and dramatic re-enactments, Caouette creates an epic portrait of a family torn apart by dysfunction and reunited through the power of love. Structured so as to evoke the film-maker's own depersonalization disorder, *Tarnation* has been variously compared to David Lynch, Andrew Jarecki's *Capturing the Friedmans* (2003) and avant-garde artists such as Stan Brakhage and Jack Smith. A personal love letter to the film-maker's mother, Renee, who spent much of her youth undergoing electro-shock-therapy for a form of schizophrenia, the film re-defines the possibilities of documentary, and of film-making in general.

A project that began when Caouette was just eleven years old, *Tarnation* was screened at the 2004 Sundance Film Festival to considerable acclaim and went on to enrapture audiences worldwide with its visual audacity and undiluted emotion. One of the main talking points at Sundance was the film's initial $218.32 budget. So how was an inexperienced film-maker such as Caouette able to bring his project to the screen and how did he manage to do it with such aesthetic distinction and for so little money?

Tarnation was edited entirely on Apple's iMovie editing software. Included free with basic system software on most Macintosh computers, iMovie allows even the least computer-savvy customers a simple means to edit their own materials into movies using their own personal computers. Since its introduction in 1999, iMovie has evolved into a comprehensive editing suite for aspiring movie-makers, with the capability to edit image, mix sound, add effects and filters, generate titles and even create screening DVDs. It was on a screening DVD that Caouette first circulated a version of his project to American festival organizers. On seeing copies of these DVDs, directors John Cameron Mitchell (*Hedwig and the Angry Inch,* 2001) and Gus Van Sant (*Last Days,* 2005) boarded the project.

By film industry standards, iMovie is a very basic program that was initially considered best suited for non-professionals learning to edit home movie footage. However, because of its affordability, accessibility and simple interface, many digital film-makers of all ages are turning to iMovie to edit their projects. *Tarnation* has ushered in a new respect and excitement for do-it-yourself film-making and is certain to force the entertainment industry to pay more attention to potent but unproven film-making talent. Talented people with distinctive voices and a desire to represent previously marginalized sensibilities and perspectives can now use inexpensive, home computer systems to create their work. *Tarnation* is representative of the kind of exciting new film that this new, accessible technology has been promising for some time and is widely considered to be the first cinematic masterpiece of outsider art. Executive producer Gus Van Sant remarks, 'I think I have always been waiting to see someone make something as moving as Jonathan Caouette's film with as little as he has had to make it. I knew something like this would appear, and I am glad that it finally has.'

JASON WOOD: *How did you originally discover the iMovie editing package and what possibilities did it immediately open up for you?*

JONATHAN CAOUETTE: My partner David's [David Sanin Paz] aunt Vicky gifted us an old iMac bubble computer and I discovered that it had on it the iMovie home editing software. This must have been about 2000, maybe 2001. I was amazed that we actually had this in our home and I was equally amazed by what I could do with it. About five years prior to getting it I had been talking with a very dear New York friend of mine, Jason Banker [an associate producer on the film], about how to edit the movie. Jason actually helped me out on *Tarnation* in regards to putting some of the montages and split-screen sequences together; these were not done on iMovie. Well, they were initially done on iMovie but then I gave them to Jason and he choreographed them in. This is the one part where I guess I cheated, but that's OK.

Anyway, I was really flabbergasted when I discovered iMovie because I cast my mind to five years prior when Jason and I had been sitting in some coffee shop discussing how it had been reported that five years from now you were going to be able to make a movie from your home. I never realized that I would be the one doing it. In retrospect, I feel like a poster boy for iMovie, and I could never have anticipated that.

I had a whole plethora of material I had saved because I was a diehard pack rat and had every format from VHS to Betamax, from laserdisc to minidisc and from eight-track to vinyl. Absolutely everything. I had also saved up all my audiotapes and my diaries. I had also kept a video diary from my time spent in a psychiatric hospital aged thirteen. I was committed for smoking angel dust. I even had answer phone messages! As soon as I discovered this software, I started digitizing everything. I would simply take my Beta footage and stick it in the Beta machine and then go out from Beta into a hi-8 camera – a consumer grade camera that my grandfather had bought me as a gift. And this is really where the budget is in the frequently quoted realm of $218.32 because all the cameras that I utilized in the film – and even the computer – was either a gift or it was on loan. Even the minidisc player came from my friend Joe; I would take little cassettes like the one you are recording us on and the proper sized audio cassettes and then go out from these mechanisms to minidisc and just make sure that it was all digital so that I could import it all via firewire into the iMovie program. Unfortunately, I was smart enough to digitize everything but not smart enough to log it.

The first thing I did was make a short film called *The Hospital* utilizing aspects of *Tarnation* and scenes of me as a child and Super-8 stuff in a fictitious story about a kid that astra-projects out of his body and remembers his past. Unfortunately, he isn't able to come back. It had a lot of music in it that would have been even more expensive than *Tarnation* to clear.

JW: *Did John Cameron Mitchell get involved in* Tarnation *after seeing* The Hospital?

JC: No, I don't think he has ever seen it. He saw an excerpt from *Tarnation* when the film was 99.9 per cent finished. We showed it to John a few days before the film premiered at the MIX Film Festival in New York. The festival is a gay and lesbian experimental film festival and I wanted to show the film to John just because we were friends at that point and I wanted his stamp of approval. Of course his stamp of approval was a little more than I anticipated because he came on as a producer. Shortly after, Gus Van Sant also came on board and they both endorsed the film and lent their names.

JW: *That must have been very gratifying.*

JC: I was doing cartwheels as soon as I found out. It was an out-of-body experience because I have been saying the name 'Gus Van Sant' since I was about seven years old as if it were a mantra. I'd seen *Male Noche* [1985] in 1987 and thought it was amazing. I also find it remarkable the way Gus did the Hollywood thing and then came back to more independent productions. His last few films are astonishing and *Last Days* continues that. You have to remember that I'm a film geek and also a big Gus Van Sant fan. When John and Gus attached themselves to *my* movie it was one of the most exciting things that had happened to me up to that point.

JW: *How daunting was the process of getting the film ready for its premiere at the MIX Film Festival? I understand that you had an original cut approaching three hours long. How did you decide what to leave out?*

JC: When I finished it, the film was actually two hours and forty minutes and I went on a maniacal coffee and nicotine editing spree and cut forty minutes out of the film. These forty minutes contained various subplots, many of which revolved around songs. I had used certain songs in their entirety and, of course, it was going to be impossible to leave them in the film in this way.

JW: *To back peddle a little, how much material did you end up digitizing?*

JC: I digitized about 160 hours of video and film that I'd been shooting. There was also a period when I was younger where I'd digitized all my Super-8 stuff to a photomac, a very lo-fi transfer. This encompassed about 15,400 reels of stuff. There's enough material still available to me for a follow up film to *Tarnation*.

Somewhere along the way I misplaced the VHS footage of the Super-8 stuff, so in the original cut of *Tarnation* that was shown at Sundance and MIX I had to project the Super-8 stuff onto the wall of my apartment and taped it on a low shutter speed to match up how I wanted it to look.

The photographs that you see in the film I had videotaped with my hi-8 camera; I would literally take the photographs, put them on the wall with a regular household light bulb underneath it and take videos of the photos. I collected four or five hi-8 tapes of our family photographs and then I would take the video of the hi-8 and import it into the iMovie program. In the iMovie program I would position each one and create a still clip from each one so that I could later do all the intricate cutting to give these kind of subliminal little inserts. I became fixated with this process because I was always a big fan of subliminal messages – anything that would come and go and leave a big impression. A key film for me in this regard is *The*

Exorcist [1973], with its famous split-second insert of the demon. When I discovered I could do that, I decided that I wanted the whole movie to be like this. I want the whole movie to spew out and regurgitate all this information to you and have you left feeling as if you have woken from a fevered dream of some kind as opposed to just sitting down and watching a regular linear story. This was when I began to add all the effects, particularly with the still photographs, to which I would add a film grain.

Making *Tarnation* did feel like a truly organic process. I remember shooting some footage of my son when he was four years old and thinking this will be great for the foster home sequence. The montage sequence cut to the Glen Campbell song was originally still photographs only, but I just felt that it was too monotonous. I wanted to break it up with a little bit of movement so that's when I realized, 'Wait, I have this great footage of Josh, I'm sure I have some angles of him where he favours me in some way.' I then added a film grain to the hi-8 video to emulate early seventies super-8 footage. Of course, when I was four and five and in foster care I wasn't filming myself. That is why the line is blurred and why I have issues with the film being pigeonholed as a documentary.

JW: *You've described it as a DIY film.*

JC: That's a sort of a trendy thing to say now but it really is. Given the DIY aspect of it, I hoped that it would be a little more prosperous for my family and I. For this reason, and because of the incredible momentum *Tarnation* has gained, I think that I am going to do another iMovie DIY film, but I think I am going to look into self-distributing it afterwards.

The whole relationship between being a film-maker and making a film is changing so rapidly and it is going to really revolutionize the way that films are distributed and exhibited. iMovies and FinalCut Pro – which I have yet to learn but will – are really at the heart of this. I can't wait to work on my next project, it's going to be really exciting.

JW: *You've released subtle details about what the next project is going to be, and from what I understand it's a kind of semi-fictional portrait of a Texan actress that will also incorporate four key films – featuring this actress – that will be entirely re-edited. Most people think that the actress is Karen Black.*

JC: Well, they're very close but no cigar. The actress is a naive, would-be scapegoat and really denotes this kind of character in all of her films and I really want to take this aspect of her and draw it out to also encompass the darker passages from some of the character pasts that this actress has portrayed. Given her incredible volume of work, I think that I'll probably draw more from the region of seven or eight films. I can't at this moment tell you who the actress is, I'm afraid. This project may never see the light of day, or it may be restricted to a festival screening. In theory, it isn't going to cost any money to make and aesthetically I intend to approach it in exactly the same way as *Tarnation*. I'll edit on iMovie, use lots of music, lots of text and lots of disparate media. If all goes well, it is going to be a fun experiment – literally – and a real tear-jerker.

JW: *Do you see parallels with* Tarnation *and its use of iMovie software with other recent technological advances in film? I'm particularly thinking of being able to shoot on smaller digital cameras, a process that has radically democratized the film-making process.*

JC: I am excited about this and feel that *Tarnation* will make cinema more accessible for film-makers and for audiences. Some people are concerned about it also. I mean, imagine the festivals' organizers and the new deluge of submissions they are going to get. I do think that being able to make movies like this is going to be another medium in itself. I don't think that everybody will necessarily be able to make good films, just like not everybody is able to make films using more traditional methods either, but this is certainly going to offer a new, more achievable way of making films for considerably less money. And thank God for it. This is a godsend for anybody that is intimidated by the film industry; I certainly was and couldn't comprehend the idea of making my first film before cheaper, more user-friendly production methods came along. I even went to acting school thinking that this may provide an entry to becoming a film-maker. It really is as easy as picking up a camera and then turning on your computer at home to make a movie.

JW: *You've also been quoted as saying that the experience of watching* Tarnation *enables you to get to meet audiences and for audiences to get to meet you. Was this also a part of your striving for accessibility?*

JC: Well, people were seeing the film and exclaiming: 'I feel that I know you already.' When I was making it, I didn't know that would be the effect it would have.

JW: *And is this particular effect slightly disconcerting? There is so much of your life and the lives of your family in there that there must come a point where you want to step back.*

JC: Absolutely. One of my biggest fears when it came to the actual distribution was that a distributor would take the film and assume, simultaneously, that the film and I are a kind of found art. That they would think that they could just put it out there and that I would ultimately become exploited. Even though it's a movie I absolutely love, I think that this is something that *American Movie* is slightly guilty of.*

JW: *I was interested to read that you not only edited to music but would also often let specific songs dictate how the editing would proceed.*

JC: I would always start with the music and then follow what was going on in the song. I initially had lots of Nick Drake

---

* Directed by Chris Smith, *American Movie* (2000) is a fascinating documentary that follows Mark Borchardt, a would-be film-maker from Wisconsin, through two years of trying to get his low-budget horror project off the ground. Far from Hollywood, Mark relies on local talent for his cast and crew, and help from his family, particularly his ageing uncle who takes a producer credit. At times funny, and at times unsettling and voyeuristic, it's a curiously compelling study of obsession.

music and whatever was going on in any particular song I would have to find video that matched that and really let the music dictate everything. Interestingly, a lot of the songs that you hear in the film were simply downloaded. There's a moment at the beginning of the film where you are told that Renee suffered electro-shock treatments and you hear some audio interference. Well, that's the sound of a download. I just really liked this sound and put in something visually to match that.

It's disappointing that there was stuff that we had to take out or in some way obscure. For example, in the scene with myself and my mother and father sitting on the couch we had Dylan's *Nashville Skyline* playing in the background but, of course, we couldn't use this so we had to cut it out. This just shows you that when I was filming I never for one moment anticipated that I would wish to put the scene in a movie one day.

Music is so important to me; I don't think I could make a film without music. Well, actually I could, but it would have to be exactly the opposite kind of film to *Tarnation*.

JW: *I understand that Lars Von Trier was an influence in terms of adopting a chapter approach to the editing.*

JC: That's right. Especially *Breaking the Waves* [1996]. The structure of my film, which has been done many times before, is that it starts in the present and then goes full circle back to where you've begun. I really like that, that's why I had to bookmark it with two re-enactments to make all the other stuff make sense. Although it got a rough ride, *Dancer in the Dark* [2000] also inspired me a little bit too.

JW: *Some of the other influences I trace back to very early American avant-garde film-makers such as Stan Brakhage and Sadie Benning. There's also your school production of David Lynch's* Blue Velvet *set to the music of Marianne Faithfull.*

JC: I'm totally inspired by David Lynch. There's even a scene in *Tarnation* where someone sings a Julie Cruise song. Remember also that I never went to film school. I acquired my influences more by being a video store geek and by developing my own notion of discerning between a good film and a bad film and my own ideas about composition. I kind of had my own passage through film school by simply watching so many movies. I know of Brakhage but I've not actually seen that much of his work.

There was also one critic, Jeff Millar, who wrote for the *Houston Chronicle*, who got involved with me at a turbulent part of my childhood. We would go to screenings at least twice a week and talk about films and critique them. By the age of fifteen I was a huge John Waters fan and checked out from the local library the book *Trash Trio** and decided that I wanted to make a film with exactly that kind of aesthetic – plus I had just met a guy who looked exactly like Divine – and Jeff Millar gave me the seed money to try and realize that project. I even wrote a handwritten cry-for-help-type letter to John Waters in which I asked for his blessing. Sadly, his attorneys wouldn't go for it. Without his blessing I wouldn't do it, so I ended up using the majority of the Super-8 footage that Jeff had paid for in *Tarnation*.

JW: *Are you still archiving materials and storing stuff up?*

JC: Yeah, I'm still archiving quite a few things. I'm not quite ready to make the transition just yet from leaving my desktop computer to working on a set, but at some point I am going to have to. That's why I want to do the Texan actress project I mentioned as a way to segue into that.

JW: *Is the $218.32 budget in danger of becoming something of an unwanted tag?*

JC: It is, but it was never intended to be a gimmick or publicity stunt. For early festival submissions forms we had to give the film a budget and at that point that was exactly what it was.

JW: *There also seems to me to be this attempt to portray you as a New York jewellery store doorman who with this film has*

---

* *Trash Trio* comprises of three collected John Waters screenplays: *Pink Flamingos*, *Desperate Living* and *Flamingos Forever*.

been transformed overnight into a prince. Is the transformation really that immediate and radical?

JC: This has given me the opportunity to be a film-maker which has been my aspiration ever since I was a child. I also have something of a dichotomy at the moment because I am so busy promoting *Tarnation* – so far I've done in the region of 800 interviews – that I can't actually spend any time working on anything new. To be honest, if I don't start creating something by July I am going to implode. I need to stop promoting this movie! But yes, it's a wonderful thing and I'm already getting ideas for a third and fourth movie. I think that after the Texan actress project, a horror movie would be a good thing for me to do. I've even written a screenplay, part of which formed the basis for *Tarnation* but which could be very easily re-augmented for a horror movie. My biggest fantasy, and this will never happen, is to direct Lynch's *Ronnie Rocket**. The crux of the story is a form of electricity that runs in reverse and which affects how people interact with each other.

JW: *You say that it will never happen but the repercussions from* Tarnation *must be such that people are now approaching you to work with them?*

JC: That's right. One night at the Mercer Hotel Gus showed me this thing he had made on his iMac using iMovie. The piece used texts that he had produced on the set of *Elephant* [2003]. Gus said that he used this approach because he was totally inspired by *Tarnation*. It feels so strange. It's too much to fathom sometimes. Ultimately, this film has been a love letter to so many people and now a lot of them are coming out and wanting to meet me. Karen Black called from Los Angeles to talk to me about the film and the feelings it inspired in her. It's amazing.

---

* Conceived soon after the release of *Eraserhead* (1976), *Ronnie Rocket* is a project that David Lynch has struggled to make for many years. In the Chris Rodley edited *Lynch on Lynch* (Faber, 1997), Lynch describes it in a pitch to a studio as being about 'electricity and a three-foot guy with red hair' (p.91). The studio ceased their interest in the project.

JW: *You earlier referred to the idea of being some kind of poster boy for iMovie – have people been coming to you as a kind of forerunner of a revolutionary moment in cinema? The publicity around* Tarnation *is quick to claim it as the first film to be commercially released that is edited on iMovie.*

JC: It's strange when you have students coming up to you from Berkeley University to tell you that they are going to be studying your film. Even weirder, I was in San Antonio last week and they did a live theatrical production of *Tarnation* in a local theatre. I think I may have created some kind of monstrosity here. It's strange, but also quite exciting.

I'd be very happy to inspire future generations of film-makers. But they have to realize that there really are no more excuses at all. Everything that you need to make a film is available to you.

JW: *Given the highly personal nature of the film's content, has making it and its subsequent release been in any way cathartic or therapeutic for yourself or for your mother, Renee? Is it also true that you no longer suffer from the depersonalization disorder?*

JC: I no longer really suffer from it now. I think the editing was an immolation of that. The choice of not holding on to cosy images of me or my mother was very premeditated because I didn't want it to seem like an exercise in narcissism. I also used brightness and contrast throughout the film to express what the depersonalization disorder experience is like. If I'd had access to more effects, I would probably have done it differently.

When Renee first saw the film she was terrified. She is still terrified, I think. It was, however, very important for her to really get her story out there. She talks about her life and how she was fucked over by the system and inadvertently fucked over by my grandparents. She certainly wants her story out there. In fact, the whole film can be perceived as a search for truth. That whole scene where I am filming my grandfather and he asks me to turn off the camera is certainly that. This notion of truth is paramount to me but I'm not sure if I'll ever actually get it. There's really nobody of sound mind in my nuclear family that I can gain information from about anything and it's very confusing and very frustrating.

JW: *And has the support of your partner David also been a comfort throughout all this?*

JC: It has. Even he appears in the film and he's just an innocent bystander. David has a very normal life compared to all this; he studies and he waits tables and he tends garden on the weekend as another side job. He's getting by in New York and we still have a very good relationship. Unfortunately, I only see him in glimpses at the moment. At times, it's made me question if I actually want to go on and make films. I'd never previously considered the responsibilities you have to endure as a film-maker.

JW: *What was the thinking behind the film's title?*

JC: I always knew that it had to have a one word title. I went through other working titles: *Lucid* and *The Day I Disappeared*, the name of the horror screenplay I mentioned. I decided on *Tarnation* because it is the compilation of two words and concepts, tarnished and eternal damnation. It's also a Southern intonation for hell. More simply, it's also the name of one of my favourite bands.*

---

* Fronted by talented singer-songwriter Paula Frazer, Tarnation were formed in 1992 with former S.F. Seals members Lincoln Allen and Michelle Cernuto, along with steel guitarist Matt Sullivan. Setting their dark ballads and love songs against a stark, ominous backdrop dominated by reverb-soaked guitars, Tarnation debuted in 1993 with 'I'll Give You Something to Cry About'. In 1995, they issued *Gentle Creatures*, their first LP for cult British label 4AD.